Folklore and Society

Series Editors
Roger Abrahams
Bruce Jackson
Marta Weigle

THE BONNY EARL OF MURRAY

The Man, the Murder, the Ballad

Edward D. Ives

University of Illinois Press
Urbana and Chicago

First published in Great Britain in 1997 by Tuckwell Press Ltd, East Linton, Scotland

Illini Books edition, 1997
© 1997 by Edward D. Ives
Manufactured in Great Britain
P 5 4 3 2 1

This book is printed on acid-free paper.

Library of Congress Cataloguing-in-Publication Data

Ives, Edward D.
  The bonny Earl of Murray : the man, the murder, the ballad / Edward D. Ives.
      p.   cm. -- (Folklore and society)
  Includes bibliographical references (p.   ) and index.
  ISBN 0-252-06639-1 (paper : alk. paper)
  1. Moray, James Stewart, Earl of, d. 1592. 2. Moray, James Stewart, Earl of, d. 1592--In literature. 3. Folklore and history--Scotland--History--16th century. 4. Murder--Scotland--History--16th century. 5. Ballads, Scots--History and criticism. 6. Scotland--History--16th century. 7. Nobility--Scotland--Biography. I. Title. II. Series.

DA790.M67194   1997
398'.358'09411--dc21   96-41869
                                        CIP

To the Memory of

RICHARD DYER-BENNET

'Casella mio . . .' (*Purg.* II, 91)

Contents

Illustrations

Preface

I STARTED SINGING 'The Bonny Earl of Murray' back in 1949, but for several years I asked no questions, knowing it only as a song, something to be sung for friends, who usually asked no questions either. It wasn't until 1954 when Roger Sherman Loomis suggested I put together a presentation for his 'Medieval Legends and Ballads' course at Columbia that I decided I'd better learn something *about* it, which led me naturally enough to Child's headnote and some brief excursions into his sources. But that was enough to get me started; the story fascinated me, and over the next few years I read whatever I could easily lay my hands on, the result being a brief article in *Midwest Folklore* in 1959.[1] Knowing how superficial that was – *all* history is superficial; it can't be anything else and still be history – I kept digging in a desultory backyard sort of way until my 1990 sabbatical gave me the chance to go to Scotland and start doing the job right, which of course led to return trips in 1992 and 1994. In sum, the origins of this book are identical to the origins of countless works by academicians: lecture notes that simply got out of hand.

The book is divided into two parts: the first concentrates on history, the second on the ballad itself. Obviously the ballad is where it all began, but once I got going the story behind it took on a life of its own. In no way will I claim that what I have written here is necessary background for understanding the ballad; the 1959 article was more than sufficient for that purpose. Nor do I offer anything that will lead to a significant reinterpretation of the known history of sixteenth-century Scotland; I can, for example, think of only one or two minor places where I differ from what Keith Brown has to say in his excellent *Bloodfeud in Scotland*.[2] But in offering these disclaimers I do not mean to denigrate my own work. What I have done is concentrate on one particular event – the murder of the Second Earl of Moray in 1592 – and realize it as thoroughly as possible, not for what it can tell us about trends or principles but for what it is in itself. If in so doing I have created a critical mass, it will inevitably shed its own light, but for now it is enough for me to hope that it tells a good story. Certainly the cast is striking: madcap Bothwell, angry Lady Doune, soldierly Ochiltree, enigmatic King James, relentless Huntly. Paradoxically enough, the least interesting character of all in this drama may well be Moray himself.

The second section, that on the ballad itself, consists of two chapters. In Chapter 4 I look at the ballad in the context of its time: when and under what circumstances it was composed and what it would have meant to a contemporary audience. In the latter section I have made great use of Flemming Andersen's study of ballad formulas and Barre Toelken's recent work on metaphor.3 At first I thought both (but especially the latter) got involved in some overly subtle interpretations of ballad language, but it is a pleasure now to acknowledge how illuminating both approaches – insofar as they differ at all – have been when applied to 'The Bonny Earl of Murray'. In Chapter 5 I have followed the ballad through the four centuries since its genesis, a task that proved far different from the usual historic-geographic sifting and arranging of variants. For the most part there *were* no variants, but that gave me a chance to explore the marches between oral and written – not to mention folk, popular, classical and revival – traditions, interesting territories in their own right. Through both chapters runs my conviction – not a very startling one, to be sure, especially to anyone acquainted with my earlier work – that how a traditional ballad becomes a traditional ballad is explained neither through some re-creative process of oral transmission (though that process will work its inevitable changes) nor through the theory of oral composition, but rather through the shaping spirit and aesthetic choices made by its original if unknown author.4

Quite obviously, most of the original documentation for Part I was written in sixteenth-century Scots, and while at first my intention was to reproduce that material exactly as I found it, several friends who read parts of the manuscript for me found that practice enough of a nuisance to make me question its utility, especially since dialect was no part of my argument. After some scholarly soul-searching I decided to make translations, but in every case I have kept as close to the original phrasing as possible. Occasionally I have kept certain dialect words when they seemed necessary either to sense or to spirit, especially when the context seemed to explain them adequately. I am, of course, responsible for all translations. The melodies I have included are taken from the sources noted and have been prepared for publication by my friend Dr. Gordon Bowie, to whom many thanks.

In the making of this book I have incurred many debts, and it remains for me to acknowledge as many of them as I can remember. Save for the unforgivable lapse of appointing me a double term as Chair of Anthropology, my own University of Maine has left me alone, telling me to go do whatever it is I do, which I have gratefully done. It also granted me a full year's sabbatical in 1989–90, which allowed me to carry out research and travel in Scotland, and awarded me a Research Grant generous enough to pay for two return trips, one in 1992, another in 1994. The staff at Fogler Library has been, as usual, very helpful, but I'd like particularly to thank Reference Librarians Mel Johnson and Chris Whittington, who spent extra time helping me hunt down certain obscurities, and Libby Soifer and her Interlibrary Loan crew, who allowed those obscurities and a good many more to cross my desk in timely fashion. And while I'm on the subject of libraries, my thanks to the staff of the William Andrews Clark Memorial Library for courtesies extended to me while I was attending the International Ballad Conference in Los Angeles in June of 1993.

My debts in Scotland are of course many, but first of all I want to thank Rosemary Bigwood, who, when I discovered I could not read the various sixteenth-century hands to be found in the Moray Muniments, transliterated something like thirty documents for me. Without her help I would have had no access to any of that valuable material.

Everyone at the School of Scottish Studies seems to have gone out of his or her way to help me in one way or another, from Senior Technician Fred Kent and Secretary Angela West to Director Sandy Fenton. Archivist Alan Bruford solved many small problems for me, and both Morag MacLeod and Emily Lyle were very generous with both their time and their expertise. Talk with Hamish Henderson – in his office, in the Meadow Bar or Sandy Bell's, or *en route* between – was worth crossing the Atlantic for all by itself. Thanks, Hamish. And heartfelt thanks to both Margaret Mackay and Margaret Bennett, good lifetime friends who looked after my needs both scholarly and personal in so many hospitable ways it's impossible to be more specific. My pro tem office mate (downstairs), Allen Simpson, on leave from the Royal Museum, gave me several useful leads, and the staff of the Dictionary of the Older Scottish Tongue office (upstairs) were pleasantly tolerant of my frequent raids on their library.

Elsewhere on the Edinburgh University campus, Dr. Julian Goodare of the Department of Scottish History spent most of one afternoon answering my many questions, and the people at the Main Library, especially those in

Special Collections, were universally helpful to an elderly American who kept getting confused by strange elevators, staircases, and catalog entries. At every other Edinburgh institution I visited I received the same quality of help – pleasant, competent and marvelously unofficious. Thanks therefore to the staffs at West Register House, particularly to Colin Johnston; at the Scottish National Portrait Gallery, particularly to Deborah Kerr; and at the Royal Commission on the Ancient and Historical Monuments of Scotland (RCAHMS). Thanks too to Dr. David Caldwell at the National Museums of Scotland and Dr. Rosalind Marshall at the Scottish National Portrait Gallery and Charles Burnett of the Scottish United Services Museum. Nor shall I ever forget the pleasure of working in the Music Room of the National Library of Scotland; thanks there to Roger Douce and most particularly to Ruzena Wood, whose song index, built up over many years, is a treasure.

Three other institutions have been very helpful. First of all, John Widdowson arranged for my appointment as Visiting Professor at the Center for English Cultural Traditions and Language (CECTAL) at the University of Sheffield in the Spring of 1990, which gave me access to their excellent libraries and the chance to try ideas out not only on him but also on people like Julia Bishop and Jeff Patton. Second, Malcolm Taylor and his staff at the Ralph Vaughan Williams Memorial Library (London) generously supplied me with several documents it would have been almost impossible for me to obtain anywhere else. Finally, my old friend Joe Hickerson of the American Folklife Center's Archive of Folk Culture (Library of Congress) was tireless and imaginative in finding material for me that it would have been rather embarrassing to have left out. Thanks to them all; of such is the world of folklore scholarship.

Special thanks are due to the Earl of Moray for granting me access to the Moray Muniments and for allowing me to study the Death Portrait at leisure. He and the Countess have maintained an enthusiastic interest in my work, and their hospitality at both Darnaway and Doune has been – and continues to be – very important to me.

To bring this to a close, there are a number of other people to whom I owe various debts for various generosities. Some of them I will specify in notes along the way. For others I hope they will accept the simple mention of their names as at least a token of my gratitude: Bill Baker, Steve Bicknell, Molly Bingham, Alaric Faulkner, Ken Goldstein, Naomi Jacobs, Bengt Jonsson, Maurice Lee Jr., Bill McCarthy, John McDowell, Tom McKean,

Jack Niles, Sandy Paton, Jim Porter, Cathy Preston, Roger Renwick, Ed Richmond, Sigrid Rieuwerts, Neil Rosenberg, Charlie Stewart, Dick Swain and Rosemary Lévy Zumwalt. To them all, *gracias.*

And then – once more and for as much of forever as is left to us – there's Bobby. Thanks. Let's do it all again.

NOTES

The following two abbreviations are used throughout this book:
C.S.P. Scot: *Calendar of the State Papers Relating to Scotland and Mary, Queen of Scots 1547–1563.*
RPC: Register of the Privy Council of Scotland.

1 "'The Bonny Earl of Murray": The Ballad as History', *Midwest Folklore* IX (Fall, 1959), 133–38.
2 (Edinburgh: John Donald, 1986). This is as good a place as any to acknowledge my debt to this book. It was my jumping-off place for serious study, and if I can't quite say it made my book possible, it certainly made my work easier.
3 Flemming G. Andersen, *Commonplace and Creativity: The Role of Formulaic Diction in Anglo-Scottish Traditional Balladry* (Odense: Odense University Press, 1985), and Barre Toelken, *Morning Dew and Roses: Nuance, Metaphor and Meaning in Folksongs* (Champaign: University of Illinois Press, 1995).
4 The best single statement of communal re-creation is still Phillips Barry's brief 'Communal Re-Creation', *Bulletin of the Folk-Song Society of the Northeast* 5 ('1933), 4–6. The most comprehensive attempt to apply the theory of oral composition to ballads is that of David Buchan in *The Ballad and the Folk* (London: Routledge and Kegan Paul, 1972). See also Albert Friedman's eloquent 'The Oral-Formulaic Theory of Balladry – A Re-Rebuttal' in James Porter (editor), *The Ballad Image* (Los Angeles: Center for the Study of Comparative Folklore and Mythology, 1983), pp.215–240.

Prologue

Memory and a sense of history weigh on me like twin copes today. Maybe it's the beautiful fall weather out there, the varying reds and golds against the brilliant blue of the distant sky, and everywhere the leaves coming down. I don't know, but while it's not an up-and-doing frame of mind, it's far from unpleasant. I look out the window, or I run my eyes over the backs of the books along the wall, glad for their presence but not wanting to read them or even take one down just now. Call it daydreaming, call it remembering. Neither is quite the right word for the welter of images and fragments of images evoked by the silent yet always singing voices in the dark at the back of my mind. I often hear them, but they don't always sing the same song. Today one voice comes in high over the others, singing of old violence, feudal fury come to the flashpoint and leading to a late afternoon's bloodletting on the north bank of the Forth across from Edinburgh four hundred years ago, a sordid and brutal business that left a handsome young lord dead and his murderer unpunished. The whole affair has very little to redeem it in terms of either heroism or noble cause, yet from such squalid stuff arose a song that has come down across more than a dozen generations.

Time, said Auden,

> Worships language and forgives
> Everyone by whom it lives,
> Pardons cowardice, conceit,
> Lays its honours at their feet.

We can never know the author of 'The Bonny Earl of Murray', nor those many singers who breathed their lives into it and sped it on its way along the centuries. Deserving of Time's honors as they most certainly are, their names are beyond all conjecture. Why they sang it or what it meant to them, these questions, too, are, as Sir Thomas Browne, said, above Antiquarism, 'not to be resolved by man, nor easily perhaps by spirits'. On the other hand, I *can* remember in some detail where and when I myself first heard it and what it meant to me, and that seems to me to make a solid platform from which to launch this excursion into another country and a past time.

It was the fall of 1949. I was a graduate student in medieval literature at Columbia University, and, when I wasn't reading Chaucer or puzzling out the subtleties of troubador poetry, I was being a folksinger, which meant learning songs from the Lomaxes' big book, Carl Sandburg's *The American Songbag* and records of the Almanac Singers, Burl Ives, and the like. Richard Dyer-Bennet, with his mastery of the guitar and his high clear head voice, was, at that time, absolutely my ideal, and I had been to hear him several times not only at Town Hall but at the YMHA and elsewhere the year before. Now here I was in Town Hall again, center orchestra, third row back, just about the best seats in the house. For a grad student on the GI Bill, I had laid out a bundle for those seats, and I rather hoped my date would be as impressed as I was. I never really had a proper chance to find out, though, for reasons which will become clear in a moment.

House lights down, stage lights up, and Dyer-Bennet walked out on the stage, impeccable as always in full soup-and-fish. He began with 'The Vicar of Bray', followed, as I recall now, by a couple of French songs and Campion's 'When to Her Lute Corinna Sings'. Great, all great. As I expected, it was going to be a good evening. Then about halfway toward intermission came 'The Bonny Earl of Murray', a piece I knew I'd read over quickly in Child at some point but had never heard sung or even imagined still *could* be sung.

I was stunned – there is no better word for it – by this angry lament that a fine young man, the Queen's love, should die so, perhaps by treachery ('Now wae be to thee, Huntly!'), all this to a powerful accompaniment that made it into something between a dead march and a war cry. For that moment I was not in Town Hall but somewhere on what might have been a moor before a swart tower from whose battlement a lone lady forever looked into the distance. Then it was over, and the program went on, but a good half of me never left that moor, and I knew I had to have that song for my own. All the rest of the evening I fought to keep that tune in my head. We met some friends afterward for a few drinks, and I did my best to keep up my end of the chitchat, but I'm sure it was a pretty poor job I made of it. I couldn't wait to get home and get at that song.

A couple of hours later I took down my Sargent/Kittredge one-volume abridgment of Child, broke out my guitar and tried quietly to see what

I could do. It wasn't long, though, before Mother asked with some annoyance if I had any idea what time it was, and that was that for then. Next morning, however, I was back at work, and by supper-time I had whomped out something that almost satisfied me. It wasn't quite 'right' – I was pretty sure of that – and it certainly wasn't Dyer-Bennet, but that was more than made up for by the fact that I now had that song inside me and could call it up for contemplation or singing any time. And I called it up often. It was my favorite song.

Or sometimes, say on a beautiful fall afternoon, it just comes to mind. And I hear Dyer-Bennet singing it once again.

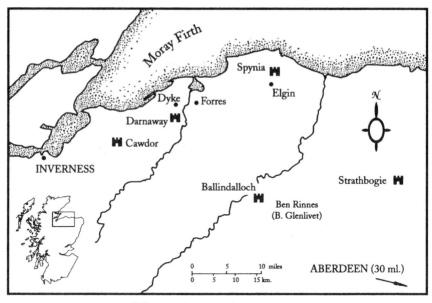

Morayshire and environs

🏰 Castle   • Town / City

Edinburgh and environs

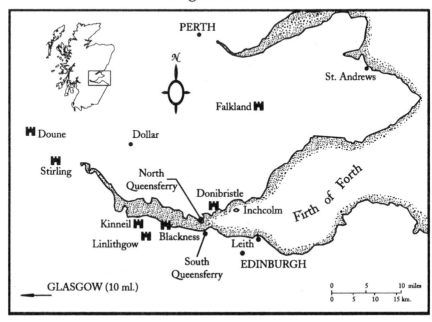

PART ONE

History

CHAPTER ONE

Background

THE SIXTEENTH CENTURY: EUROPE

THAT THE SIXTEENTH century was a time of fierce dynastic European wars is true enough. Habsburgs in Spain, Germany, and Austria struggled first with the French Valois and then with the Bourbons – the favorite battlegrounds being Italy and the Low Countries. But such wars were nothing new. They had been going on for centuries and would continue for centuries to come. What *was* new was Protestantism, a fierce and effective challenging of the ancient authority of the Catholic Church to act as mediator between sinful humanity and God. Trumpeted by men like Luther and Calvin, it led to whole kingdoms breaking from Rome and others being torn by savage religious strife. As might be expected, the two thrusts, the dynastic and the religious, often fell together in ways that make it hard to tell which was uppermost, if indeed either one was, at any one moment.

It was a confused and bloody time, but at least Don John of Austria had broken the back of Turkish seapower at Lepanto in 1571. Things had quieted down in Italy, too, and, as the century rolled towards its final decade, France was so convulsed with its own internal upheavals – both religious and dynastic – that center stage was pretty much left to the struggle between Catholic Spain and Protestant England. Philip of Spain, for reasons far more political than religious, tried to invade England, only to see his huge fleet, the Great Armada, ignominiously destroyed by storm and the Protestant likes of Howard, Drake, and Hawkins. Its invincible wreckage washed up on the rocky shores of the North and Irish Seas for months, and that, it might seem, was that.

But the Armada was only the latest politico-religious challenge Elizabeth had faced in her more than three decades as Queen of England. Ireland was in constant turmoil, and even at home in England her situation was by no means secure. She could never be certain how many of her subjects were really Catholic and how those that were would line up if push came to shove. Seditious Jesuit 'missionaries' seemed to be everywhere, even though Parliament had outlawed them and declared it a felony to harbor them, and the machinations of Mary Queen of Scots with France and Spain continued even while she was a prisoner in England and ended only with her execution in 1587. The Armada's defeat was a welcome breather, but Philip never stopped plotting, and Elizabeth knew that one of his favorite plotting grounds had been and probably would continue to be Scotland. France too – otherwise occupied as she might be – had a long history of interest in Scotland, the so-called 'Auld Alliance', and while French influence there was minimal after Mary's downfall, it was still something to be reckoned with. All of which meant that the whole situation north of the Cheviot Hills bore careful watching, especially since the young Scottish King, James VI, was the leading candidate for the English succession.

SCOTLAND: KING, KIRK, AND COURT

James had his own problems, but they were the same basic ones other European monarchs of the time had to deal with: religion and political power.[1] In one way the religious problem had been 'solved', in that the 'Reformation Parliament' of 1560 had not only broken from Rome by establishing the Kirk of Scotland, it had thoroughly proscribed practice of the Catholic religion. Even so, perhaps as many as a third of the powerful nobles remained Catholic,[2] some secretly, some quite openly, and while that would raise awkward problems, as we shall see, James's larger struggle was with the newly established and very feisty Kirk.

Strongly Calvinist as it was, the Kirk made it clear through the *Second Book of Discipline* (1578), chiefly the work of Andrew Melville, that it was God's spokesman for Scotland and the King should heed it in all matters. 'The preachers,' says Andrew Lang, 'desired the State to be wholly ruled by God's Word, of which they were the infallible interpreters.'[3] James, on the other hand, young as he was, had been doing some thinking of his own, and he had come to believe that he ruled by Divine Right. Thus he was pleased when Parliament in 1584 declared him head of the Kirk, confirmed the institution of Crown-appointed bishops, and declared that affairs of state were not to be dealt with from the pulpit.[4] The Kirk, of course, was furious, calling these decrees 'The Black Acts' and doing all in its power to nullify them. Kirk and King collided in many ways both large and small. When, for example, James had his Queen anointed with oil at her coronation, the Kirk predictably howled its disapproval of such a pagan and Jewish (read Catholic) custom.⁵ It was perfectly clear to James that what was at stake in this confrontation was not merely some theological nicety but his political power itself. 'Reformation Scotland,' says Wormald, 'was in a microcosm only an extended version of the great medieval struggle between the spiritual and temporal powers, with Melville and James VI playing the rôles of pope and emperor.'⁶ As time moved on, though, it was not always clear which of them was standing barefoot in the Canossan snows.

On the more directly political front, James had to deal with a fractious and factioned nobility. It is true that Scotland had been a kingdom for centuries, but it is also true that the real power remained with a landed aristocracy, any faction of which might see fit to kidnap the King (that had happened several times) to further its cause. Such abductions were demonstrations of royal weakness, to be sure, but they also demonstrated that the King's person, as symbolic of a higher authority, had considerable value. But no question about it, that higher authority – in terms of a body of laws and the machinery for their enforcement – had fallen into much disrepair, as a series of premature royal deaths vitiated the necessary strong royal leadership. To begin with, James's grandfather (James V) was only a child in 1513 when his father died at Flodden, and the various administrations of his minority were less interested in Scotland than in their own particular factions. When he died at age thirty in 1542, his infant daughter Mary, James's mother, became Queen. She 'ruled' in absentia for her first nineteen years, and the turbulence of her six-year personal reign needs no rehearsal here. When James became James VI at her abdication in 1567, Scotland was once again ruled by a series of regents with their own agendas. It is safe, therefore, to say that by the time James began his personal rule in 1585, the idea of a strong central government was hardly even a memory, and it was certainly not a memory everyone was interested in reviving. The Borders were notoriously unruly, the clans ruled the Highlands, and the great families – Gordons, Stewarts, Campbells, and the like – held most of the real power and spent a good deal of time plotting, making alliances, and lunging at each other's throats.

LAW AND JUSTICE: KING VS. NOBLES

Yet it would not be right to think of Scotland as a land without law. There *was* statute law and a King's justice to which one could appeal, but they were all too often ignored. The Privy Council complained bitterly about 'the multitude of deadly feuds through which all parties having interest therein spares not to take their private revenge and advantage of others, disdaining to seek remedy by the ordinary form of law and justice, without fear of God or reverence of his authority'.[7]

The *idea* of kingship was always very strong in Scotland, but obviously men simply found the familiar and to-hand mechanisms of direct action through feudal and kinship ties more satisfactory than anything provided 'by the ordinary form of law and justice'. Redress was almost entirely in the hands of the local lords, and a mix of feudal and clan loyalties prevailed. As Keith Brown says, 'strong kinship was thought to be the best protection a man could have', and that kinship worked both ways: a lord's tenants supported him and he supported them.[8] Willingness to invoke the law or to accept any kind of outside arbitration could be interpreted as evidence that a man had no place else to turn, and that – in a society in which personal and family honor were extremely important – was an admission that reflected poorly on both man and lord.

The weakness of the central government vis-à-vis its landed nobility can also be seen in the general expectations a citizen might have of military service in his lifetime. There was no standing army as such, but it was expected that all men would be both ready for duty when called and able to arrive appropriately armed. As far back as 1535 there were laws setting out what weapons a man should have according to the value of his property, and sheriffs held regular – and rather unpopular – 'wapinshawings' (*i.e. musters*) to see to their enforcement.[9] Such service was always a possibility, but it was far more common for a man to serve his immediate lord as a retainer when that lord traveled to Court or otherwise had need of him. A lord's retinue could range from a handful to a sizeable army, depending on the circumstances. At Bothwell's trial in 1567 for the murder of Darnley, for example, the Earl of Argyle, acting as Lord High Justice, 'had a guard of two hundred hackbutters, with matches lighted, to enforce the authority of the Court', while the defendant appeared in Court fully armed, and '*four thousand* of his followers were drawn up at the door'.[10] Even if those figures are inflated, and they very likely are, it should still be noted that the authority of the royal Court was not only being challenged by an earl's retinue, it was being enforced by one, too. Attempts were made to limit by law the size of these retinues. Thus, in 1590 an earl was to be allowed no more than a dozen retainers, all of them unarmed, but such restrictions were widely disregarded.[11]

FEUDING AND VIOLENCE

Basic to all that has been said is the importance of honor, personal honor and family honor, leading to vengeance for slight, itself both leading to and aggravating those long-standing bloodfeuds that were the curse of sixteenth-century Scotland. James recognized early on that the settling of such feuds would be one of his major tasks as King, and in the end he was largely successful. We shall see how he dealt with perhaps the greatest feud of the time, that between Huntly and Moray, but in the 1580s and '90s that feud and many others were at their bloody worst. As an afterthought – but a relevant afterthought – it is worth keeping in mind that the average age of all the nobility of Scotland was about twenty-seven, and while that is not exactly the hot blood of youth, it is certainly the full flow of young manhood and all it implies.

Given, then, that bloodfeud was common, that there were a lot of aggressive young men around – touchy about their honor and skilled in the use of both sword and pistol – and that risk of punishment under law ranged from low to non-existent, we should not be surprised to find a high level of rather adventitious violence. In Edinburgh, where practically everyone carried weapons on the street and a pistol at the belt had become an item of high fashion,[12] we hear time and again of 'frequent slaughters, bloodshed, arson and open robberies, thefts, and oppressions',[13] or of how 'the laird of Airthe and the laird of Wemyss met upon the high street of Edinburgh; and they and their followers fought a very bloody skirmish, where there was many hurt on both sides with shot of pistol.'[14] That the duly appointed officers of the law were not always in control of the situation is made especially clear by the following incident:

> . . . a great number of wicked and seditious persons, craftsmen, inhabitants, of the burgh of Edinburgh, upon the xiii day of May instant, under silence of night, convened themselves together in arms, and, in most treasonable, barbarous and shameful manner, attacked the houses of the provost and one of the bailiffs of the said burgh, struck the dwelling house of the same bailiff with forehammers [*i.e. sledgehammers*], entered therein perforce, and with awful countenance and boasting words compelled him to put at liberty from the tolbooth of the same burgh a malefactor being therein for the time.[15]

Finally, the bloodfeud fury and the need for vengeance often drove men beyond mere killing, as when a party of Gordons dragged their victim outside, shot him dead, and then 'with their drawn swords, cut him all in pieces; and as monsters in nature, left not six inches of his body, arms, legs, and head undivided and cut asunder'.[16] Another victim they killed 'by hanging of him by the bagstones, binding of his head and feet together on the pothook, smoking him to death'.[17] It is hard to imagine men of this kidney ever acceding to arbitration or being satisfied with any sentence meted out by a mere court. Blood called out for blood, which called yet again for blood, and nowhere was that call louder than in the great feud between Huntly and Moray.

THE HUNTLY-MORAY FEUD

It is not possible to trace the Huntly-Moray feud back to any one particular incident, but in a general way there were causes enough to set these two houses against each other. First of all, George Gordon, Fourth Earl of Huntly, had been made Earl of Moray in 1549, but he fell out of favor with the Queen Dowager and was forced to renounce that earldom six years later. However, though stripped of the title, he continued to profit from many of that earldom's revenues. After Mary came to Scotland in 1561 to begin her personal rule, she increasingly saw the powerful Huntly, Catholic though he most certainly was, as unreliable to the point of being dangerous, a judgment that was to prove totally correct. Ultimately Huntly openly opposed her, only to be defeated by her half-brother James Stewart at Corrichie Burn near Aberdeen the next year, at which point Mary conferred the earldom of Moray on James.[18] There was reason enough for animosity between the two families on this head alone, but we can be sure that the Gordons of Huntly being the leading Catholic family in Scotland and the Stewarts of Moray one of the leading Protestant ones added no small aggravation.

There were other annoyances, like the right to certain monies from the bishopric of Moray. The lordship of Spynie was also in dispute, as were certain valuable fishing rights both in Loch Spynie and along the Spey. To sum it all up, the Gordons had been the power in the Northeast for a long time, and the new Stewart house of Moray represented a serious challenge.

The chief Gordon we will be dealing with in the next two chapters is George, Sixth Earl of Huntly. Succeeding his father in 1576 at age fourteen, he was educated in France and became in every way a highly cultivated man, deeply interested in the arts, who in time built his castle at Strathbogie into one of the showplaces of the nation. By very astute maneuvering (including his marriage to the young Duke of Lennox's sister) he became an important person at court. The King loved him deeply, lavishing affection on him in a manner few others, before or since, ever enjoyed, even granting him free access to the royal chamber. Captain of the guard and lieutenant of the north, Huntly sought power, gained it, and knew how to use it effectively, even if that meant that a cultivated gentleman had to ride down his enemies like a savage. 'He butchered the Earl of Moray in a foul murder,' says Willson, 'captured two cooks from an enemy clan and roasted them alive, and adorned the turrets of his castle of Strathbogie with the severed limbs of his foes.[19]

But that gets us ahead of our story.

NOTES

1 An excellent brief survey of Scotland in the sixteenth century can be found in Maurice Lee, Jr., *John Maitland of Thirlestane* (Princeton: Princeton University Press, 1959), pp. 3–20.

2 Jenny Wormald, *Court, Kirk, and Community: Scotland 1470–1675* (Edinburgh: Edinburgh University Press, 1991; first published 1981), p. 133.

3 Andrew Lang, *A History of Scotland from the Roman Occupation*, in four volumes (New York: Dodd, Mead, 1902), vol.ii, p. 351.

4 David Harris Willson, *King James VI & I* (New York: Oxford, 1967), p. 93.

5 Willson, p. 93.

6 Wormald, p. 76.

7 J. H. Burton (editors), *Register of the Privy Council of Scotland* (Edinburgh, 1877–98), vol. iv, p. 686 (3 Nov. 1591). Henceforth, all citations to this source will be abbreviated *RPC*.

8 Brown, *Bloodfeud*, p. 16.

9 David H. Caldwell, 'Royal Patronage of Arms and Amour Making in Fifteenth and Sixteenth Century Scotland.' In David H. Caldwell (editor), *Scottish Weapons and Fortifications 1100–1800* (Edinburgh: John Donald, 1981), p. 73. An excellent picture of the numbers available and the state of their armament can be gleaned from the report of a wapinschawing held in Moray 2 February 1595. See *RPC*, xiv Addenda 1545–1625, pp. 376–380.

10 *Cassell's Old and New Edinburgh*. In three volumes (London: Cassell, n.d.), vol. i, pp. 167–68.

11 Brown, *Bloodfeud*, pp. 251–52.

12 Caldwell, p. 82.

13 *RPC*, iii, p. 524 (3 Nov. 1582).

14 Robert Birrel, 'The Diary of Robert Birrel', in J.G. Dalyell (editor), *Fragments of Scottish History* (Edinburgh, 1798), p. 13. The incident is dated 24 Nov. 1567.
15 *RPC*, iii, p. 567 (15 May 1583).
16 Brown, *Bloodfeud*, p. 32 See *ibid.* and p. 30 for further examples of this sort of excess.
17 William Fraser, *The Chiefs of Grant* (Edinburgh, 1883), vol. iii, p. 178.
18 For a more detailed account of this opposition, see Antonia Fraser, *Mary Queen of Scots* (New York: Delacorte, 1969), pp. 192–203.
19 Willson, p. 99.

CHAPTER TWO

The Road to Donibristle

DOUNE AND MORAY: BEGINNINGS

IN 1528, one William Edmonstone fell from favor, and James V conferred his captaincy of the Castle of Doune on a new favorite, Sir James Stewart of Beath. Unfortunately Edmonstone grudged Sir James his good fortune to the extent that when the two men and their retainers 'met in the High Street of Dunblane' thirteen years later 'a serious fray ensued' in which Sir James was slain.[1] Then in 1563, after almost twenty years of non-entry, Sir James's son, also named James and already Commendator of St. Colme, finally received custody of the castle, and things began to happen to him thick and fast. In January of 1564 he married Margaret Campbell, eldest daughter of the Fourth Earl of Argyle, to begin with; then in 1565 he was knighted by Darnley, and before he knew it he was caught up in the turbulent events of the last two years of Mary's reign. In 1567 he was suspected along with Moray, Morton, Ruthven and others of having had a part in the murder of Riccio. Then, after Mary's abdication in 1567, he was further suspected of being one of her sympathizers and ordered to surrender Doune Castle. He refused, whereupon Lennox attacked and wrested it from him in three days.[2] Ultimately it was returned to his keeping, and in 1581 James VI created him a Lord of Parliament with the title of Doune. He came to hold other offices, such as Member of the Privy Council, a Commisioner of Justiciary, and Collector-General of Revenues. He died in 1590 and is buried at Doune.[3]

It was during those years around the time of Mary's abdication that Sir James's first child was born, and not surprisingly he named him James. Almost certainly he was born at Doune Castle, and while it is impossible to pinpoint the year – the available documents allow a range from 1564 to 1568 – my best guess would be 1567, and from here on all my statements about his age at the time of any particular event will be based on that estimate.[4]

Of his education and upbringing we know nothing, but we can be sure that whatever he got he got at home, not in France like the sons of more prestigious Scottish noble families, notably his future bloodfeud enemy George Gordon of Huntly. But minimal formal schooling would not have set him distinctly apart from other high-born young men of his time. True, the Education Act of 1496 required all substantial barons and freeholders to send their eldest sons to grammar school and even to a university 'so that they may have knowledge and understanding of the laws',[5] but how much that represented the realities of the 1570s is hard to say.

If there is nothing in the record that speaks directly to young James's education, there is a fair amount to show how deeply his father was interested in providing for his fortune. From the beginning right on through the end of his minority (say from 1568 through 1588) we find Sir James acting as 'administrator' or 'tutor' on behalf of 'his son and apparent heir', asserting his right to specific 'teind sheaves' (tithes) or the fruits of certain vicarages, warning tenants and townsmen 'to refrain from meddling with them', taking possession of lands in his son's name, instructing the sheriff in regard to 'forthputtings' and removals, and so on. It is of course possible that young James made many of his own decisions,[6] but at the very least he had the benefit of his father's advice and skill, which meant that by the time of his marriage in 1580 he had land and income from Menteith, Glenfinlas, Donibristle, Aberdour, Dalgety and several other places – rather commodious arrangements for a thirteen-year-old boy.[7]

MARRIAGE AND MINORITY (1580–1587)

If it was Sir James who was largely responsible for building his son's estate, it seems highly likely that he also had a leading part in arranging for his advantageous marriage. It has been suggested that the Earl of Arran had an important hand in this matter,[8] and that may well be, but Sir James was extremely ambitious for his son and very likely set about to exploit for him a neat set of contingencies. When the 'Good Regent' James, First Earl of Moray, was assassinated in 1570, he left a wife and two daughters. His widow soon remarried, this time to the Earl of Argyle and while the Moray earldom stood vacant it was pretty clear that whoever married the eldest daughter Elizabeth would become the Second Earl of Moray *jure uxoris*. In this connection, it will be remembered that Sir James of Doune had married Argyle's sister, and I have no doubt that, seeing the possibilities, he set about to convince his sister-in-law that his thirteen-year-old son James would make an excellent match for her fifteen-year-old daughter Elizabeth.

He was successful, and in January of 1580 young James received from the King a gift of the ward and marriage of the Regent's daughters,[9] and just a year later on 23 January 1581 he married Elizabeth himself. It does not seem to have been a universally popular marriage, it being 'to the great misliking of the best part of the Earl of Moray's friends to see his daughter so meanly married as to the Abbot of St. Combe's son',[10] but even so James appears to have been recognized immediately as Second Earl of Moray, and the couple received a pension of £500 a year from the King out of the bishopric of Aberdeen. However, both he and his wife were still decidedly minors, and for the next five or six years all of their legal documents were either executed 'with the consent of Lord Doune' or by the young Earl as 'son and apparent heir to Sir James Stewart of Doune'.[11] Not only, then, had Sir James become a Lord himself, but he had no small leverage over an earl.

Clearly Doune was an aggressive and ambitious man, an extremely active councillor to the King,[12] and, recognizing that his son's new eminence considerably augmented his own, he was to put a great deal of energy over the next decade into attempting to direct and control the young Earl's activities. But the young Earl seems to have had ideas – not very surprising ones – of his own. All the chroniclers agree that he was extremely well-favored, one contemporary speaking of him as 'the lustiest youth' and another going well beyond that, claiming that 'Moray was the most warlike man both in courage and person, for he was a comely personage, of a great stature and strong of body like a kemp (*i.e. champion*)'.[13] These are, to be sure, descriptions of the man at the time of his death, but even a more contemporary account describes him as 'a young man of xvii years of age; of a very tall stature but', it adds by way of qualification, 'of little proof,' and a 1582 survey of those who stood for or against the Duke of Lennox simply dismisses him as 'very young'.[14] I don't think it is stretching matters to see him in his late teens as a young buck, the world in his pocket, flexing his considerable muscles and wanting to be where the fun and action were while not being particularly interested in the humdrum aspects of lordship or even of being a husband – those very things his father was of course deeply concerned about. At any rate, although the details are not always entirely clear, that is how I read a rather remarkable series of letters from Lord Doune to his son in March of 1582.

In the first letter, Doune is in Edinburgh, Moray in Doune. Moray had recently failed to keep an appointment with his wife, but, Doune says, 'I have made your excuse so well to your wife that the same is marvelously well accepted'. She looks forward to meeting him next week in Campbell – probably Castle Campbell near Dollar – where 'my Lord and my Lady' (his mother-in-law and her present husband, the Earl of Argyle) will also be. He goes on:

> Therefore I pray you that you ride not to Kinneil nor to any other place . . . for if ye be absent when she looks to meet with you, ye will crab her at the heart, for my lady her mother and I are grown very great (*i.e. close*) again. And the point of her coming to Campbell is to make a new appointment with me, which you will cast into confusion [*if you don't show up*] . . . Therefore, son, I pray you stir not out of the place where you are till I make you new advertisement. In the meantime be merry and blithe, and command Andrew Stewart to get men to the park dyke before the sowing comes on. And . . . look that ye see them at work and that they be busy until my homecoming.[15]

Fatherly advice (with a certain clear self-interest involved) plus some instructions about farm work. But the Earl never received this letter since he was already at Kinneil, whence he evidently complains in a second letter that he is ill-provided with money. The father's reply the next day (8 March) shows clear annoyance. He is glad his son is short of money, he says, and his having given false excuses to his wife will anger her. However, he agrees to send him what little money he has, 'not to play at cards and dice but to do necessary small business with', a line which could be no more than all-purpose fatherly admonishment but is more likely aimed directly at what he knows to be the case. Do not fail, he concludes, to come to Doune Monday, lest matters with your mother-in-law be seriously upset.[16]

Lord Doune is obviously trying hard to make everything work the way he knows it should, but he is getting precious little help from his son, who, as the next letter dated a week later makes clear, not only hasn't shown up for the Monday meeting but plans to go back to Kinneil. The exasperated father goes on about family relations and agriculture:

> You know that the last time that you were there your good mother and wife were both angry because ye came not forward to visit them. Wherefore ye shall come hither to this town [*i.e. Edinburgh*] to visit your wife and be in Kinneil one night on the way and another night going home again.

I marvel that you did not set the men to work on the park dyke before sowing time, seeing I wrote to you for that same . . . Your wife is very angry . . . as you will know at meeting.[17]

Another letter perhaps a month or two later suggests that since his wife cannot come south – presumably they are both at Darnaway – until eight days after Whitsunday, he himself should not come before then but wait and be her convoy, 'for in doing that you shall do yourself both honour and profit and close the mouths of your enemies that speak largely on that behalf.'[18] I take that statement in two related ways: first, that the word is out that all is not well between the Earl and the Countess – and it should not be forgotten that he held his title only through that marriage – and, second, that he is not spending as much time as he should at his seat in Darnaway, being too much at Court or at his pleasure elsewhere (a letter from his mother a year later regretting that he has gone to court and desiring him to hasten home again suggests much the same thing).[19] Meanwhile, the letter concludes, ask your wife 'to speak to her mother and get you the silver to get you your clothes and other necessaries that you have difficulty with' – probably a fatherly rebuff of another request for money.

The Earl's irresponsible and absentee ways may have been putting a strain on his marriage, but the fact remains that sometime in the early 'eighties Elizabeth bore him a son, and a contract dated 22 September 1586 makes it clear they were to have a second child soon. It is an interesting document:

James Lord Doune and Dame Margaret his spouse promise . . . to entertain in board and bed, with necessaries apertaining thereto accordingly, the said James Earl of Murray and Dame Elizabeth Stewart with four gentlemen to serve them and one boy to fill the cup to them, one gentlewoman to serve my lady, their eldest son with his nurse and one woman to wash their linen . . . and straw to feed seven horses.[20]

The contract is to continue 'until the said Dame Elizabeth shall be delivered of her bairn presently in her womb or so long as the said James, Earl of Moray, and his spouse pleases or can agree with his said father and mother, so that it exceed not one year'. For this service the Earl is to sign over his £500 pension for that year and, as a final touch, 'to follow the counsels and admonitions of my said father in all things apertaining to his honour and mine'. There is always a danger of reading too much into such a document – such carefully spelled-out family arrangements may, for instance, have been quite common at the time – but knowing the parties involved I see Lord Doune protecting himself from a son and daughter-in-law whose expensive tastes and demands as higher nobility could prove excessive. There are several examples available not only of the younger couple's extravagance but also of how often that extravagance came to roost on Doune's shoulders. One in particular – a Pittarro merchant who writes Doune regretting he can no longer stay execution of letters against Moray and his wife for 'great sums of money which they owe him' – could well have been on the father's mind at the very time the contract was drawn up![21] Further, demands that Elizabeth 'agree' with her in-laws and that her husband – for all his being an earl – play the part of dutiful son, suggest by their very presence that the two couples' relationship was problematic at the time.

Even so, in the next year (1587) other letters show Lord Doune continuing to be active in his son's affairs. He has arranged a £1000 loan for him 'with your good friend and mine Andrew Abercrombie and Alan Cowtis . . . which they have freely granted and will have for their security my handwriting and my wife's'. He has also arranged for three thousand merks to be 'delivered to Mr. Robert your servant on Tuesday', so long as Moray makes a meeting with the lender at Donibristle Sunday night. Therefore 'haste you the sooner to take away all occasion of delay on his part', and come a day early so we may consult 'on your hard turns that fall in great heaps'. He closes with 'hearty commendations to your bedfellow', who has not been well, 'and pray her to good hearting and give her strength to get on her feet for to meet the perilous turns that are practised against her and her bairns'. It is not, by any measure, a cheerful letter.[22] There is no way of knowing what specific unpleasant 'turns' Doune is referring to, but we can be quite sure they involved George Gordon, Sixth Earl of Huntly.

TROUBLES WITH HUNTLY, THE ARMADA, BRIG O'DEE (1587–1589)

In November Lord Doune writes to the Countess of Argyle that there is trouble with Huntly over the baillery of Spynie.[23] As for Moray, he requests and is granted license to 'pass forth of the realm to France, Flanders, Germany, or other parts beyond the sea for the space of three years',[24] and a letter from his father telling him to stand not 'but go forward, and by the grace of God I shall keep trust'[25] may well refer to this proposed venture, though it seems strange to me that under the circumstances he would encourage it. The trip never came off, but a letter to Moray from his Countess saying that she has 'spoken with all the gentlemen in this country [*i.e. Darnaway*] who have promised to do very well in your absence'[26] may indicate how seriously Moray was considering it. In that same letter, she pleads with him to attend to a certain matter, the neglect of which 'will cause many here to have an evil opinion of you'. Everything suggests Moray's rather low level of concern with his responsibilities, and the paired facts that no letter *from* him is datelined Darnaway and that many letters *to* him are so dated support that suggestion rather well.

On the other hand, the threat of the Great Armada *did* bring him north for a while in mid-1588 under a commission to watch the coast between Inverness and the Water of Spey 'both Highland and Lowland'.[27] Huntly too – in spite of anxieties about his loyalties – had such a commission, and rumors about what was going on in the Northeast were plenty. In fact, according to an English intelligencer, word was brought to King James on August 11 'how the Spanish fleet is landed in the Firth of Moray, in the Earl of Moray's country, 100 miles from Edinburgh', and the Earl, 'always suspected as a papist . . . is now in his own country'.[28] The report of the landing was mistaken, of course, as for all practical purposes was the designation of Moray as a papist (we will return to the question of his religion later). Meantime the Armada disappeared, and the so-called Northern Earls could get back to the serious business of squabbling among themselves, which they most certainly did.

In spite of his general absenteeism, and young and inexperienced as he was, Moray seems to have taken hold of the idea at about this time that he was in a position to challenge Huntly and even possibly to replace him as the generally acknowledged Lord of the North,[29] and it must be admitted that at first Huntly played right into his hands. To begin with, in February of 1589, a young man by the name of Pringle was captured in England bearing letters from Huntly both to the Duke of Parma and – worse yet – to Philip of Spain lamenting the Armada had not landed in Scotland, where it would have found countless allies. No question about it, the documents are very damning, and Elizabeth in understandable and unmistakeable fury sent them to James with a note of dismay that he seemed to hold such traitors 'near and dear . . . Good Lord,' she said, 'methinks I do dream. No king a week could bear this!'[30]

Undeniably, though, James bore it, but just as undeniably he was badly shaken. At first report he refused even to read the letters; then, when he did, he insisted they were forgeries, but finally, accepting them as genuine, he confined Huntly to Edinburgh Castle (though he let his wife and servants join him and even dined with him there himself).[31] A letter he wrote him at the time has more of a disappointed lover's sorrow about it than the fury of a monarch betrayed.[32]

Moray saw a chance here and moved quickly to have Huntly put to the horn – that is, declared an outlaw – but his servant who carried the message to Banff barely escaped with his life at the hands of the Gordons there.[33] In addition, Moray found that his own people were constantly being harassed by 'limmers' and 'broken men', and it doesn't take much imagination to see that Huntly, angered at being horned, was behind a good share of these raids. If Moray had been counting on some kind of popular revulsion against a traitorous papist lord, he had been mistaken: Huntly was still in charge on the land. And, since all the King did was put Huntly in ward for eight days, Moray had gained nothing from his constant presence at Court either.[34] As 'an advertiser from Scotland' wrote to Walsingham, 'My lord of Huntly is indeed a great courtier and knows more of the King's secrets than any man at this present moment does'. He wrote that back in 1587, but, in spite of such exasperations as the letters just mentioned, it was still true in 1589.[35] Moray had not yet learned – if in fact he ever did learn – how dearly the King loved Huntly, nor how, like a true lover, he could forgive him anything.

Moray was to have another even more dramatic chance to learn that lesson a month later. So sure of his power was Huntly that – along with Errol, Crawford and Bothwell – he mounted an open rebellion, raising an army of three thousand and taking over Perth and Aberdeen, evidently fully expecting that the King would panic into abject capitulation. But the King did no such thing. Penniless as he was, and with no more authority than adhered to the name of King (which at the moment wasn't all that much), James raised his own small army and headed north to confront the rebels at Brig o'Dee to the south of Aberdeen. The odds were three to one against him, but he surprised everybody by standing his ground. 'His Majesty would not so much as lie down on his bed,' wrote a member of the expedition, 'but went about like a good captain encouraging us.'[36] Huntly and the others figured the consequences of open battle with the King and, deciding against it, allowed themselves to be taken back to Edinburgh and tried for treason. They could justly have been beheaded, but all got off with pardons, remissions, or, in Huntly's case, a few months of easy confinement.

Again, love played a major part, but James was also shrewd enough to realize that Huntly would be useful to him in another struggle. As Andrew Lang put it, 'in a country where the pretensions of the preachers were really the most threatening danger to the Crown, Huntly, a Catholic, could be relied on against the preachers'.37 Moray might reasonably have hoped that some advancement would come his way from his rival's expected downfall, but clearly that hope was vain. He gained nothing from Brig o'Dee (why, I have wondered, did he not seize the opportunity to march north with his King?). Soon Huntly was as powerful as ever – and the raids on Moray's lands and tenants continued and even increased.

TROUBLES AT DARNAWAY

A series of letters from servants to their absent Lord show rather clearly what things were like around Darnaway at this time. William Douglas writes from nearby Earlsmill asking about the three thieves they had caught:

> Your Lordship has promised to send me a commission to give them a trial. The keeping of them does no good . . . Therefore I desire your Lordship to send me a commission with this bearer, and God willing they shall be punished according to their offenses.

He goes on to say there is a rumor that some 'broken men' [*i.e. outlaws*] will be released locally soon, and he 'desires your Lordship to advise me, in case they come onto your Lordship's lands, what your Lordship's will is that I do therein'. The letter is full of questions and housekeeping matters like 'Haste the seeds home to the gardener with this bearer'.38 That same day Douglas, in an even longer letter to the Countess, says that 'loose men' have threatened to kill him if he tries to gain entry to some land that had been given to his wife.39 The tone suggests that the Countess is far more in touch with Darnaway matters than her husband is.

Another servant, James Torrie of Logie, says that raiders drove off his cattle while he was away with the Earl in February:

> They took them the space of two miles beyond the Water of Findhorn through the Forest of Drumine, and were it not that good friends and neighbors within the Forest of Darnaway roused and rode and followed them until they were compelled to leave the cattle for fear of their lives, I had never gotten one beast of them again.40

He is 'daily in fear of my own life by limmers', he says, 'but if your Lordship was in the country they would stand in more awe and I would fear them the less'.

A letter from one George Dunbar continues this sad litany:

> I am daily cumbered with complaints of your Lordship's poor folks how they are molested by great and small who are neighbors to your Lordship's lands, and no man to find fault with the same. Your bailiff is out of the country and no man here knows where he is. Your Lordship's chamberlain will . . . concern himself only with such things as will make his wife's bairns sure of some rent.

One such neighbor, he continues, has caused ditches to be made on his Lordship's land and appropriates the same to the tenants' injury. Another man, 'young Garnside', troubles tenants in their pasturage, and 'the men of Rothes' seek to appropriate a glen called Corremel. Dunbar says he has told the tenants 'to defend their marches', but they are overwhelmed. 'This is one part of the news of this country,' he concludes, 'but I am more angry that your Lordship's land is lawless than anything that ever I saw!'[41] It is a long and careful letter, and while Dunbar's exasperation with his master's lordship never actually breaks through, neither is it ever very far beneath the surface.

In all evenhandedness, I should raise the objection that it may be unfair to judge Moray's lordship on the basis of this handful of letters. Is it possible, for instance, that they represent the exception and not the rule of his behavior, emphasizing as they of course would what happened in those rare times when he was away? It *is* possible, to be sure, but since their details are so consistent with his character as we have already come to know it, it is not likely. As another servitor said, 'his Lordship has too few Stewarts dwelling upon his lands of Moray'.[42] That criticism is couched in general terms, but perhaps the writer was saying as specifically as he felt he could that the Earl was too much away, that Huntly's people were encroaching on his lands, and that his own officers weren't doing their jobs.

THE KING'S MARRIAGE AND BOTHWELL'S 'STEWART FACTION' (1589–1590)

In no way can 1589 be thought of as a good year for Moray's cause, even though it represented something of a bad year for Huntly, what with the

Spanish letters and Brig o' Dee. Moray still found himself outmaneuvered at Court and overpowered on the land, and 1590 was to be no better for him. He began it by being charged to enter himself in ward in Stirling. The specific charge is not clear, but he went to the house there of one Giles Graham, 'accompanied by nine or ten horsemen, his servants'.43 How long this ward continued we do not know, but evidently he was soon clear of it, because in March he was appointed a Commissioner to enforce the Acts against Jesuits and Seminary Priests in his lands.44 It was nothing much, there being several score such appointments nationwide – Huntly, for example, held such an appointment for *his* lands – but at least it shows that Moray was out of ward and in his country by then.

During these early months of 1590 the King was out of Scotland, having gone to bring back his Queen-to-be, the Princess Anne of Denmark. That venture had several strange aspects. First of all, in late 1589 Anne had actually made three attempts to reach Scotland, each time being turned back by storms that the Danes – well ahead of the Scots in their interest in the powers of darkness – attributed to witchcraft. Then, as Admiral of Scotland, Francis Stewart, Earl of Bothwell, was ordered to go after her, but his estimates of the cost of such an expedition were so high that Chancellor John Maitland dismissed the plan, suggesting instead that the King go himself. Uncharacteristically, considering the danger involved, James agreed, and – considering that the Chancellor had opposed the marriage in the first place (something the Queen never forgave him for) – he decided to take Maitland with him. But perhaps the final strangeness was that Bothwell was given considerable advisory power – perhaps the chief advisory power – in the King's absence.45

It seemed then, and still seems today, an odd choice for the King to make – Bothwell being, as we shall see, very much of a loose cannon – but made it was, and Bothwell set about exploiting his new power by increasing his efforts to establish a strong Stewart faction at Court, in which venture he counted heavily on the support of Athol and, especially, his cousin-german Moray. It was not a new alliance – an English intelligencer having noted back in November that the three lords seemed to be forming some sort of a head 'against the Earl of Huntly, who of late has moved some quarrel against the Earl of Moray, which caused him and his wife to retire to the south'46 – but it had promise of being a powerful one.

Moray and his wife got right to work. There was evidently a rich salmon fishery along the River Spey to which they had a traditional claim, and when Huntly put boats and nets in there they not only had him put to the horn but had letters of treason issued against him. There was a good deal of legal back-and-forth on this matter, but in June Huntly went to the Privy Council and declared that since he had 'passed personally to the shore or waterside of the said fishing and had his cobbles [*a kind of boat*] drawn from the said water and discharged his fishers of any further fishing with the said cobbles, nets or coracles', the letters of treason and horning should be suspended.47 They were, and, what is more, after the Maytime excitement of both his homecoming and the coronation of his Queen had died down, the King was not long in letting Moray know that he 'mislikes no order in the realm worse than that of passing to the horn'.48 Stewart though he was, he had no interest in encouraging a Stewart faction in his court. Nor was Maitland ready to get involved, as Ambassador Bowes reported back to London:

> The Earl of Moray hath dealt effectually with the Chancellor [Maitland] to draw him to subscribe the bond with the Stewarts. The Chancellor acquainted Bowes with his refusal to enter into that association, which shall one day stir some trouble in this realm.49

The Ambassador was right, and the trouble would not be long in coming.

MORE TROUBLE WITH HUNTLY OVER SPEY AND SPYNIE

The Spey fishing rights continued to rankle. In August Moray's cousin William Stewart of Seton wrote him a long letter that – while it nowhere specifies its subject – certainly has to do with that matter, although it is so bristling with anxious instruction and encouragement that it may well refer to a good deal more. Moray's enemies, he says, are very busy taking such steps, evidently both in the courts and elsewhere, as will serve their turn. 'They talk a great deal about how their possession shall serve them for a good claim, and that they shall cut your tent ropes if you come there.' He continues angrily:

> I cannot abide the proud speaking of these snafflers . . . My Lord, you had never the like to do since you came to manhood, so that by the handling of this turn you shall get esteem or simple contempt of all men, and [*if you don't take strong measures*] it shall give occasion to every man bordering your lands to oppress your tenants and shame your self . . . For as God lives, rather than have you not do this turn

as you should, I had rather for my own part be banished from the country all my days . . .

My Lord, I will request you to consider this letter . . . and provide remedy, for I see what they are doing daily, and shall advise you thereof, so that I will not be at fault, and if after advisement you neglect the same yourself, the burden will lie on your own shoulders.[50]

That anyone should feel compelled even to send such a letter to his Lord shows deep concern that that Lord may *not* do what has to be done, and the record suggests that in the present instance that concern was justified. To be sure, toward the end of August Moray and his Countess had letters of inhibition issued against Huntly, but that lord quite predictably ignored them.[51] Then, as if in further answer, Huntly turned over Spynie Castle, another contested property, to Alexander Lyndsay, who, according to an English intelligencer, was 'the King's best beloved minion – a proper man and,' he adds significantly, 'Huntly's wholly'.[52] Moray was unable – or unwilling – to challenge him, seeming to be, as Keith Brown says, 'paralysed into inaction'.[53] Stewart of Seton must have thrown up his hands in despair, but, as he says, the burden was on Moray's shoulders.

THE RESTIVE CLANS AND THE DARNAWAY INCIDENT (1590)

Even so, all was not going smoothly for the mighty Huntly, as long-standing local and clan squabbles began to heat up considerably. The Macintoshes were restive with his lordship, and so were the Grants, among whom a recent incident brought things to a boil. John Gordon had married the widow of Grant of Ballindalloch, and the tutor of that house, John Grant, killed one of Gordon's servants in a quarrel. Spottiswoode tells the story of what followed thus:

> Gordon pursuing him before the justice, for not appearing he [*the tutor*] was denounced rebel, and commission given to the earl of Huntly as sheriff of the county to apprehend him. The earl making search for him cometh to the house of Ballindaloch, and after some resistance taketh it by force, but findeth not the tutor. This the family of the Grants interpreting to be done in their disgrace, they betook themselves to the patrociny [*i.e patronage*] of the earl of Moray, and with them the clan Chattan and divers of the surname of Dunbar did join.

These defections to the enemy were a far more serious matter than the death of a servant, and Huntly treated them very seriously indeed:

> Huntly offending that any in those parts should make head against him, and having understood that the earls of Athol and Moray were to meet these clans in Forres, for making up a confederacy, did assemble his friends, and went thither to dissolve the meeting.[54]

Macintosh, Grant, ClanChattan, and Calder [*Cawdor*] were working hard to convince Moray that now was the time for him – with their strong support – to make head against Huntly, and evidently he was paying close attention.[55] But when the conspirators received word that Huntly was on his way with several hundred men they wisely decided to disperse in order, as Ambassador Bowes put it, 'to provide better for him'.[56] Moray withdrew to Darnaway, and Huntly chose to follow him. Whether or not he planned to attack is not quite certain, but what is certain is that some of his men started riding around the castle firing off shots and generally hallooing. Not surprisingly, those within the castle returned the fire, and John Gordon – he who had married the widow of Ballindalloch! – was killed, 'shot in the mouth with an harquebuss'.[57] Huntly's own account of what happened when he reached Darnaway is rather interesting:

> Petitioner [*i.e. Huntly*] had directed thither an officer of arms, with a dozen of witnesses, to ask delivery of certain malefactors; but before the officer and witnesses approached within half a mile of the castle, there issued forth of the same a certain [*number*] of the said Earl of Moray's and the Laird of Grant's, Caddell's, and McIntosh's servants, of their special cause, who pursued the officer and witnesses, discharged pistolets at them, and then entered again within the said Castle, forth whereof they shot and discharged great pieces of artillery, harquebuses of found [*i.e. of cast metal*] and culverins, notwithstanding any signs of peace and holding up of napkins in token thereof; and at last slew the late John Gordon, brother to Sir Thomas Gordon of Cluny, knight.[58]

'A BROYLL HATH FALLEN OUT . . .' (1591)

A furious Huntly withdrew, but only to regroup. 'To be revenged of this affront,' says Spottiswoode, 'Huntly gathereth forces to invade the earl of Moray; and he [*Moray*], assisted by the earl of Athol, his cousin, prepareth to

defend. The convocations,' he adds, 'were great on either side.'[59] Chancellor
Maitland was concerned enough to write directly to Lord Burghley that
there had 'a broyll fallen out . . . which has set the whole north in two parts,
having taken arms on both sides'.[60] This shooting could well have been
the cap to set off the whole Northeast powderkeg, but the King stepped
in, and for some reason everyone involved listened. Huntly's commission
to apprehend John Gordon's killer was revoked, both sides were ordered
to discharge their forces, and the two principals were commanded to
ward, Huntly at St. Andrews, Moray at Stirling. 'Charges were directed
to command Athol home,' says Spottiswoode, 'and inhibit Huntly from
coming west of the river Spey and Moray not to come on the east of
Findhorn. This course did restrain them,' he concludes, 'but gave not
an end to these troubles.'[61] Huntly never actually got to St. Andrews,
however, and by mid-December all three principals – Huntly, Moray
and Athol – were in Edinburgh, having been sent for by the King,
but they came 'with greater numbers than the proclamation appointed'.[62]
Bothwell was there too with his retainers, which means that the streets of
Edinburgh were alive with Stewarts, confident of their strength, armed
to the teeth, and spoiling for a fight with the great Earl of Huntly.

The King and his Council were unhappy with the situation but found
they could in no way settle it. What they did was to order both Huntly
and Moray to give caution (*i.e. security*) of £2,000 Scots to keep the
peace. Further, in an attempt to defuse the local powderkeg, they sent
Huntly home while restraining – albeit against their will – the Stewarts
in Edinburgh. But while they were there they tried to cajole English
Ambassador Bowes into lobbying the King in their favor, a move in
which they were at least moderately successful.[63] Nevertheless, things
remained tense, as Bowes reported to Burghley in late January of 1591:

> The griefs amongst Huntly against Moray, Athol, and others in the
> north continue and are increased by the cuff that Moray gave openly
> in the Tolbooth before the Council to John Drummond, servant to
> Huntly and in especial credit [*with him*]. Moray and Athol remain
> still here, seeking to have leave to return [*home*], which hitherto they
> can not obtain.[64]

And if Huntly had been raiding Moray's lands, it is clear that Moray had
been doing at least some raiding of his own, since one Walter Kinnaird of
Cubbin complained that Moray and his servants had frequently cast down
his dykes, broken in the doors of his house, and threatened his life.[65]

Huntly, meanwhile, evidently decided to return to Court, accompanied, much to the King's displeasure, by a sizeable armed band. 'The King's goodwill towards him continues,' wrote Bowes, 'but he likes not of his repair hither in this forcible sort.' Moray and Athol liked not of it either and began right away to make preparations. Again Bowes:

> Moray and Athol hearing of his coming sent to all their friends, and Moray rode off to Bothwell at Kelso, whereat the King is much offended. Bothwell and other Stewarts have warned their friends to attend here, but the King has given order to restrain them, and sent to Bothwell to remain at home. He likewise sent John Drummond – Huntly's servant in great credit [*and the man Moray struck in the Tolbooth!*] – to Huntly to will him to retire to his house: it is uncertain what he will do. Moray and Athol, seeking this day to have spoken with the King, could not have access, wherewith they are deeply wounded.[66]

The whole affair was a desperate muddle, with no satisfactory solution in sight. By mid-February Moray and Athol were finally permitted to leave Edinburgh, whereupon they headed north to Forres, where, with the support of the lairds of Grant, Caddell, Macintosh and others, they again considered themselves 'strong enough to encounter Huntly in his own bounds without the aid of the King'.[67] Huntly, meanwhile, had not been idle, having established his forces at Elgin, just twelve miles away. 'He has increased his retinue by fifty gentlemen,' said Bowes, 'allowing to every one of them two geldings. He has drawn to Elgin many of his Highlanders, who daily spoil all passengers and many inhabitants thereabouts.'[68] Not only that, he ordered the old cathedral fortified and manned, which brought impotent howls of protest from the burgesses.[69]

With the whole Northeast once again ready to explode, the King had to do something, and on 16 March the Privy Council issued the following order:

> George, Earl of Huntly, not to pass bewest the Water of Spay, James, Earl of Moray, not to cross be-east the Water of Findhorn, and John, Earl of Athol, not to repair benorth the Skarkeith, till they have his Majesty's licence, nor yet to invade or pursue each other in any way, under pain of rebellion.[70]

I doubt that the requisite shifts actually took place this time any more than they had taken place three months earlier – Huntly, for instance, would have had to desert Elgin and pull back eight miles. Nor is there evidence of any reconciliation growing out of this order, but the King's intervention does seem to have cooled things down once again for a couple of months.

BOTHWELL OUTLAWED

Enters on the scene again the enigmatic and energetic figure of Bothwell, who in April of 1591 suddenly found himself accused of complicity in witchcraft and even of having participated in the notorious North Berwick Hallowe'en Sabbat of 1589.[71] Bothwell claimed the whole business was a plot by Maitland to ruin him, and he may well have been correct, but, be that as it may, he was summoned to answer for it and warded meantime in Edinburgh Castle.

Whatever Bothwell's motives were for involving himself in witchcraft, and however large or small that involvement may in fact have been, the King – always morbidly fascinated by witchcraft – was instinctively and totally convinced that he *was* involved, and for ever after he both hated and feared Bothwell beyond all men. 'All the king's energies were henceforth directed toward punishing him for his alleged crime,' said Maurice Lee, 'and anyone who spoke well of him or was in any way connected with him was apt to find himself unpleasantly implicated.'[72] Unfortunately for Moray, though, he was Bothwell's cousin-german, and the King could never entirely forget that unpleasant little fact. Both furious and desperate, Bothwell tried to rally his friends to come to his aid, but it so happened that most of them had been urged – perhaps forced is a better word – to leave Edinburgh. On May 27 he wrote to Moray, his 'very good lord and brother', complaining that 'matters here go otherwise than I looked for' and that he is to be put on trial:

> I understand your Lordship has a promise of his Highness that he shall be present at that trial which will in no way be closed to you, and therefore I must request your Lordship for my cause to be present here, to the end that you may see my innocence made known to all the world. Not that you should request any benefit for me at his Highness's hands but that I may receive the most extreme trial that can be had tending to equity, law and good conscience. . . . And if from this trial your Lordship and other friends shall absent

yourselves I doubt not God shall try the same to his glory and my perpetual honour and comfort.[73]

If that last sentence suggests that Bothwell was a bit dubious how many of his friends would actually show up, his dubiety about Moray was on the money, as can be seen by that lord's waffling response:

My servant Andrew Stewart has shown me that your Lordship is desirous that I should come to Edinburgh with diligence for your cause. I have such earnest causes of my own to do that it is not possible to me to come so shortly, as this bearer Andrew Stewart will show your Lordship. I understand that there will be a sufficient number of your friends in Edinburgh to be cautioners for you. And if the matter stands on my presence and cannot otherwise be settled, I shall be ready to come on your notice.[74]

'So shortly' does not ring quite true three weeks after the request, especially since Moray was not at Darnaway but at Doune, no more than a good day's ride from Edinburgh. Clearly he did not wish to place himself so openly at cross purposes with his King, but at least he got a letter off to Maitland asking that 'this action not depend upon my presence, but that others of my Lord Bothwell's friends may stand cautioners'.[75] I am sure that no-one was fooled by the young Earl's trimming. Certainly Bothwell read the wind, and three days later, after a visit from Maitland, he 'escaped' the Castle and spent the next several months as an outlaw, raising his own particular kind of hell and keeping everyone just a little off balance. He will re-enter our story directly again before too long.

THE FIGHTING INTENSIFIES: SPEY FISHINGS AND SPYNIE'S MEN (1591)

Meanwhile the fighting in the Northeast intensified, and Huntly was having by far the better of it. He launched yet another attack on the Spey fishings in July. 'Huntly,' Ambassador Bowes reported, 'hath caused the cobbles of Moray's fishings to be cut to his great loss', and apparently all Moray was able to do about it was file an official complaint.[76] To be sure, the fighting went back and forth, and both sides were dealing in brutality and just plain nastiness. An English correspondent has left us a vivid picture:

In the north the Earl of Moray, the Lord of Grant, a great man in the Highlands, besides Macintosh and such-like, gathered, killing eighty or a hundred men in one day of Huntly's friends, not even sparing the beasts and cattle that they cannot carry away, but killing three or four hundred a day. Whereupon Huntly got leave from the King . . . to go against them with fire and sword. Huntly treacherously sent to a principal great man to say that a certain Earl known to be his friend was hunting near his house, and would come but to his door, not alighting, and drink. The gentleman, simple, not distrusting, himself, three sons and servants came out, with bread, ale, and wine to give him entertainment: but who should it be but the Earl of Huntly, who with his company shot and slew with pistols the nobleman, three of his sons and some servants . . . In revenge, the friends of those persons that were slain have sought out young of Huntly's friends learning abroad at schools, cruelly killing them.[77]

Moray seems to have remained in the south at Doune, but a couple of letters from his servant John Leslie show what things were like at Darnaway during the summer of 1591. Both have to do with problems with Lord Spynie, but it should be remembered that Spynie, Alexander Lindsay, was given his place by Huntly and owed him manrent. In the first letter, Leslie says that one of Moray's tenants, David Ross, had switched his allegiance to Spynie, and a few days later another tenant came to him 'having in his hand six arrows that David Ross's son had shot at him but had not hurt him'. That was too much for Leslie, who immediately took out after Ross and, having caught up with him, whipped him 'with a belt four and twenty and so beat his men that I trow they shall not be well before Whitsunday'. When Spynie got word 'that the first man that ever he gave maintenance to in Moray had gotten the greatest shame that ever was done to a gentleman', his fury knew no bounds, and, says Leslie, 'he thought there was nothing to content him but my life', adding that he will have to bear this feud until his Lordship comes north. But he needs advice immediately:

Therefore, My Lord, send word what thinks Your Lordship best to be done with David Ross, for if Your Lordship suffer this opposition it will cause greater men than he to mistake Your Lordship. If Your Lordship would have his life, send me word and I shall either get it for you or get you one as good.[78]

Obviously Leslie is ready – and small wonder! – to go for blood, but not without his master's backing, and he seems concerned that Moray may hang back, thus encouraging Spynie or, worse yet, Huntly to make the next move. That concern surfaces more directly in the next letter. He and George Dunbar have taken Spynie's men, John and David Ross, 'limmers . . . who had oppressed your poor men of the thanedom', but he has heard that Moray has been asked to let them go on caution. 'If you so do,' Leslie warns, 'the country will cry out on it, for they are guilty in six or seven points!' He regrets that His Lordship had not left a commission for the execution of such men, but even so, he has written to Mr. Andrew ten days ago 'to have him come here to execute them, but I've received no answer yet'. He complains that Moray is 'over slow of your instructions, making Your Lordship to be ill-served'. As for other news, 'my Lord of Huntly has all his people in readiness with nine days' provisions, but where he goes to God knows. The rumour here is he is going to Inverness to hold a court, and in his homecoming again he'll take up a Mackintosh escheat.' In closing, Leslie 'marvels much why you send not the harquebuses you promised, knowing the place to be so desolate.'[79]

We caught the limmers! Let's get them hanged! You're too slow in writing! Huntly's on the move! Where are those harquebuses? No doubt in my mind that Moray has an excellent servant here, one who is both on the job and ready to speak his mind, nor have I any question that Leslie feels his master is not as interested as he should be in what's happening up in Moray. And things were getting worse fast, as Leslie's next letter – dated only five days later – makes very clear indeed:

> On the twelfth day of this month James Gordon, accompanied with the number of sixteen Gordons – gentlemen all – came to Your Lordship's boats and cobbles of Spey and have broken them and cut Your Lordship's nets and laid all your coracles on land and beaten Your Lordship's servants that work at your fishing – and Joakie Maweir escaped very narrowly with his life.

There is nothing but trouble, he continues, and there is deep concern that Huntly may attack Darnaway either on his way to Inverness or on the way back:

> My Lord, this is a masterless country at this present, for there is no man in Moray that may put twenty men together. There is no man here but has received sure warning of Huntly's journey and has put all his gear aside. Therefore, My Lord, haste you home . . .

For if they get this house [*Darnaway*] we shall be all hanged over the wall.[80]

'HUNTLY RULES ALL IN THE NORTH'; MORAY AND ATHOL RESPOND (1591)

Huntly did not attack Darnaway, but neither did Moray hurry home, because two months later Leslie wrote again, trusting, as he says, that his Lordship will come soon, as otherwise his continued absence may be 'misinterpreted by the new Lieutenant',[81] which is to say Huntly, who was once again Lieutenant of the North. And that appointment could make matters far worse for Moray and his friends.

It will be recalled that as a consequence of Brig o' Dee Huntly had lost his commission as Lieutenant of the North, but he had recently petitioned for its return. That return had been 'prepared and made ready for him', in early August, according to Bowes, 'but not delivered for wise and good councillors impugn the same in regard of the troubles that shall arise thereby in the north'. Bowes was quite specific:

> It is said that Athol, Moray, and the rest of that fellowship, hearing of this great authority given him and doubting [*not*] that he shall annoy them and their friends by the color thereof, have lately knit themselves together by band to withstand all wrongs to be offered or done to them by Huntly, and they think them able to put him to foil in case [*i.e. so long as*] the King shall hold off his hand betwixt them: so as it is looked that new troubles shall arise there in case Huntly shall obtain the lieutenancy he looketh for.[82]

But the wise and good councillors did not long prevail, and by mid-September Huntly had his commission again – a mighty convenience that would give legitimacy to any raid he might decide to mount (after all, he could say he was merely punishing or forestalling breakers of the King's peace).

Moray, Athol, and certain clients of Argyle met at Dunkeld and 'agreed to party one another' against Huntly, but it was whistling in the dark. 'Blood is drawn daily in the north between Huntly's friends and the followers of Athol, Moray, and Grant,' said Bowes, and there is no question whose blood was flowing most freely. Moray's party complained that Huntly had obtained a commission of justiciary – a kind of trial court – over their lands

'under colour and pretense to punish trespassers and malefactors . . . [*but*]
meaning no other thing but to be cruelly revenged upon us . . . [*and*] for
uttering and execution of every hatred and injury conceived by the said earl
against us'. They had even obtained a court order 'by occasion of the many
slaughters, murders, robberies and oppressions' to limit his jurisdiction,
but Huntly simply acted as though that piece of paper didn't exist. They
petitioned for and received a second exemption a year later, which appears
to have been no more effective. No doubt about it, Huntly was riding his
enemies down.[83]

Not only was Moray losing the battle on the ground, he was also losing
support at Court. First of all, his father had died the year before, and while
Lord Doune was not one of the major powers at Court, he had been a very
solid source of support for his son. Worse yet, though, was the death on
18 November 1591 of his wife, the Countess Elizabeth, and it should be
remembered that it was only through his wife that he held his earldom.
Finally, Huntly was hard at work hacking away at Moray's clan alliances,
and he had been quite successful: both the Grants and the Macintoshes –
on whom Moray had depended heavily over the past few years – signed
new agreements with Huntly and left the field. Athol was in disgrace,
Bothwell was an outlaw, and, as Bowes wrote to Burghley, 'Huntly rules
all in the north, and over Moray, who since his wife's decease finds little
favour at court'.[84] Quite simply, for Moray, the jig was up.

BOTHWELL'S HOLYROOD RAID (1591)

But the final curtain was not yet, though act five had begun, and it
was Bothwell who opened it with typical flamboyance. As Cowan says,
ever since his forfeiture in May, he had been hard at work creating his
own legend:

> He flitted back and forth between Crichton [*his home*] and Edinburgh,
> riding beneath the city walls and dining openly and ostentatiously at
> Leith. In a series of hairsbreadth escapes he eluded capture to return
> like a moth to the flame. His name was linked with that of Queen
> Anne who also loathed Maitland.[85]

On that latter note, an English intelligencer – writing from Berwick in
words he said he would not have felt safe writing while he was in Scotland
– claimed 'that Earl and Queen had some unlawful manner betwixt them

so that none in Scotland dare name the Earl to the King, he is so odious to him'.[86]

Maitland's devotion to good government and the fact that he himself was not a peer had always seriously distanced him from many of the powerful nobles of the time, but Bothwell truly and passionately hated him, calling him that 'puddock-stoole of a night' compared with himself – 'an ancient cedar' – and blaming him for just about all of his troubles.[87] Bothwell's murderous intentions toward the Chancellor had been rumored for some years, and when the double opportunity not only of realizing them but also of capturing the King himself was presented to him by 'some that envied the Chancellor's credit with the King and others whose hopes wholly depended upon the troubles of the State', he did not find it hard to be persuaded. In fact he *was* persuaded.

Therefore, on the evening of December 28, 1591, he and his followers, carrying with them 'certain great forehammers' with which to break down the King's and Chancellor's doors, arrived at Holyrood Palace and were let in at a back passage. Things moved along nicely until one of the conspirators seized an opportunity along the way to beat down a door behind which some friends of his were imprisoned, and the resultant racket raised the whole palace. Bothwell, seeing the enterprise endangered, called for fire. Spottiswoode describes the ensuing confusion well:

> But ere they could find any, Sir *James Sandilands* . . . with a number of people of *Edinburgh* . . . did beat him and his company from the doors, and was in possibility to have taken them all, if there had been any lights; but those being all extinguished, Bothwell with the principals of his company made shift in the dark and escaped.[88]

He lost some nine of his followers, 'men of small note', says Spottiswoode, 'who were executed the next morning'. But, much to the King's exasperation, Bothwell himself rode off into the night and disappeared once again.

Both King and Chancellor were understandably shaken by the Holyrood raid and both called for and received support from those about them. But not from the Kirk, with which of course James had been conducting a running battle over just who was really in charge. The preachers decided the raid would make a stout and nubbly stick with which to beat some Presbyterian sense into the rather-too-Episcopal James, and they got right to work employing it. Two days later, for example, a Mr. Craig, preaching before the King, said that since he 'had lightly regarded the many bloody shirts presented to him by his subjects craving justice, so God, in his providence had made a noise of crying and forehammers to come to his own doors'.[89] Needless to say, this was not the kind of help James felt he needed at the time. What he really wanted was Bothwell's hide nailed to the palace door, and when he heard that he was in the west preparing to sail to Spain he evidently gave Huntly, in his capacity of Lieutenant of the North, a commission to head him off and bring him in. How wide-ranging that commission was and exactly what its terms were – or even whether it existed at all – will become important to our story shortly. Bothwell didn't go to Spain, but once again – in spite of Huntly's best efforts – he and his retainers disappeared into the countryside. There was a strong suspicion that Moray might be hiding him.

THE MURDER OF CALDER (1592)

Meanwhile the Huntly-Moray feud went on apace, with Huntly clearly gaining strength at every turn, but he knew that one turn he would have to be very careful about was Moray's alliance with Argyle. Moray was doubly related to Colin Campbell, Sixth Earl of Argyle, first through his mother (the Earl's younger sister) and second through his mother-in-law, the Earl's wife, and he had been able to count heavily on this relationship. Naturally, in bringing about any final solution to his problems with Moray, the last thing Huntly wanted was to bring Argyle might down on himself. But he had a plan.

When the sixth earl died in 1584, he named his eight-year-old son Archibald as his successor, also appointing a council of six Campbells to advise his widow in all matters. As might be expected, violent dissensions broke out amongst these advisers, but finally the real power narrowed down to two: Campbell of Calder [Cawdor], who had Moray's support, and Campbell of Ardkinglas, who did not. The death of the latter in 1591 left Calder essentially in sole control, but it also left a number of Campbell lairds and barons out in the cold. What Huntly decided to do was to approach these malcontents with a plot to dispose of both Calder and Moray, and there are those who believe that Maitland was a party to this plan, distrusting Moray as he did on account of Bothwell.[90] At any rate, plans were made and set in motion that would lead to Calder's being shot to death at Knipoch in Lorne on 4 February 1592, just three days before the death of Moray. In a reflective mood two years later Bowes claimed it was 'commonly said that Huntly durst not have slain the Earl of Moray in the life of Calder'.[91] Maybe not, even probably not, but with Calder out of the way and the remaining Campbell lairds at least not aligned against him, Huntly certainly could make his next move against Moray more confidently.

MORAY BROUGHT TO DONIBRISTLE (1592)

There can be some question whether Huntly choreographed that next move or simply took advantage of an opportunity that presented itself, but I agree with Keith Brown that 'the evidence seems to point to a plot',[92] and to make that plot work he first of all had to have Moray in a position where he could easily attack him. To achieve this, he enlisted the aid of Maitland, whose job it became to convince the King both that something should be done to bring Huntly and Moray to agreement and that Huntly himself – weary of so many years of bitter, bloody and wasteful feud – very much desired such a rapprochement. Maitland was successful, and the *Historie of King James the Sext* tells the story of what happened next:

> Therefore he willed the King to send my Lord of Ochiltrie unto Moray, and desire him to repair to any part near the court, because Huntly was then present with him [*i.e. with the King*], to the end that his Majesty might the more easily reconcile them. Moray having heard the message, simply believed the same, and the messenger knowing nothing of the fraud, they came both together to a part in the province of Fife called Donibristle, which Moray had chosen for his residence.[93]

As far as I can see, they could not have chosen a better man for their go-between than Andrew, Third Lord Ochiltree. He was, first of all, a Stewart and Moray's long-time good friend, but – even more important than that – he was an honest and straightforward fighting man to whom things were what they seemed to be. He had also just become Lord Ochiltree, his father having died in December, and therefore probably would have been unfamiliar with any plots that might have been hatching at court.[94] At any rate, with him as the messenger, Moray saw no reason to suspect foul play, and I am sure that, considering the precariousness of his position vis-à-vis Huntly at that time, he would have been very interested in any kind of honorable relief the King might be able to arrange.

His choice of Donibristle for his stay is also a measure of his good faith, a manor-house belonging to his mother, about four miles from North

Queensferry and fourteen miles from Edinburgh on the north side of the Firth of Forth. Had he been at all suspicious, he could have stayed safely behind the walls of Doune, but Donibristle was just a house, a pleasant seat on a little rocky bay. In the background of the Death Portrait – a work we can reasonably take as authoritative – it appears as a collection of low-roofed buildings, possibly thatched, surrounded by a gated wall enclosing a stack yard, fully justifying the English intelligencer Aston's description of it as 'not able to be kept'.[95] Certainly it could not have been kept by the retinue Moray had with him: his friend Patrick Dunbar, Sheriff of Moray, and a handful of servants – probably no more than a dozen men altogether. There is some question whether or not his mother was in residence at the time, and at least one source, Bowes, claims his sister was there too with her family. At any rate, it was a most unwarlike ménage.[96]

A letter to Moray from his servant Andrew Abercrombie in Edinburgh dated 25 January suggests that Moray had been at Donibristle for some time, perhaps since the middle of the month or even earlier. It further suggests that he had left Darnaway both suddenly and secretly. 'I find great fault with much that your Lordship does,' says Abercrombie, 'and especially of keeping such things close from me . . . not advising me of Your Lordship's journey to Donibristle.' This has caused certain important letters to be misdirected:

> There are letters directed to the north to Darnaway to summon everyone there before the secret council one day as I shall tell you in my next letter to appear before them under pain of horning for receiving of my Lord Bothwell on a day of December.

Ochiltree has written, too, he says, 'and will take up the matter betwixt Your Lordship and him'. But he too is somewhat dismayed: 'He strongly urged me to write to Your Lordship and marvels that Your Lordship sent him no advisement concerning Your Lordships' meeting as you promised'. Abercrombie ends much as he began, complaining that Moray had failed to keep him informed of his whereabouts, something he only found out via 'the bruit of the town'.[97] It is a type of complaint we have heard before from others.

Once he had seen Moray to Donibristle, Ochiltree 'departed from him toward court, to inform the King and the Chancellor of his sudden obedience'.[98] Although his official task was now done, it is evident he wanted to get together with Moray once again before the Court arrived in Edinburgh on 31 January, but that second meeting never took place, perhaps because of Moray's procrastination, perhaps because there were those at Court who didn't want it to happen. At any rate, it never took place. The next move – step two in the plot – was to be Huntly's.

HUNTLY MOVES ON DONIBRISTLE

We should remember that Moray came south because he believed the King would attempt an honorable end to the feud, but – once James had settled himself in at Provost Nicoll Edwards' comfortable house at Niddry's Wind – Huntly and Maitland seem to have begun worrying him with Moray's Bothwell connection: that the two were, after all, cousins; that Moray had received him after the Holyrood raid; and, worse yet, that he was even rumored to have been one of the raiders. The whole business was serious enough for Moray to have been called to appear before the Council, and he may even already have been at the horn for not appearing. It is not entirely clear what James's reaction was to this pressuring, and particularly it is not clear whether he gave Huntly a new commission to bring Moray in or whether Huntly decided that his earlier commission to 'pursue by fire and sword the Earl Bothwell and all his partakers'[99] was sufficient. However it was, Huntly presented himself to his Sovereign on that Monday morning of 7 February at the head of a sizeable body of armed men.

The King was indulging in his favorite pastime of hunting as Huntly and his men rode up. Aston tells the story as follows:

> That morning Huntly told the King he had a purpose to ride in pursuit of Mr. John Colville and some others that were with the Earl Bothwell, and for that cause he was to pass over the water. Yet the King fearing the inconvenience that might ensue by reason of the Earl of Murray being on the other side, forbade him ride, which he promised to obey.[100]

According to Moysie, on the other hand, Huntly claimed he was on his way to a horse-race at Leith. Either way, the import of these passages is that he left the King satisfied that he was up to no mischief that day. How much the King actually knew, or how much he suspected, are matters that have never been settled, nor will they be; yet, while I find it hard to believe he was one of the plotters, I am sure he was quite aware that the Earl of Moray's days were being numbered – and who was doing the counting.

If, in fact, Huntly ever started for that horse-race in Leith, he soon changed direction and led his troop to Queensferry. An embargo of sorts had been in force in all the Forth ports since January 21, when the Privy Council ordered that no boats 'depart forth of the ports where they are now lying till they give up the names of the persons to be transported by them',[101] probably to make things more difficult for Bothwell. However, some of the contemporary sources suggest that the King and the Chancellor gave *special* orders closing the ferries to all *except* Huntly – and even to have all the boats from both sides ready and available to receive him and his retinue on the south side that morning – and true it is that shortly thereafter Ochiltree was forbidden a crossing, as we shall see.[102] No such order has been found, and the King expressly denied having issued one, but the fact remains that Huntly and his troop had no problem getting across the Forth and were soon on the road to Donibristle four miles away.

They must have made a formidable group. How many there were depends on who one reads. Moysie speaks of 'six or seven score', but he probably let his considerable indignation get the best of him. A Privy Council document lists twenty-seven by name, but that would include only men of quality, and the same would be true of Aston's claim of 'forty horse of his servants'. My own estimate would be something like eighty men, horse and foot. One source speaks of them bearing 'jacks, steelbonnets, long culverins, harquebuses, pistolets, swords and other weapons invasive',[103] and even if we make allowances for this being an after-the-fact list by a lawyer for the plaintiff – therefore 'worst case' – we can still speak of this group as being so heavily armed that only the most charitable observer could have concluded that they were headed for a horse-race at Leith or anywhere else.

THE ATTACK AND THE DEATH OF MORAY

Moray could not have been anything but shocked when he saw what was coming into the open land surrounding Donibristle: fourscore men in heavy battle array led by his bloodfeud enemy – and he himself with less than a dozen men in a house he couldn't possibly defend. The usual parley followed. Huntly sent John Gordon (brother to the Laird of Gight) 'to desire the Earl of Moray to give over the house and to render himself prisoner'.[104] In no way was Moray going to turn himself over to Huntly, who of all men alive he most hated and distrusted. How the parley might have gone if it had continued there is no way of telling, because a shot rang out as one of Moray's servants – probably in a moment of pure funk – mortally wounded Captain Gordon, and the fight was on for fair.

James Melvill in his *Diary* claims the action took place 'in full daylight', while most other sources make it appear it was night. We should remember it was early February, and while the fighting did probably start in the daylight of mid-afternoon, it surely ended in the early dark, even though, according to one source, it only lasted 'for the space of one hour or thereby'.[105] The English intelligencer Aston describes the early action:

> They that were within came forth sundry times, and discharged their pistols and slew some of Huntly's men ... Thereupon they [*i.e. Huntly's men*] took the corn stooks and laid them to the house so that the extremity of the fire forced them that was within to come forth.[106]

All the sources agree that the house was fired – the Death Portrait shows it consumed in flames – and of course once that had occurred all was lost.

Still there was no surrender, but before the end came there were things to be done. 'When Moray found himself void of all hope of life,' says Ambassador Bowes, 'he committed his children and the revenge of his death to Lord Ochiltree, praying his sister then with him, and now saved, to make the same known to Ochiltree.'[107] Now he had a nasty decision to make, but he was not without a courageous friend's help in making it. Birrel tells the story this way in his *Diary*:

> The Earl of Murray being within, knew not whether to come out and be slain, or be burned alive: yet, after advisement, this Dunbar says to my Lord of Murray, I will go out at the gate before Your Lordship, and I am sure the people will charge on me, thinking me to be Your Lordship; so, it being dark of night, you shall come out after me, and see if you can fend for yourself. In the meantime, this Dunbar, Tutor to the Sheriff of Murray, came forth, and ran desperately among the Earl of Huntly's folks, and they all ran upon him, and presently slew him.[108]

Some say 'this Dunbar' was the Sheriff himself, while others claim it was the Tutor, the Sheriff having been killed earlier in the fighting. Sheriff or Tutor or whoever he may have been, may holy St. Jude of the Lost Causes cast incense on his name.

After his spirited telling of Dunbar's story, Birrel's account of Moray's escape is low-key indeed: 'During this broil with Dunbar,' he says, 'the

Earl of Moray came running out at the gate of Donibristle, which stands beside the sea, and there set him down among the rocks, thinking to have been saved'.[109] In other words, under the diversion of the attack on Dunbar, Moray dashed out quickly and hid – pretty much as his friend had planned it. Aston tells much the same story, but with more drama:

> The Earl himself, after he was so burnt that he was not able to hold a weapon in one of his hands, came through them all with his sword in his hand, and like a lion forced them all to give place, and so got through them all, and with speed of foot outran them.[110]

But his freedom was short-lived. Huntly's men soon found him among the rocks by the shore. One story has it that as he was escaping from the burning house, the plume on his helmet caught fire unbeknownst to him, and his pursuers were able to trace him by that to his hiding place and kill him.[111] The historian Gordon claims that Huntly had commanded that Moray be taken alive, 'but the Laird of Cluny (whose brother was slain at Darnaway) and the Laird of Gight (who had his brother lying deadly wounded before his eyes) . . . killed him among the rocks of the sea', unable in the heat of battle to restrain their feud-born fury.[112] 'The report went,' says Spottiswoode, 'that Huntly's friends fearing he should disclaim the fact (for he desired to have taken him alive) made him light from his horse and give some strokes to the dead corpse.'[113] A century and a half later, Bishop Percy would tell the story this way in his *Reliques*:

> It is a tradition in the family, that Gordon of Bucky gave him a wound in the face: Moray half expiring, said, 'You hae spilt a better face than your awin.' Upon this, Bucky pointing his dagger at Huntly's breast, swore, 'You shall be as deep as I;' and forced him to pierce the poor defenceless body.[114]

On the other hand, Sir Walter Scott reassigned speech and sword-cut as follows in his *Tales of a Grandfather*:

> As Moray was gasping in the last agony, Huntly came up; and it is alleged by tradition, that Gordon pointed his dirk against the person of his chief, saying, 'By Heaven, my lord, you shall be as deep as I,' and so compelled him to wound Moray whilst he was dying. Huntly, with a wavering hand, struck the expiring earl on the face. Thinking of his superior beauty, even in that moment

of parting life, Moray stammered out the dying words, 'You have spoiled a better face than your own.'[115]

How one arranges the details is a problem more aesthetic than historical, but, as we shall see, the accomplices had good reason to be concerned about how Huntly himself might later arrange them.

It was over. Huntly and the others sheathed their swords and, mounting their horses, rode off into the night. Moray lay by the water, his hot blood crimsoning the rocks of the shore. Donibristle was in flames. Nothing remained to say or do.

But tomorrow's wind would blow the horrid deed in every eye.

NOTES

1 Sir William Fraser, *The Red Book of Menteith* (n.p., 1880), vol ii, p.484.

2 See *C.S.P.Scot.*, iii, p.323 (Lennox to Cecil 24 Aug. 1570); iii, p.325 (Randolph to Hunsdon 5 Aug. 1570); *Act. Parl.*1581, pp.229, 234.

3 Fraser, *Red Book*, II, pp.471ff; Sir James Balfour Paul, *The Scots Peerage* (Edinburgh: David Douglas, 1906), vol.iii (Doune).

4 *C.S.P. Scot.*, ix, p.226; *Scots Peerage* v.6, p.317; Moray Muniments 1/1/168.

5 Grant G. Simpson, *Scottish Handwriting* 1150–1650 (Aberdeen: Aberdeen University Press, 1977), p.12. The entire section pp.6–26 is helpful.

6 On this matter of age, it is interesting that an English intelligencer in 1580 felt that by that time the King ought to govern by himself, 'being now near the age of fourteen years.' *C.S.P.Scot.*, v, p.396 (Bowes to Walsingham 16 Apr. 1580).

7 See Moray Muniments, 1/1/29, 168, 328, 370, 372, 387, 390, 391, 396.

8 Brown, *Bloodfeud*, p. 145. In regard to this point, there is a letter in the Moray Muniments (217/3/239, dated 12 Feb 1582) from the Earl of Arran, Lord Chancellor, to the Earl of Moray, expressing his esteem and goodwill towards him.

9 Moray Muniments 1/1/281 (5 Jan. 1580), 1/1/275 (13 Jan. 1580), 1/1/297 (19 June 1581). See also *Act Parl*, 1581, iii, p.230.

10 *C.S.P.Scot.*, v, p.611 (Thomas Randolph to Hunsdon 4 Feb.1580/1).

11 Moray Muniments 1/1/275, 281, 297, 370. For the royal pension, see *R.P.C.* iii, p.450.

12 See *C.S.P.Scot.*, vi, p.583 (Bowes to Walsingham 8 May 1583); p. 686 (Bowes to Walsingham 29 Dec. 1583).

13 David Moysie, *Memoirs of the Affairs of Scotland* (Edinburgh: The Bannatyne Club, 1830), p.89; *The Historie and Life of King James the*

Sext (Edinburgh: The Bannatyne Club, 1825), p.246. Later chroniclers are probably following these citations; see William Robertson, *The History of Scotland* in *The Works of William Robertson* (London, 1822), vol iii, p.98; Sir Walter Scott, *The Tales of a Grandfather* (London: Adam and Charles Black, 1898; first published 1827–9), p.353; John Hill Burton, *The History of Scotland* (Edinburgh and London: William Blackwood, 1897), vol.v, p.289; Charles Rampini, *A History of Moray and Nairn* (Edinburgh and London: William Blackwood, 1897), p.155; *Dictionary of National Biography*, vol. 18, p.1194; Brown, *Bloodfeud*, p.145.

14 *Bannatyne Club Miscellany*, i, p.57; *C.S.P.Scot*, vi, p. 159 (Sept 1582).

15 Moray Muniments 2/3/261 (7 Mar. 1582).

16 Moray Muniments 2/3/262 (8 Mar. 1582).

17 Moray Muniments 2/3/263 (16 Mar. 1582).

18 Moray Muniments 2/3/266 (undated, but, since Whitsunday fell on June 3 that year, probably some time in late April or May).

19 Moray Muniments 2/3/266 (dated 5 August 1583).

20 Moray Muniments 1/1/79 (22 Sept. 1585). A note says that the contract was not completed, yet there is a discharge for it dated 3 June 1587 (Moray Muniments 1/1/53).

21 Moray Muniments 12/43/190 (16 Oct. 1586).

22 Moray Muniments 2r/3/267 (26 May 1587).

23 Moray Muniments /15/351 (19 Dec, 1587).

24 Moray Muniments 2/3/148 (1587).

25 Moray Muniments 2/3/268 (24 Nov. 1587).

26 Moray Muniments 2/3/255. The letter is datelined "Darnaway 26 May", but no year is given.

27 *R.P.C.* iv, p.307 (1 Aug. 1588).

28 *C.S.P. Scot.*, ix, p.595. Report from Sir Henry Waddyngton, 11 Aug. 1588.

29 W. Croft Dickinson, *Scotland from the Earliest Times to 1603* (third edition, Oxford Univ. Press, 1977), pp.386–87.

30 Lang, ii, p.343. For complete texts of these letters, see *C.S.P.Scot*, ix, pp.682–97 (20 Feb. 1589).

31 *C.S.P. Scot.*, ix, p.702 (Asheby to Burleigh 2 Mar. 1589).

32 *C.S.P. Scot.*, ix, pp.699–700 (Feb. 1589).

33 Moray Muniments 2/3/227 and 230 (both dated 14 March 1589).

34 *C.S.P. Scot.*, x, pp.1,5 (Wm. Asheby to Burghley 14 March 1589); Lang, ii, p.344; Brown, *Bloodfeud*, p.148

35 *C.S.P. Scot.*, ix, p.174 (13 Aug. 1587); p.481 (Ogilvy to Walsingham Aug. 1587).

36 Willson, p.102.

37 Lang, ii. p.347.

38 Moray Muniments 2/3/227 (14 Mar.1589).

39 Moray Muniments 2/3/226 (14 Mar.1589).

40 Moray Muniments 2/3/229 (16 Mar.1589).

41 Moray Muniments 2/3/232 (dated 14 June.1589?).

42 Moray Muniments 2/3/14 (5 Jan. 1589?) Alexander Stewart, a burgess of Elgin, was writing to Archibald Stewart, one of the Earl's servitors, complaining of injury done to him by a Scott, 'my Lord's officer'.

43 Moray Muniments, 2/3/280 (9 Jan. 1590).

44 R.P.C., iv, p.464. (It is interesting that once again he is spoken of as being a Catholic.)

45 Edward J. Cowan, 'The Darker Vision of the Scottish Renaissance: The Devil and Francis Stewart.' In Ian B. Cowan and Duncan Shaw (eds.), *The Renaissance and Reformation in Scotland* (Edinburgh: Scottish Academic Press, 1983), p.127.

46 C.S.P.Scot., x, p.202 (Alexander Hay to William Ashby, 28 Nov. 1589).

47 R.P.C., iv, p.496 (24 June 1590). See also Moray Muniments 2/3/295 (12 Apr. 1590), 2/3/274 (19 May 1590), 2/3/287–288 (23 May 1590), 2/3/292 (23 May 1590), 2/3/57 (27 May 1590), Brown, *Bloodfeud*, p.151.

48 Moray Muniments 2/3/249 (30 June 1590).

49 C.S.P. Scot., x, p.392 (Bowes to Burghley 4 Sep. 1590).

50 Moray Muniments 2/3/304 (4 Aug. 1590).

51 Moray Muniments, 2/3/292.

52 C.S.P. Scot., x, p. 17. (Bowes to Burghley).

53 Moray Muniments, 2/3/270 (2 Oct. 1590) Brown, *Bloodfeud*, p. 151.

54 Spottiswoode, ii, p.410. See also *The History of the Feuds and Conflicts Among the Clans* (Glasgow, 1818), pp.36–39. In *Miscellanea Scotica*.

55 *History of the Feuds*, p.38; Gordon, *Sutherland*, pp.214–215; Browne, *History of the Highlands*, pp.218–219; Alexander Mackintosh Shaw, *Historical Memoirs of the House and Clan of Mackintosh and of the Clan Chattan* (London: R. Clay and Taylor, 1880), pp.241–252.

56 C.S.P. Scot., x, p.425 (Bowes to Burghley, 28 Nov. 1590).

57 C.S.P. Scot., x, p.428 (Bowes to Burghley, 7 Dec. 1590).

58 R.P.C. iv, pp.569–570 (23 Jan. 1590/1). See also Spottiswoode, p.382; Moysie, p. 85.

59 Spottiswoode, ii p.410.

60 C.S.P. Scot., x, p.431 (enclosed in a letter from Bowes to Burghley 7 Dec. 1590).

61 Spottiswoode, ii p.411.

62 C.S.P. Scot., x, p.436.

63 C.S.P. Scot., x, p.438 (18 Dec. 1590), 442 (26 Dec. 1590), 462–463 (23 Feb. 1590–1).

64 C.S.P. Scot., x, pp.456–457 (Bowes to Burghley, 3 Feb. 1590–1).

65 Moray Muniments, 2/3/332 (12 Jan. 1591). This same Walter Kinnaird died in 1613 and is buried in Dyke churchyard. See Charles

McKean, *The District of Moray* (Edinburgh: Scottish Academic Press, 1987), p.56.

66 *C.S.P. Scot.*, x, pp. 456–57 (Bowes to Burghley, 3 Feb. 1590–1).

67 *C.S.P. Scot.*, x p.462 (Bowes to Burghley 23 Feb. 1590–1). See also p.469 (Bowes to Burghley 23 Feb. 1590–1) and p.460 (Bowes to Burghley 13 Feb. 1590–1).

68 *C.S.P. Scot.*, x p.469 (Bowes to Burghley 23 Feb. 1591).

69 Moray Muniments 2/3/296 (26 Nov. 1590).

70 *R.P.C.*, iv, p.597 (16 Mar. 1590/1).

71 E.J. Cowan, 'The Darker Vision', pp.128–31. The whole article, pp. 125–40, is a splendid discussion of Bothwell's career.

72 Lee, *John Maitland*, pp.229–30.

73 Moray Muniments, 2/3/251 (27 May 1591).

74 Moray Muniments, 2/3/252 (18 June 1591).

75 Moray Muniments, 2/3/254 (18 June 1591). See also *C.S.P. Scot.*, x, p.531 (Bowes to Burghley 19 June 1591); Brown, *Bloodfeud*, p.155. There is, however, no reason to accept Brown's statement that in spite of his excuses he *was* in Edinburgh three days later, when he struck Huntly's servant. That little contretemps took place five months before (see above, p.25).

76 *C.S.P. Scot.*, x, p.541 (Bowes to Burghley 6 July 1591); Moray Muniments, 2/3/155 (3 July 1591).

77 *C.S.P. Scot.*, x, pp.572–73. The correspondent was writing from south of the border, claiming he would not have felt safe sending such a letter while he was still in Scotland.

78 Moray Muniments, 2/3/309 (n.d.). Honesty compels me to admit that my assigning this letter and the two succeeding ones to the summer of 1591 is a matter of judgment. None of them are year-dated.

79 Moray Muniments 2/3/327 (dated only '12th instant').

80 Moray Muniments 2/3/236 (17 June 1591).

81 Moray Muniments 2/3/237 (7 Aug. 1591).

82 *C.S.P. Scot.*, x, pp.557–58 (Bowes to Burghley 8 Aug. 1591).

83 *C.S.P. Scot.*, x, p.572 (23 Sept. 1591), pp.586–87 (10 Nov. 1591); Moray Muniments (2/3/347).

84 *C.S.P. Scot.*, x, p.593 (Bowes to Burghley 4 Dec. 1591), p.601 (Bowes to Burghley 20 Dec. 1591).

85 Cowan, 'The Darker Side', p.131.

86 *C.S.P. Scot.*, x, p.574 (9 Sept. 1591).

87 See Maurice Lee, *Maitland of Thirlestane and the Foundation of Stewart Despotism in Scotland* (Princeton: Princeton University Press, 1959). See also Brown, *Bloodfeud*, pp.127–30. James finally created him Lord Thirlestane on the day of Anne's coronation, 17 May 1590.

88 Spottiswoode, v, pp.386–87.

89 Calderwood, v, pp.142–43.

90 For an opposing view, see Lee, *Maitland*, pp.239–242.

91 *C.S.P. Scot.*, xi, p.338 (Bowes to Burghley 18 May 1594). For full accounts of the Calder affair, see 'Papers relating to the Murder of the Laird of Calder', *Highland Papers* (Edinburgh: Scottish History Society, 1914), Vol.I, pp.143–93; Donald Gregory, *The History of the Western Highlands and Isles of Scotland*, Second Edition (London and Glasgow, 1881), pp.244–52. See also Mary Caperton Bingham, 'Two Murders in One Act: The Murders of the Bonny Earl of Moray and the Thane of Cawdor' (Unpublished Honors Thesis: Harvard, 1990).

92 Brown, *Bloodfeud*, p.156.

93 *Historie of King James the Sext*, p.247. See also Lang, ii, p.357; Moysie, p.88; Spottiswoode, vi, p.387; Melville, *Memoirs*, p.407.

94 See Bingham, p.60.

95 Lang, ii, p.357.

96 *C.S.P. Scot.*, x, p.641 (Bowes to Burghley 17 Feb. 1592). See also Aston in Lang, ii, p.357n; *Historie of King James the Sext*, p.248; Moray Muniments 2/4/58 (3 June 1592). According to the present Lord Moray, there is a family tradition that the mother was not there but came down only after the murder.

97 Moray Muniments 2/3/356 (25 Jan. 1591/2).

98 *Historie of King James the Sext*, p.247.

99 Melville, *Memoirs*, p.407. See also *C.S.P. Scot.*, x, p.640 (Bowes to Burghley 17 Feb. 1591/2); Spottiswoode, vi, p.387.

100 Lang, ii, p.357n.

101 *R.P.C.*, iv, pp.718–19 (21 Jan. 1592).

102 Lang, ii, p.357n; *C.S.P. Scot*, x, p.640 (Bowes to Burghley 17 Feb. 1592). See also *Historie of King James the Sext*, pp.248–49; Moysie, p.88; Moray Muniments 2/4/58 (3 June 1592).

103 A 'jack' was body armor; a 'steelbonnet' was obviously a metal helmet; a 'culverin' was a handgun; a 'lang culverin' would have been something like a musket; a 'hagbut' was an harquebus, a long-barreled firearm heavy enough so that the barrel was supported by a crotched stand near the muzzle. Moray Muniments 2/4/58 (Supplication to the King by James, Third Earl of Murray: 3 June 1592).

104 Gordon, *Sutherland*, p.216.

105 Moray Muniments, 2/4/93 (15 July 1595).

106 Lang, ii, 357n.

107 *C.S.P. Scot.*, x, p.641 (Bowes to Burghley 17 Feb. 1592).

108 Birrel, p.27.

109 Birrel, p.27.

110 Lang, ii, p.357n.

111 Spottiswoode, vi, p.387; *C.S.P. Scot.*, x, p.639 (Aston to Bowes 10 Feb. 1592); Birrel, p.27.

112 Gordon, *Sutherland*, p.216.

113 Spottiswoode, vi, p.387; Brown, *Bloodfeud*, p.157.

114 Thomas Percy, *Reliques of Ancient English Poetry* (New York: Dover,

1966), vol.ii, p.226. Originally published in 1765. Henceforth, unless another edition is specified, all references to this work will be to the Dover edition.

115 Scott, p.354 (Ch. 33). See also Lang, ii, p.357; *RPC*, iv, p.725n (Masson); Brown, *Bloodfeud*, p.157.

CHAPTER THREE

The Road To Strathbogie

HUNTLY, AFTER FINISHING his deadly business at Donibristle, probably planned to return to Edinburgh, but since it was late he and his retinue went only as far as Inverkeithing, less than two miles along the way to the ferry, and there they spent Monday night. However, he sent Gordon of Buckie on ahead to carry the news to the King. We will return to Buckie's adventure shortly, but first it is necessary to backtrack a bit to pick up on Andrew, Lord Ochiltree.

It will be recalled that ever since his bringing Moray south, Ochiltree had intended meeting with him again, but for various reasons that second meeting had never taken place.[1] Evidently, though, he was on his way to meet with Moray on the morning of the murder, but when he came to the ferry he was stopped, commandment having come from the King that no boats should pass. According to Roger Aston, Ochiltree dutifully returned to Edinburgh, 'thinking there had been some enterprise to have been done by the King that day'.[2] Yet, since he still wanted to see Moray, he went to James to get his warrant for passage. The King evinced surprise, saying he knew nothing of any such restraint on the ferries, but he nevertheless commanded Ochiltree to stay with him all day and even 'carried him on hunting' the next morning. Moysie tells basically the same story, but he depicts Ochiltree as less trusting and the King as far more suspect:

> The Lord Ochiltree, hearing the rumour whereof he had no certainty, being accompanied at the time with forty or fifty horse of his own, by reason of his deadly feuds that he stood under, placed them all in arms, and made themselves ready to go over to Donibristle to see the manor: likewise the Earl of Morton promised to send some of his men with him also. Whereof the King being informed, sent for the said Lord Ochiltree with all diligence to come unto him, and in the meantime caused close the ports, and gave command to the bailiffs to stay all his [*i.e. Ochiltree's*] horses within their stables. Likewise at his coming to

His Majesty, after long conference His Majestie charged him by no means to set off, or to ride contrary to his knowledge. The said lord after some speeches to His Majesty retired to his own lodging.[3]

By 'some speeches' I take it that Ochiltree was angry at being detained and told the King exactly what he thought. That would not have been much to the King's liking, but it would have been Ochiltree's way.

Buckie, coming over from Inverkeithing, went directly to Nicoll Edwards' house where the King was staying, but he was prevented from delivering his message in person. Having, therefore, done all that he could do, he started on his way back across the Firth. Ochiltree, however, had learned of his presence and swung into action. Moysie continues:

> Whereof knowledge coming to Lord Ochiltree and some of the Duke of Lennoxes' servants, and the Earl of Mar's, he went and sought him [*i.e. Buckie*] very diligently in the Canongate; and hearing he had taken horse at a backside and ridden away, the Lord Ochiltree sent for his horse with all diligence, and followed after him; but he escaped very narrowly.[4]

Tuesday morning the King went off hunting again, this time up around Wardie, and he had Ochiltree with him. They were in easy sight of the Firth, and the King, seeing the smoke of Donibristle, asked what place that was. Ochiltree, dead certain that he knew, asked the King's leave to go to the rescue, but James refused him.[5] Ochiltree was in a bind: he had been commissioned by the King to bring his kinsman south, and it was on his word that Moray had come. He knew something was very wrong, yet the King – either through feigned or honest innocence – prevented him from doing what he knew should be done. It was a brutal dilemma for this straightforward warrior, but, inexperienced as he was in the ways of the Court, he chose at that moment not to disobey his King.

It would have been too late by far for him to have saved Moray, but had Ochiltree pursued Huntly that morning he almost certainly would have caught him at Inverkeithing. Who would have killed who passes all reasonable conjecture, and we can leave it at that. According to Moysie, though, Huntly was eating when he got word from Buckie of imminent pursuit, and he 'rose therefrom, and slipped away without paying for his drink'.[6] Perhaps we should attribute that last little dig to lawyer Moysie's strongly protestant bias, but there need be no question that Huntly got on his way in a hurry.

Huntly headed north, almost certainly returning to Strathbogie, and settled in to await developments. He didn't have to wait long. Word of the murder spread through Edinburgh like fire in dry grass, and the popular outrage was both deep and genuine, not simply a product of the machinations of the ministers or the stirrings-up of Moray's friends, although certainly both contributed. Clearly Huntly had struck down someone Edinburgh loved, and like a true lover Edinburgh was angry beyond all measure. On the very next day, for example, Roger Aston wrote to Bowes that 'the people cries out of the cruelty of the deed', adding that 'we look for nothing but mischief', and on the following Sunday Bowes himself wrote back to London that the murder had set the people in great rage and caused many in Edinburgh – nobles, ministers and burgesses alike – to sue the King for speedy punishment of the murderers.[7] Nor was this outrage a thing of the moment, for we find Bowes a fortnight later deeply concerned that the discontent of the nobles and 'the general rage of the people' may tear the country apart and draw in foreign troops, and even in April he writes that 'the people's murmur and rage daily increases'.[8] Moysie may have been an outspoken protestant, but we can safely take his anger as representative of Edinburgh's:

> The said Earl of Huntly with his bloody retinue most treasonably raised fire, burned the house of Donibristle, and most unworthily and shamefully murdered and slew the said late Earl of Moray, being the lustiest youth, the first nobleman of the King's blood, and one of the peers of the country, to the great regret and lamentation of the whole people.[9]

At first that anger was directed at Huntly, but it wasn't long before it came to include both the King and the Chancellor. As Keith Brown points out, James's reaction was one of 'official outrage but actual indifference',[10] a stance exhibiting both his personal love for Huntly and his realization that that Earl was too politically valuable to allow him to be sacrificed for what amounted to a simple bloodfeud killing. Brutal as he most certainly was, Huntly offered the best chance for keeping order in the tumultuous north, and he could serve as a useful counterweight to the ambitions of the Kirk.

At the same time, James knew he had to body out his official outrage, and he did so in two ways. First, on 8 February he cancelled both Huntly's commission for pursuit of Bothwell and his lieutenancy of the north; second, he had a proclamation sent out to gather an army to pursue both Bothwell and Huntly himself.[11] There was great enthusiasm for this latter move, and the army was supposed to head north on the 11th, but at the last minute the King put the expedition off until 10 March, claiming that the necessary forces could not be levied in so short a time. 'What effect this sudden delay shall bring,' Bowes wrote to Burghley, 'I leave to your lordship's consideration.'[12]

LADY DOUNE'S OUTCRY; CAPTAIN GORDON'S FATE

There is some question as to where the Earl's mother, the Lady Doune, was at the time of the murder. According to the present Lord Moray, the historian Sir John Moncrieff claimed she was at Donibristle, and her subsequent death was the result of severe burns she had received in the fire. On the other hand, the story that has come down in the family is that she was at Doune but went down to Donibristle as soon as she got the news the next day. The family account is surely the correct one, but wherever she was, she went into action immediately.

First of all, she tried to appeal to the King for justice, but he conspicuously avoided her. According to Moysie, he 'passed out to the hunting' in order not to meet her, but Calderwood's account – and it is in the main supported by one of Bowes' dispatches – is the most complete:

> Upon the ninth of February, the Earl of Moray's mother, accompanied with her friends, brought over her son's and the Sheriff of Moray's dead corpses, in litters, to Leith, to be brought from thence to be buried in the aisle of the Great Kirk of Edinburgh, in the Good Regent's tomb; and, as some report, to be made first a spectacle to the people at the Cross of Edinburgh. But they were stayed by command from the King . . . The Earl of Moray's mother caused draw her son's picture, as he was demeaned, and presented it to the King in a fine lawn cloth, with lamentations, and earnest suit for justice. But little regard was had to the matter. Of the three bullets she found in the boweling of the body of her son, she presented one to the King, another to ** [*sic*] the third she reserved to herself, and said, 'I shall not part with this, till it be bestowed on him that hindreth justice.'[13]

Along with the two dead bodies, Lady Doune brought the mortally wounded Captain Gordon, who had been left for dead by the Donibristle raiders. 'His hat, his purse, his gold, his weapons were taken by one of his own company,' says Calderwood indignantly, adding however, that 'he was taken in to the Earl of Moray's mother, and was cherished with meat and drink and clothing. A rare example!'[14] Her intent, of course, was not so much humanitarian as it was to bring him to public justice for his part in her son's slaughter, but according to Moysie Lord Spynie had already procured a warrant to have him taken from her 'to have eschewed the present trial of law'. That was too much for Ochiltree, who – already feeling himself compromised and even betrayed for his part in bringing Moray south – gathered up his thirty or forty men 'well horsed in their armor' and rode to the King to speak his mind.

Quite characteristically, the King was out hunting, but Ochiltree, coming on him while he was stopped for drink, told him in no uncertain terms what a bad idea the Spynie warrant was, 'declaring to His Majesty how far the murder touched His Highness, whereof he besought him most humbly to consider, and what great wrong he [i.e. Ochiltree] had received herein His Majesty best knew'.[15] Ochiltree was angry enough on his own behalf, but through his anger the King evidently felt the hot breath of the general outrage over the deed of Donibristle, and he saw that he might cool it by a token punishment. Therefore he granted Ochiltree's request – a warrant to bring Gordon 'to the trial of an assize that same day'.

Ochiltree lost no time. Whether he received the Captain from Lady Doune or had to take him from Lord Spynie the record does not say, but he brought him to trial in Edinburgh, where he was speedily condemned and publicly beheaded at the Mercat Cross. His servant, who had also been at Donibristle, was hanged at the same time. According to Calderwood, Gordon 'condemned the fact [i.e. the murder of Moray] as horrible, protesting that he was brought ignorant upon it; but confessed the Lord had brought him to this shameful end for his many other great offenses'.[16]

Later historians have commented on this travesty of justice. James Browne, for instance, points out that Gordon was put to death 'for having assisted the Earl of Huntly acting under a royal commission. The recklessness and severity of this act,' he goes on to say, 'were still more atrocious as Captain Gordon's wounds were incurable, and he was fast hastening to his grave.'[17] Hindsight can allow us to agree, but given the temper of the time, it is perhaps merciful that the Captain wasn't hanged, drawn and quartered!

THE KIRK RESPONDS

'The fact that Huntly was a Catholic and Moray a Protestant was irrelevant to the murder, but not to its aftermath,' said Maurice Lee, and he is quite right.[18] Although there is no record that Moray had even a nominal interest in the Kirk – curiously he had often been reported by English intelligencers to be a papist[19] – the paired facts that he was the son-in-law of that most protestant of protestants the Good Regent and that his murderer was the most notoriously Catholic lord in Scotland were more than sufficient for the ministers not only to champion his cause but to scourge the King for not championing it more vigorously. Almost immediately they began calling for Huntly's punishment and – since for political reasons he had allowed himself to become a member of the Kirk – his excommunication. The Rev. John Row in his *History* gives the following example of how they dealt with the King:

> Some few days after the murder, Mr. Patrick Simson, preaching before the King, Gen. iv. 9, 'The Lord said to Cain, Where is Abel, thy brother?' said to the King, before the congregation, 'Sir, I assure you in God's name, the Lord will ask at you where is the Earle of Moray your brother?' The King replied, before all the congregation, 'Mr. Patrick, my chamber door was never shut upon you; you might have told me any thing you thought in secret.' He replied, 'Sir, the scandal is public.' And after the sermon, being sent for to the castle, went up with his Bible under his oxter, affirming that would plead for him.[20]

James was still smarting from the Kirk's refusal to excommunicate Bothwell and the others involved in the Holyrood raid of six weeks before, forgetting, as Lang says, that Bothwell was 'a Protestant and had only attacked a king'.[21] The Kirk had its own agenda, to which Bothwell could be useful as 'a sanctified plague', but Huntly was the Whore of Babylon incarnate, and not to seek his destruction for Moray's murder was certainly the blasphemy against the Holy Ghost! Rather than caving in, though, the King tried to reason with the ministers, as Calderwood suggests:

> The King sent for five or six of the ministers, made an harangue to them, wherein he did what he could to clear himself and desired them to clear his part before the people. They desired him to clear himself

by earnest pursuing of Huntly with fire and sword. A proclamation was made, with beating of the drum, to declare the King innocent, but no word of pursuing of Huntly. The King alleged his part to be like David's, when Abner was slain by Joab.[22]

Good biblical scholar that he was, James could not have hit on a more apt parallel for his predicament, but while David's mourning and fasting for Abner pleased the Israelites, nothing James did in response to Moray's murder seemed to calm the rising storm of Edinburgh's anger. The obvious fact is, of course, that he did very little, and people were becoming more and more impatient for some action on Moray's behalf.

THE FLIGHT FROM EDINBURGH; MAITLAND'S FALL

Things soon reached a point where both the King and Chancellor Maitland decided it would be best to leave town for a while. At first, the King evidently tried to make it look as if he were pursuing Bothwell, but if so no-one believed him for long. As Robert Aston wrote to Bowes, James – following the Chancellor's advice – was fleeing the fury of the people. And, of course, so was the Chancellor.[23] According to Calderwood, their journey had an unpropitious beginning:

> The King and the chancellor went from Edinburgh to Kinneil, to the Lord Hamilton, to eschew the obloquy and murmuring of the people. Hardly could they be assuaged. The provost and magistrates of Edinburgh with great difficulty stayed the crafts from taking arms, to stay the king from riding, and to threaten the chancellor. The soldiers of the king's guard being miscontent their wages were not paid, took the chancellor's trunks and coffers off horseback into the guard-house, till Carmichael made a solemn promise that they should be paid.[24]

The whole court moved frequently over the next five or six weeks: from Kinneil to Linlithgow, then to Glasgow, Dumbarton, back to Glasgow again and then finally to Linlithgow before returning to Edinburgh in the beginning of April.[25]

Through all this time, Maitland found his position at court deteriorating as, rightly or wrongly, more and more of the weight of Moray's murder was loaded on his shoulders. Several rather nasty allegations had been circulating – some even nailed to his chamber door – and, wrote Bowes back to London, 'it is seen that he has now to walk warily, otherwise his life will be in peril'.[26] In addition, the Queen – who owed him a grudge going back to his not favoring James's marriage to her in the first place – evidently seized the opportunity and worked quite effectively to help bring him down. Worse yet, Bothwell – outlawed but always a squall in the offing – fired off a letter to the ministers and elders of Edinburgh that blamed Maitland for just about everything. Not only, he claimed, had he recently 'hounded out the Earl of Huntly most cruelly to murder the Earl of Moray', but he had done everything he could to stir up trouble between Lord Hume and himself, 'esteeming the destruction of both, or any of us, should have made him elbow room, and given an occasion to a puddock-stool of a night to occupy the place of two ancient cedars'.[27] Although he was certainly more outspoken than the rest, Bothwell was far from alone in seeing Maitland as an upstart. He had never been either popular or truly accepted by the generality of the nobles, whatever their faction. The pressure mounted, and by the end of March Maitland was forced to leave the court. Perhaps the King felt that sacrificing him at this point would be seen to some extent as an act of exorcism, but its effect was minuscule, and it left the King standing more alone than ever.

MORAY'S FRIENDS ON THE MOVE

All this time Moray's friends had been far from inactive. 'All men are bent for revenge of this cruel murder,' wrote Roger Aston, 'chiefly the friends of Moray as Mar, Morton, Argyle and Athol with all the Stewarts and the Duke [*of Lennox*] as earnest as any.'[28] It will be remembered that Lady Doune had commissioned Moray's full-length death portrait – with all his wounds agape and Donibristle burning in the background – to be painted and sent to the King. Typically, James refused to look at it, but according to Bishop Percy it was 'carried about, according to the custom of that age, in order to inflame the populace to revenge his death'.[29]

However that may be, Moray's body itself lay unburied in the Kirk at Leith, but his friends were planning a funeral to be held in Edinburgh on 3 March. Almost certainly what they had in mind was a lavish state funeral – catafalque, effigy, banners and all;[30] in fact, the Death Portrait Lady Doune commissioned was probably intended as part of the funeral 'furniture'. Then, once the cortège had reached the Mercat Cross, Moray's mother and friends would present their petitions 'craving earnestly that the King would both punish Huntly's fault', claimed Bowes, 'and also clear his own honour for the pacifying of his grieved subjects'. Bowes saw this funeral as a possible turning point: 'the burial of Murray,' he said, 'will be the birth either of resolution for these motions intended, or else for some other course of revenge to be attempted'.[31]

Bowes may have been right. Had that funeral gone off as planned, it could have dangerously focused the anti-Huntly energy, possibly bringing it to the flashpoint and badly burning the King in the process. But for various reasons it never did take place. Even so, there is no doubt that the old Stewart faction had, as Keith Brown says, 'found a rallying cause',[32] and it could ride on the wave of public indignation, which was by no means slackening. One Robert Stewart, for example, disguised himself well enough to get into Huntly's company, intending to kill him with his pistol, but he was discovered at the last moment. He made his escape, but, said Bowes, he was still resolved 'to exchange lives with Huntly',[33] At the same time, over 160 protestant noblemen signed a declaration that they would have no dealings whatsoever with any of the Donibristle conspirators, 'and neither receive, supply, nor entertain them, nor yet furnish them meat, drink, house, nor harbory, nor otherways have intelligence with them, privately nor publicly, by letters, missives, nor no other manner of way'.[34] Kirk-sponsored, it was admittedly a rather toothless document – in no way a hue and cry after Huntly – but even so it shows the temper of the time.

HUNTLY REACTS

What, then, was Huntly himself doing through all this time? Quite simply, having taken care of his business at Donibristle, he went home to Strathbogie and very likely took care of whatever business had presented itself there in his absence. It was all part of what it took to be an earl, especially the most powerful earl in the north. That is not to say he took the killing of Moray lightly – as on a par with hanging a thief or captured limmer. He knew that what he had done would have serious consequences, and I am sure he had weighed those consequences carefully beforehand. He went home to await their development, that's all.

He had expected, for example, that an angry Kirk would cast the killing in the usual papist/protestant mold, and he knew he would have to deal with whatever the fury of men like Athol, Mar and Ochiltree might mount against him. The King would have to show official anger and even mete him out some token punishment, but once again he knew that

James both needed and loved him. What he hadn't taken into account was the true extent of Moray's popularity and how the hot wind of anger over his murder might drive everything into a firestorm beyond control. Neither, of course had the King, and a letter he wrote Huntly before he left Edinburgh shows his concern both for the Earl's safety and his own. It is worth quoting in full:

> Since your passing herefrom, I have been in such danger and peril of my life, as since I was born I was never in the like, partly by the grudging and tumults of the people, and partly by the exclamation of the ministry, whereby I was moved to dissemble. Always I shall remain constant. When you come here, come not by the ferries; and if you do, accompany yourself, as you respect your own preservation. You shall write to the principal ministers that are here, for thereby their anger will be greatly pacified.[35]

As we have seen, the King did 'dissemble' official outrage by revoking both Huntly's lieutenancy of the north and whatever commission he may have had to pursue Moray – a rather futile post-theft locking of the barn.[36] Taking all things into consideration, Huntly decided not to conciliate but to brazen it out, and to that end he sent the Master of Elphinstone to say that his act was justified by a commission granted him by the King. Since Moray had disobeyed his orders, he claimed, he was forced to assault him in his house, and now he asked only to be tried by the laws of the realm.[37] His saying that he was only following orders threw extra heat on the King, and James agreed to a trial, a move that he felt certain would show his interest in expediting justice.

The trial was set for 7 March, but no-one was quite sure Huntly would show up for it. If he didn't, the military expedition against him, postponed from 11 February, was set to begin on the 10th, setting out from Perth, and all men were commanded to be in readiness. The betting was that Huntly wouldn't come, but all anyone could do now was wait and see.[38]

WARD IN BLACKNESS

Huntly came alright, and in typical Huntly style, moving south to Perth with three hundred horse just a few days before the army for his pursuit was to convene there. Ostensibly he was on his way to his trial, but at this point he was ordered to ward himself in Blackness Castle, an imposing pile shaped rather like a ship and standing on a neck of land out into the Firth of Forth about six miles from Linlithgow (where the court was at the time). Huntly agreed to ward, and as a consequence the expedition against him was again called off.[39] Those who had joined him in the Donibristle raid were supposed to ward in Edinburgh Castle, but they turned out to be less cooperative – some of them suspecting that they might well wind up taking the rap for their leader – and went their separate ways home.

Ward or no, when Huntly entered Blackness on 12 March he took with him enough men to make him master of the place. Moray's friends were furious about this travesty of punishment, and there was talk among them of doing justice in the time-honored way of the feud. Huntly, on the other hand, had expected his ward to last no more than a day or so, and, when he found himself still in Blackness a week later, he too was furious and fired off a remarkable letter to the King, claiming that he was innocent of the slaughter of Moray, and that the Lairds of Cluny, Gight, and Innermarky, having an especial deadly feud against Moray, killed him against his express will, and adding that he himself could not rescue Moray or scarcely save himself from the rage and violence of those lairds.[40] Whatever truth there may have been in his charge, this bit of arrant buckpassing must have vindicated for those lairds the wisdom both of their refusing to go into ward themselves and their fabled insistence that Huntly deliver the *coup de grâce* at the time of the murder.[41]

Since Huntly was in ward pretty much at his own pleasure rather than in true durance, it was suspected that one of his servants like the Master of Elphinstone might come at any time to convoy him home. Should that happen, Argyle, Athol, and Mar planned to get the King's permission to apprehend him and, failing that permission, to apprehend him anyway.[42] In addition, Ochiltree and Athol refused a royal order to come to court until they saw what was going to happen next.

They didn't have to wait long, because on 20 March the King released Huntly from ward, a move that was 'expressly against all justice or equity, and in particular against the common laws of Scotland' according to the indignant author of the *Historie and Life of King James the Sext* some years later.[43] Moysie gives a more contemporary – and, surprisingly for Moysie, less indignant – account:

After he had remained five or six days in ward, he gave in a bill to the council and desired to be freed upon caution that he should appear upon the third day of the next justiciar [*i.e.court*] within the shire where he dwelt, or sooner upon fifteen days warning, and submit to the law for said murder: which . . . was granted by the King and most part of the council, and his release was put in the King's own hands; and so was freed quietly by his Majesty.[44]

To say the least, it was not a popular move. According to Roger Aston, the King's excuse for it was that it had been impossible to gather eight earls to serve as a jury of his peers. In addition, though, Huntly was willing to deny in writing that he had any royal commission for Moray's capture or slaughter, thus getting the King off *that* hook. Finally, while Moray's friends were sure to be angry about Huntly's release, there was very little chance that they would in fact take out after him. Even without throwing the King's personal love for Huntly into the balance – and we can be sure it weighed heavily – there seemed no point in continuing a ward that was both expensive and laughable. Therefore Huntly and his servants left Blackness on 20 March, staying first with his ally the Earl of Crawford until well into May,[45] then heading north to Strathbogie. Ostensibly the Earl was under heavy caution, but, says Moysie, that was never truly established.[46] No question about it, Huntly had survived the worst of the blaze he had kindled in February, but the Affair of Donibristle would continue to smoulder – and even burst into brief flame – for some time to come.

THE GOLDEN ACT

Meanwhile the Lady Doune, according to Calderwood, 'seeing no justice like to be obtained for the murder of her son, left her malediction upon the king, and died in displeasure'.[47] Ambassador Bowes sent the following back to London:

The Lady Doune is dead, by the passion, some think, of her griefs conceived that she was denied to bury the Earl her son honourably in Edinburgh. She has in her testament and with her own hand left an especial note to the King to do justice to preserve himself from violence. Her death and actions and the denial of this burial, have quickened the late murmur amongst the people for Murray's murder.[48]

Meanwhile Moray's body, having been refused interment in the Good Regent's tomb in St. Giles Cathedral, lay in its lead coffin at Leith, an abeyant focus of foment;[49]

Meanwhile Moray's friends continued both to form new alliances and to pressure the King for justice – Ochiltree even saying to the King's face 'that he would embrace and refuse no friendship that would assist and take part in the revenge of that murder';[50]

Meanwhile, as Masson says, 'the rebel Earl Bothwell was zigzagging in arms over the country as he chose, not only defying capture and meditating no one knew what wild new demonstrations of his own, but drawing to him the sympathies of many';[51]

And meanwhile the Kirk kept up its agitation not only for the banishment of all papists but 'for punishment of murder, especially in the persons of Huntly and his accomplices guilty of Moray's slaughter'.[52]

All of which is to say there was still a great deal of Donibristle anger about, and if Huntly could bide his time the King could not afford that luxury.

But what was he to do in order to restore his badly failed popularity and authority? Releasing Huntly from Blackness after only eight days had certainly made matters worse, but, short of completely reversing his field and mounting a full-scale punitive expedition – something he had neither the facilities nor the heart for – he appeared to have no effective options.

However, Chancellor Maitland had recently returned to court after his brief banishment, and he had a plan that should at least get the Kirk off James's back. It called for an act of Parliament that, among other things, ratified all the Kirk's present privileges, granted it the right to call General Assemblies, abolished the ecclesiastical jurisdiction of the bishops, and granted new powers to the presbyteries. Those last provisions must have been especially bitter pills for the strongly episcopal James to swallow, but swallow them he did, along with a provision that repealed most of the hated 'Black Acts' of 1584.

Inevitably this new legislation became known as the Golden Act, 'The Ratification of the Liberty of the True Kirk, of General and Synodal Assemblies, Presbytries, and Discipline; and Laws in the contrary Abrogated'. Passed by Parliament in June of 1592, it gave the Kirk just about everything it could have wanted. 'Mr. John Maitland, chancellor, was a chief instrument to induce the king to pass it at this time,' says Calderwood, 'and that to win the hearts of the ministers and people, alienated from him for his hounding out of Huntly against the Earl of Moray. But the king repented after that he had agreed to it.'53 Calderwood is quite right about that. James hated the act, and in the years to come he not only hindered its application in every way he could, he managed ultimately both to emasculate it and to get his bishops back in power. As Dickinson puts it, 'by a combination of astuteness, subtlety and plain common sense, as well as by bribes, flattery, threats, and some chicanery . . . James was able gradually to graft an episcopal form of government upon a presbyterian church'.54

That James was in time able to recover what he knew he had lost is clearly a measure of his growth in 'kingcraft'. But that he consented in the first place to a piece of legislation as incompatible with his principles as the Golden Act is just as clearly a measure of how desperate he saw his situation to be in the late spring of 1592. And just to make matters worse, less than three weeks later Bothwell, apparently inspired by this latest demonstration of the King's weakness, launched another raid on his person, this time at Falkland. He was beaten off, but still the attempt represented just one more humiliation for James.55

In spite of its recent victory, then, the Kirk kept up its hammering for Huntly's punishment. Later that summer, for example, when James grumbled that the ministers and the people were making a great fuss over Moray's death while seeming not at all exercised over the Earl of Eglinton's recent slaughter, even though Eglinton was of a far higher degree, he was answered that not only was Eglinton killed 'for former feud' in open combat but his killers had been duly punished. What was needed now was 'like justice done on Huntly and his accomplices guilty of the murder of Moray, slain in the King's sight in odious manner and with no little touch to the King's own honour'.56 The Golden Act seems to have bought James very little, if any, good will.

'A REGIONAL CIVIL WAR'

After Blackness and a sojourn with Crawford, Huntly was not long inactive. As early as June Bowes reported that he was 'assembling great forces in the north of persons ready to obey him for love or fear', adding that 'the purpose is not yet known'.57 What was happening was that the feud was becoming, as Keith Brown says, 'a regional civil war',58 with the likes of Athol, Argyle, Macintosh, Grant, and of course Moray on one side, the likes of Huntly, Angus, Errol, Mar and Crawford on the other. A good deal more was involved in the ensuing complex of struggles than simple bloodfeud revenge, and since my purpose is only to follow out the main consequences of Moray's murder to their ultimate resolution, the account of the next decade given in the following pages will suffer from some foreshortening. Happily, though, Keith Brown has covered the broader developments admirably for those who want the more complete story.[59]

To begin with, if Huntly had ever in fact lost his standing as the greatest lord in the north, he was well on his way to regaining it, but even so, all was not entirely well in the summer of 1592 between him and his friends of the Donibristle raid. They were, as Bowes put it, 'at some dryness' with him, because he had allowed them to be put to the horn for Moray's slaughter while he himself clearly remained in the King's good graces.[60] That dryness increased when Huntly received the King's permission to travel abroad, a move that they felt would have left them at the mercy of Moray's friends, and they evidently breathed a collective sigh of relief when he decided not to go.[61] Meanwhile Moray's son and heir – or whoever was acting on his nine-year-old behalf – had recently sent an angry supplication to the King and Parliament calling for proper action against Huntly:

> And [the murder was committed] so openly in the sight of all . . . and so near unto your majesty's own present principal residence and seat of justice that the like was never heard of within this realm nor in any other Christian kingdom before. And therefore deserves to be met and punished and revenged with the most severe extraordinary and most manner of justice and punishment for removing of God's heavy plaints threatened in his law and hanging above this realm and all its inhabitants if this barbarous cruelty be not speedily revenged.[62]

But quite predictably the king did nothing at all. Fighting continued, raid and counterraid, all that summer and fall and well into the winter. Then came the affair of the Spanish Blanks.

Around New Year 1592–3, some blank sheets signed by Huntly, Errol, Angus, and Gordon of Auchindoun were found on the person of a Scottish Jesuit named Ker on his way to Spain. Under torture Ker revealed a plot to bring Spanish troops to Scotland, and indeed the Catholic earls *were* on the verge of revolt. James, while still wanting to keep Huntly and the others as a counterbalance to the Kirk, decided he would have to move against them – however token such a move might be – both to satisfy his own people and to keep good relations with Elizabeth of England. Therefore on 5 February 1593 the Catholic earls were denounced as rebels, while the King moved north with a small army, entering Aberdeen unopposed a week later.

And that was about it. Huntly and his supporters simply melted into the countryside. A few arrests were made, and a high-sounding document was created stating that the subscribed nobility would have no traffic or intercourse with those 'that shall be denounced to the horn, or declared fugitives from his Highness's laws for the treasonable fire raising and burning of the place of Donibristle and murder of the late James Earl of Moray'.[63] But in a matter of weeks Huntly was released from the horn, and later that summer the King suspended the above-mentioned act in view of the 'great incursions by fire-raising, murder of women and bairns and innocent people' Huntly and others were suffering at the hands of 'Clan Chattan and other broken men'.[64] In other words, things had returned to normal, and the King's Aberdeen expedition turned out to be something between a futile gesture and a fraud.

It must have become increasingly clear to everyone – Huntly especially – that the King was not going to mete out any punishment for the Donibristle raid. If anything was going to be done, it would be done the old-fashioned way, and the summer of 1593 does seem to have been especially brutal on both sides. We read that at one point Huntly came 'with an open host and displayed banner . . . and used the greatest cruelty that ever we heard was ever used on Scottish people, with fire & sword, slaughter of men, wives & bairns to the number of ninescore persons . . . and also consumed & dissolved by fire many buildings, places and houses'.[65] In May Huntly decided to repossess once more the fishing rights long in dispute between him and Moray. In the fighting he captured one of Athol's servants 'whom he caused to be hanged and afterwards his head, arms and legs to be cut off in his own presence at Strathbogie and to be put up on poles'.[66] Later in the summer he gave further scope to his macabre brutality. Finding where Athol and Macintosh had sent their cooks a day ahead of them to prepare for their coming, he 'made toward the house where the cooks were and burnt them both, sending the Earls word he had left two roasts for them'. In response, according to the same dispatch, the two earls carried out a raid on Huntly's land where they allegedly slew 158 persons – men, women and children.[67]

Crops laid waste, homes burned, animals driven off or wantonly destroyed, not to mention the angry shapes of death and mutilation war always visits on the innocent – 1593 was an especially unpleasant year for the northeast of Scotland.

GLENLIVET AND ITS AFTERMATH

Nor was there to be any improvement during 1594. In fact, the countryside found itself oppressed by larger and larger armies as young Argyle more and more took over the anti-Huntly leadership from Athol, bringing perhaps 8,000 men into the field. Hearing of his approach, Huntly, with a force of somewhere between a quarter and a half of that number, met him on the slopes of Ben Rinnes in Glenlivet on 3 October and – in a battle Keith Brown describes as 'defying all the military science of the period' – inflicted on him a stunning and decisive defeat.[68] For Huntly, though, Glenlivet was a rather pyrrhic victory, because, while he lost only about twenty men, every one of them was a man of substance, and the number included eleven of the Donibristle raiders.

Meanwhile the King, having finally lost patience with the rebel Catholic lords, came north with a small army on a second punitive expedition. But Huntly and Errol, considering themselves in no position to oppose him, disappeared across the Moray Firth into Sutherland for a while. Perhaps the expedition's most dramatic achievement was a raid on an undefended Strathbogie in which the old tower house was destroyed but the main castle itself was left virtually untouched.[69] Once again, a royal venture north of the Dee fizzled out. James and his army were back in Edinburgh by the end of November, and by early 1595 Huntly was once again unquestionably Cock-of-the-North.

PEACE WITH THE KIRK

Cock-of-the-North he may have been, but he was in no way clear of all his troubles. The Kirk had never let off demanding both his punishment for Moray's murder and his abandonment of the Church of Rome. Early in 1596 he agreed to go into exile in France. There, together with Angus and Errol and the already-exiled Bothwell, he continued to plot Spanish aid until, seeing how futile this was, he and Errol returned to Scotland that summer – 'exile' in this case amounting to no more than a convenient continental junket! However, once he had returned he knew that, like it or not, he would have to make his peace with the Kirk, and making that peace would, at the very least, involve an abject apology for Moray's murder. Needless to say, Huntly was not a man who was much given to making apologies of any sort.

The bargaining got under way, and evidently Rome – or at least Spain – was concerned enough about Huntly's possible 'conversion' to send a Mr. James Gordon, Jesuit, 'of intention to divert him from giving obedience',[70] but the Earl knew full well what it was he had to do. Early in 1597 the General Assembly of the Kirk drew up a list of eleven articles detailing such matters as his Confession of Faith, his willingness to accept instruction, and his agreement to drive out all priests, Jesuits and excommunicated persons from his lands. The seventh article read as follows:

> Anent the slaughter of the Earl of Moray, that he declare his grief and repentance for the same, and promise to make reparation to the party, when the same may be conveniently accepted of, and utter his aforesaid repentance and grief therein, at the time of his public satisfaction aforesaid.[71]

In March Huntly met with the ministers in Aberdeen as they required, and they found him 'obedient and willing to satisfy in all humble manner' all the articles in question. However, the record also speaks of 'long conference and ripe advisement',[72] which I take to mean that Huntly fought hard for the best bargain he could get. It is worth comparing the document accepted at the May General Assembly with the one just given:

> He declared his unfeigned grief for the slaughter of the Earl of Murray, and will satisfy the party at the pleasure of the Kings Majesty, the Kirk, or of godly and indifferent friends, will make offers to that effect; furthermore he has given a blank to his Majesty to be filled up with particular reparation, and that [*to be taken care of*] after his absolution.[73]

Nothing about 'repentance', nothing about 'public satisfaction', and the King would handle whatever reparation there was to be. I have found no record of any reparations, and my guess is that there never were any.

Thus, on 26th June 1597 in the Church of Aberdeen,[74] that most Catholic George Gordon, Sixth Earl of Huntly, was received as a member in good standing of the Kirk of Scotland, and a member he remained for the rest of his long life. Such membership was obviously a political necessity – or at least a tactical convenience – for him, but how deep his conversion ran may be guessed at by the magnificent three-storey sculpted 'frontispiece' he placed over the main doorway to Strathbogie in the early 1600s, some of the imagery of which was so clearly Roman that when the Covenanters briefly took over the castle in 1640 they immediately and virtuously hammered the offensive parts into oblivion.[75]

THE KING ENDS THE FEUD

So much for the Kirk, but the King still had two serious Huntly-related problems. First of all, there was continuing and even growing enmity between Huntly and Argyle – James's two most powerful nobles – and, second, there was still the old Huntly-Moray feud and that matter of reparations. True, Athol had died and Ochiltree's interests were deflected elsewhere, but there were others gathered around Moray – still in his early teens – who remained hot for revenge. What with his accession to the English throne in the offing, James set to work on both problems.

They were tetchy problems for sure, and English intelligencers followed the King's progress – or lack of it – in solving them with great interest: 'The King never was so earnest as now to prepare Argyle and Moray to agree with Huntly (14 March 1601) . . . The King has taken great pains this last week for the agreement of Huntly and Moray, but prevailed not (25 August 1601). . . . The King has travailed much in the agreement . . . yet can neither prevail by entreaty nor threatening (20 April 1602) . . . If it go the worst, it will divide his whole country and till it be agreed the King cannot for any service whatever bring 10,000 of his people in arms together (4 May 1602)'. The man who came in time to be known as Britain's Solomon was obviously suffering a heavy and early tax on his wisdom.[76]

Things went back and forth on both problems for some years, but by February of 1603 James seems to have arranged the general outlines of a remarkable settlement. The details – financial arrangements and the like – are not clear, but the main thrust was brilliant: Huntly was to marry his son and heir to Argyle's eldest daughter, while Moray was to marry Huntly's eldest daughter. As a demonstration of the good will engendered by this agreement, Huntly went to Stirling, where he feasted with both Argyle and Moray, and, said English intelligencer Nicolson in a letter to Lord Cecil, there was 'nothing but kind feasting and company keeping with and among them, one with another, as lovingly as brethren'.[77] For all practical purposes, both problems were solved, and the Northeast could be at peace.

On 24 March 1603, James VI of Scotland became James I of England. Young Moray was one of those attending him on his trip to London. Four years later, on 20 October 1607, Moray did in fact marry Huntly's daughter Anne. The marriage proved both fruitful and – from all we can tell – happy. King James had wrought well.[78]

As for Huntly, on 17 April 1599 James created him a Marquis. Naturally there was some surprise both in England and amongst the Scottish clergy over this advancement, but James asserted it was a thing promised to Lennox at Huntly's marriage to his daughter, 'which promise was now performed unto him to comfort him in that good course of loyalty and conformity in religion, which he doubts not he will continue'.[79] He lived long and prospered. Over the next dozen years he built Strathbogie into one of the most magnificent and luxurious castles in all Scotland. Across the south front these words appear:

GEORGE GORDOVN FIRST MARQVIS OF HVNTLIE
HENRIETTE STEVART MARQVESSE OF HVNTLIE

He died on 16 June 1636 in his seventy-fifth year. 'The marquis was a valiant, provident, and politic man, successful in all his enterprises,' says latter-day genealogist Sir Robert Gordon, and surely we can agree with his assessment. '[*He was*] a great favorite of King James the Sixth,' he continues, 'who loved him entirely', and surely we can agree with that too.[80]

It is perhaps appropriate that he died in the saddle in Dundee, coming from Edinburgh, on the road home to Strathbogie.

CODA I: THE DEATH PORTRAIT

There are two loose ends that ought to be tied off before we close this story, and the first has to do with the so-called Death Portrait. It will be recalled that the King not only refused to look at it, he refused to allow Lady Doune to display it in Edinburgh.[81] There is no further mention in contemporary records of what happened to it then, but later sources, Bishop Percy for one, claim that it was 'carried about, according to the custom of that age, in order to influence the populace to revenge his death'.[82] Since there are records of other pictures being used in this way, that may well be true. For example, shortly after the Regent Moray's assassination in 1570, 'there was hanged forth in the open street an ensign of black satin, on which was painted the King [*i.e. Darnley*] as he was found dead, the Regent in his bed as he died, with his wound open, the King [*i.e. James*] on his knees crying, "Judge and revenge my cause, Lord".'[83] Then in 1595 the Earl of Mar, on the occasion of the feud killing of one of his servants, had his picture painted 'with the number of the shots and wounds, to appear the more horrible and rewthfull [*ruthless?*] to the beholders'.[84]

Three years later that same Earl, declaring the Laird of Johnstone a 'breaker of assurances', had *his* picture – 'drawn in blood to signify a murderer and hung with his heels upwards with his name set under his head and INFAMY and PERJURY written athwart his legs' – displayed 'very solemnly by trumpets and heralds of arms' at the Cross in Edinburgh.[85] In still another instance, such a banner was actually carried in the Laird and Lady of Bargany's funeral procession:

> His Honours being borne by the Goodman of Ardmillane, the Goodman of Kirkhill, with sundry more of the friends. His nephew, young Auchindrayne, bearing the Banner of Revenge, wherein was painted his portraiture, with all his wounds, with his son sitting at his knees, and the phrase written betwixt his hands, 'JUDGE AND REVENGE MY CAUSE, O LORD!' And so, conveyed to Ayr; by all very honourably, to the number of one Thousand horse, of Gentlemen; and laid in the aforesaid tomb.[86]

That, by the way, is probably the kind of funeral Lady Doune and Moray's supporters had in mind.[87]

But – carried through the countryside, borne in a funeral procession, displayed in a public place – whatever was done with them, such pictures could serve but one major purpose: to keep a cause alive. Certainly that was what was behind the creation both of the extant sketch of Darnley's murder at Kirk o'Field in 1567 and the 1568 Darnley memorial painting done for his parents by de Vogeleer.[88] Indeed the latter, with its historical 'window' inset and its speech scrolls, may even have been something of a model for the Moray painting. Interestingly enough, the scrolled call for revenge is shown as if spoken by the infant James in at least three contemporary renderings.[89] Granted that it was obviously a traditional phrase in such paintings, I doubt that the irony of its presence in the Moray Death Portrait would have been lost on the King.

But the Death Portrait is in sharp contrast with the Darnley painting. Where the latter is calm and prayerful, showing the dead lord in full armor atop his medallioned tomb, the former is brutal and direct. Rather than being simply the central point in a careful composition, Moray's naked and muscular body fills the whole seven-foot canvas, with all his wounds – gaping sword cuts on leg and face, right ear a bloody mess, bullet holes in chest and gut – graphically displayed. The inset shows not only Donibristle in flames but, once again, Moray's body lying on the rocks by the shore, his head in a pool of blood. 'GOD REVENGE MY CAUS', reads the scroll. It is hard to imagine a more savage and uncompromising call to action.

After four hundred years is it still possible to determine who the painter of this remarkable work was? No, not for certain, but since it had to be done in a hurry we can be sure it was a local product. There were several Edinburgh painters of that time who specialized in heraldic work – banners, armorials, and the like – and it turns out that one of them, John Workman, was contracted with to prepare 'all ceremony's furnishings thereto belonging and pertaining such as timber, buckram taffeta and other materials given as well as workmanship' for Moray's funeral.[90] Whether that contract included the present painting is open to question, but, since we know that such paintings *were* sometimes carried in funeral processions, it is at least an interesting possibility.

There are some problems, though. The contract is dated 25 April 1592, more than a month after the date for which Moray's funeral was originally planned, and Workman's fee of £53.9.0 was to be paid by 3 August, which makes it sound like *that* was the planned date for the event. Furthermore, on 30 January 1592/3 Workman had to start legal proceedings to get his money, and in fact there is no evidence that he ever did get it, probably because no funeral ever took place! Finally, on 17 February 1592 – well before the date of Workman's contract – Robert Bowes wrote to Lord Burghley that 'the picture of Murray's naked body and wounds is drawn and intended to be shown at the Cross in Edinburgh'.[91] Now of course it is perfectly possible that at first Workman felt that a verbal agreement was sufficient and only went the legal route when he began to have some doubts. Obviously we can't get a true bill either way, but, given the available evidence, John Workman – 'painter, burgess and indweller in Edinbuirgh' – is our most likely candidate for the creator of this painting.

Once it was completed, and once it had served whatever its immediate uses may have been, what happened to it? The first report of it comes in 1765 from Bishop Percy, who, in his headnote to the ballad, said it was in the possession of the present Lord Moray, though he himself made no claim to having seen it. Nor did Rampini over a century later, though he described it rather well (if a little over-dramatically when he refers to its 'blue shades of decomposition'[92]). Apparently it was one of those things that everyone knew *about* and knew was around *somewhere*, but, according to the Randolph Hall Account, it wasn't until around 1912 that Morton, 17th Earl of Moray, discovered it 'rolled up in an ordinary deal box, where presumably it had lain unnoticed for centuries in the Charter Room at Donibristle'.

Today, at Darnaway Castle, it is one of the two main attractions to be seen in Randolph Hall – the other being the magnificent hammer-beam ceiling. It is protected by a heavy wooden frame and case, the panels of which, according to Morton, 17th Earl of Moray, 'are made from the wood of the "Gallows Tree" which stood on the banks of Argaty Burn on the east side of Doune Castle. Tradition has it that prisoners were hung there after trial in the Justice Hall'.[93]

The panels are kept closed most of the time now.

CODA II: THE BODY

The other loose end is the intriguing question of what became of the Earl of Moray's body. Recall that his mother brought it across the Firth from Donibristle to rest in the Kirk of Leith until preparations could be made for its final burial in his father-in-law the Good Regent's tomb in St. Giles.[94] The record shows that James Henryson, surgeon of Edinburgh, received £100 for the embalming of the deceased, and that Quintin Weir, burgess of Edinburgh, received £65 for preparing two lead chests, presumably one for the Earl and one for the Sheriff.[95] Plans were made, as we know, for his funeral to be held on 3 March, but the King would not permit it and the plan was aborted. Over the following years there are occasional references to the Earl remaining unburied, but where was the body sojourning? Still in the Kirk in Leith? There is no way of telling for sure, but so long as it was above ground it remained a symbol of unfinished business for the Stewart faction and a political focus of trouble for the King. Nevertheless, nothing was done until 1598, six years later, when the Privy Council finally got around to ordering his son and his brother (Harry, Commendator of St. Colm) to bury the late Earl 'in the accustomed burial place of their predecessors, within twenty days next after they be charged thereto, under the pain of rebellion and putting of them to the horn'.[96] Presumably that order was carried out.

But *where* was he buried, and where is he now? No-one knows for sure, but according to the present Lord Moray there are three possibilities. The first is a family plot in Dyke churchyard near Darnaway. Family tradition has it that while the Third, Fourth and Fifth Earls are buried there, the Second is not. 'This is/ the/ Burying Place/ of/ The Family of Moray' is all the monument there has to say. The second possibility – again, though, no records – is the old local Kilmadock Cemetery on the estate at Doune. Lord Moray feels that this is the most likely place, and somehow I'm inclined to agree.

The third possibility is that he is in the Good Regent's tomb in St. Giles, which, of course, is where Lady Doune intended he should be, but unfortunately the evidence for his presence there ranges between confounding and hopeless. Back in 1829–33 architect William Burn was commissioned to carry out some extensive restorations to the church, in the course of which he obliterated much of the old architecture. Then in April of 1879 a search was made for the old vault, and the polymath Sir William Chambers reported the results as follows:

> The search was to a certain extent disappointing. No coffin of any kind could be found containing the remains of the illustrious Regent. Three leaden coffins were discovered in a bad condition. The most perfect of these coffins, as seen by the arms and inscriptions, contained the remains of Alexander, fourth Earl of Galloway, born 1670, died 1690. The other two leaden coffins bore neither arms nor inscriptions, and seemed to pertain to persons of a slight figure. It was the opinion of a medical authority present that the remains in one of the coffins were those of a young man; and that the remains in the other were those of a female of middle age . . .
>
> To all appearance, a coffin of some kind had been emptied of its contents, which now lay as a confused heap of bones. A skull picked up from the heap was viewed with much respect. Massive, and with craniological indications of mental superiority, it was believed to be that of the Regent Moray. Such, at least, was our own belief, and that of one or two other persons present. The skull was carefully replaced in the heap of bones alongside the leaden coffins, and to prevent intrusion the vault was immediately built up.[97]

In 1981–82 an archaeological dig rediscovered what must have been the same tomb, finding there 'three lead coffins and fragments of a wooden one', all unidentifiable.[98] Finally, there's the account that has come down in the family. According to the present Earl, some work on the cathedral foundations required that the vault be opened once again in the early 1930s, and several coffins were found within it. The oldest and largest of them was assumed to be the Regent's, but no-one could identify the others.

And there the matter rests. Two lead coffins? Three? Several coffins? A massive skull and a pile of bones? A plaque on the wall of the alcove could identify the 'female of middle age' as the Regent's wife Anne, who became Countess of Argyle after his assassination. She died in 1588. But the others? 'A young man?' Yet the Bonny Earl could hardly be described as 'of slight figure' . . .

The secret is safe, and here we walk away from it. Kilmadock is more likely; but St. Giles is more poetic, and it is gratifying to imagine that fierce old Lady Doune had her way at last.

Sic transit gloria mundi.

NOTES

1 See above, pp.35–37.
2 Lang, ii, p.257n.
3 Moysie, p.89.
4 Moysie, pp.89–90.
5 *C.S.P.Scot.*, x, p.640 (Bowes to Burghley 17 Feb.1592).
6 Moysie, p.90.
7 For Aston, see Lang, ii, p.357n; for Bowes, see *C.S.P.Scot.*, x, p.637 (Bowes to Burghley 13 Feb. 1592).
8 *C.S.P.Scot.*, x, p.643 (Bowes to Burghley 27 Feb. 1692); x, p.663 (Bowes to Burghley 4 Apr. 1592).
9 Moysie, p.89.
10 Brown, *Bloodfeud*, p.157.
11 *R.P.C.*, iv, pp.725, 733n.
12 *C.S.P.Scot.*, x, p.637 (13 Feb. 1592); *R.P.C.*, iv, p.725.
13 Calderwood, v, p.145. See also Moysie, p.90; C.S.P.Scot., x, p.641 (Bowes to Burghley 17 Feb. 1592).
14 Calderwood, v, p.145.
15 Moysie, p.90.
16 Calderwood, v, p.146.
17 Browne, i, p.220. See also Gordon, *Sutherland*. p.216.
18 Maurice Lee, *Great Britain's Solomon* (Champaign: Univ. of Illinois, 1990), p.74.
19 See, for example, *C.S.P.Scot.*, ix, p.595 (11 Aug. 1588), p.666 (7 Jan. 1589), p.703 (5 Mar. 1589); x, p.611; *R.P.C.*, iv, p.464 (6 Mar. 1590).
20 Rev. John Row, *The History of the Kirk of Scotland from the Year* 1558 *to August* 1637 (Edinburgh: The Wodrow Society, 1842), pp.144–45. See also Melvill, *Diary*, pp.309–13.

21 Lang, ii, p.358.

22 Calderwood, v, p.145. For the story of Abner and Joab, see Samuel II:3.

23 C.S.P.Scot., x, p.648 (27 Feb 1592).

24 Calderwood, v, p.146. See also C.S.P.Scot., x, p.642 (Bowes to Burghley 17 Feb. 1592).

25 Moysie, pp.91f.

26 C.S.P.Scot., x, p.642 (Bowes to Burghley 17 Feb. 1592).

27 Calderwood, v, pp.155–56.

28 C.S.P.Scot., x, p.636 (Aston to Hudson 11 Feb. 1592).

29 Percy, Reliques, ii, p.226. See also Charles Rampini, A History of Moray and Nairn (Edinburgh: Blackwood, 1897), p.157. Both men's sources for this statement are unclear.

30 See below, pp.66–69. For another description of the kind of funeral they surely had in mind, see Pitcairn, Kennedy, pp.136–37.

31 C.S.P.Scot., x, p.644 (Bowes to Burghley 27 Feb. 1592).

32 Brown, Bloodfeud, p.157.

33 C.S.P.Scot., x, p.657 (Bowes to Burghley 22 Mar. 1592).

34 Acts and Proceedings of the General Assemblies of the Kirk of Scotland (Edinburgh, 1845), ii, pp.822–23.

35 Calderwood, v, pp.146–47. Calderwood is our only source for this letter.

36 For the uncertainty about what commission or commissions he had, see above, pp.34, 37.

37 C.S.P.Scot, x, p.637 (Bowes to Burghley 13 Feb. 1592); p.648 (Aston to Bowes 27 Feb. 1592). See also Moysie, pp.91–92.

38 C.S.P.Scot., x, p.652 (Aston to Bowes 2 Mar. 1592).

39 C.S.P.Scot., x, p.653 (Bowes to Burghley 17 Mar. 1592); R.P.C., iv, p.733.

40 C.S.P.Scot., x, p.655 (Bowes to Burghley 18 Mar. 1592).

41 See above, pp.40–41.

42 C.S.P.Scot., x, p.656 (18 Mar. 1592). See also Calderwood, v, p.149.

43 Historie, p.248.

44 Moysie, p.92.

45 C.S.P.Scot., x, p.674.

46 Moysie, p.92.

47 Calderwood, v, p.149. See also Moray Muniments, 2/4/58 (3 Jun. 1592).

48 C.S.P.Scot., x, p.679 (Bowes to Burghley 29 May 1592).

49 Moray Muniments, 1/1/202 (15 Nov. 1592), 12/43/195.

50 Moysie, p.93.

51 R.P.C., iv, p.749n.

52 C.S.P.Scot., x, p.679 (Bowes to Burghley 29 May 1592).

53 Calderwood, v, p.612.

54 William Croft Dickinson, Scotland from the Earliest Times to 1603

(London and Edinburgh: Thomas Nelson, 1965), p.358. See also Agnes Mure Mackenzie, *The Scotland of Queen Mary* (Edinburgh: Oliver & Boyd, 1957; first published 1936), pp.227–29; Gordon Donaldson, *Scotland: James V to James VII* (Edinburgh: Oliver & Boyd, 1965), pp.198–201; Willson, p.109; Lang, ii, p.359.

55 Moysie, p.94; *C.S.P.Scot.*, x, pp.708–09 (Bowes to Burghley 28 Jun. 1592); Melville, *Memoirs*, pp.408–09.

56 *C.S.P.Scot.*, x, p.746 (Bowes to Burghley 6 Aug. 1592).

57 *C.S.P.Scot.*, x, p.705 (Bowes to Burghley 24 June 1592).

58 Brown, *Bloodfeud*, p.161.

59 *Ibid.*, pp.161–73.

60 *C.S.P.Scot.*, x, p.719 (Bowes to Burghley 4 Jul. 1592).

61 *C.S.P.Scot.*, x, pp.741, 748, 760 (Bowes to Burghley 30 Jul., 6 Aug., 17 Aug. 1592).

62 Moray Muniments 2/4/58 (3 Jun. 1592).

63 *C.S.P.Scot.*, x, p.662 (Mar. 1593); xi, p.70 (13 Mar. 1593).

64 *C.S.P.Scot.*, xi, p.153 (22 Aug. 1593).

65 Moray Muniments, 2/4/180 (1602).

66 *C.S.P.Scot.*, xi, p.91 (Bowes to Burghley 20 May 1593).

67 *C.S.P.Scot.*, pp.165–66 (Aug. 1593).

68 Brown, *Bloodfeud*, pp.167–68, 180 (n.200); *C.S.P.Scot.*, xi, pp.456–60.

69 W. Douglas Simpson and Christopher J. Tabraham, *Huntly Castle* (Edinburgh: HMSO, n.d.), p.7.

70 *History of the Church of Scotland*, p.61.

71 *Acts and Proceedings*, ii, p.897.

72 *C.S.P.Scot.*, xii, p.550 (14 May 1597).

73 *Acts and Proceedings*, iii, p.919. See also pp.922, 929, 934.

74 *History of the Church of Scotland*, p.62.

75 For a good picture and a detailed diagram and explanation of this doorway, see Simpson and Tabraham, *Huntly Castle*, pp.24–25.

76 *C.S.P.Scot.*, xiii, pp.788, 870, 967, 978 (all Nicholson to Cecil).

77 *C.S.P.Scot.*, xiii, p.1106 (1 Feb.1603).

78 Doubleday, ix, p.186.

79 *C.S.P.Scot.*, xiii, pp.450–51 (Nicholson to Cecil 20 Apr. 1599); p.489 (31 May 1599).

80 Gordon, *Sutherland*, p.479.

81 See above, pp.50, 54.

82 Thomas Percy, *Reliques of Ancient English Poetry* (New York: Dover, 1966; originally published in 1765), ii, p.226.

83 *C.S.P.Scot.*, iii, pp.92–93 (Randolph to Cecil 1 Mar. 1570).

84 Duncan Thomson, *Painting in Scotland 1570–1650* (Edinburgh: National Galleries of Scotland, 1975), p.34. Quoted from *Historie*, pp.346–47 (T. Thomson 1825 edition).

85 Brown, *Bloodfeud*, p.29. Quoted from *Border Papers*, ii, p.538 (Bowes to Burghley 5 Jun. 1598).

86 Pitcairn, *Kennedy*, p.68. Quoted in part in Brown, *Bloodfeud*, p.30.

87 See above, p.54.

88 See Dana Bentley-Cranch, 'Effigy and Portrait in Sixteenth Century Scotland', *Review of Scottish Culture*, 4 (1988), pp.11, 13. For better reproductions, see Rosalind K. Marshall, *Queen of Scots* (Edinburgh: HMSO, 1986), pp.145, 148–49.

89 See Marshall, *Queen of Scots*, pp.145, 148–49, 159.

90 Scottish Record Office, Register of Deeds, 1/43, fol.103–04 (30 Jan 1592). See also Thompson, *Painting in Scotland*, p.34.

91 *C.S.P.Scot.*, x, p.641.

92 Rampini, p.157.

93 Randolph Hall Account.

94 See above, p.50.

95 Moray Muniments, 1/1/202 (23 Mar. 1592, 20 Nov. 1592).

96 *R.P.C.*, v, pp.444–45 (16 Feb. 1598). This order was a double one, commanding not only Moray's burial but also that of John, Lord Maxwell, a victim of the Johnston–Maxwell feud in the borders, who had been killed 6 December 1593. See *R.P.C.*, v, pp.112–13 (22 Dec. 1593); Child, iv, pp.34–38 (Child 195: 'Lord Maxwell's Last Goodnight').

97 William Chambers, *Historical Sketch of St. Giles' Cathedral, Edinburgh* (Edinburgh: W.&R. Chambers, 1890), pp.li–lii. I am extremely grateful to Mr. J. Campbell Penney, Elder of St. Giles', for his help in this matter.

98 'The Archaeological Dig in St. Giles' 1981–82: Provisional Report', p.4.

The Ballad

CHAPTER FOUR

The Murray Ballads

THE FIRST 'BONNY EARL'

IN THE EARLY 1700s, a young Scots musician by the name of William Thomson settled in London, just in time to catch the wave of enthusiasm for 'Scotch songs' that was breaking over the English capital.[1] He appears to have become a rather fashionable singer and teacher, and in 1725 he published *Orpheus Caledonius or a Collection of the best Scotch Songs set to Musick by W. Thomson* fifty songs with their melodies and a bass accompaniment. Apparently this edition was very successful, because in 1733 he brought out a second, this one in two volumes and including fifty more songs, one of them being 'The Bonny Earl of Murray':

Ye *Highlands* and ye *Lawlands*,
Oh! where ha'e ye been:
They ha'e slain the Earl of *Murray*,
And they laid him on the Green.

Now wae be to thee Huntly,
And wherefore did ye sae;
I bad you bring him wi' you,
But forbad you him to slae.

He was a braw Gallant,
And he rid at the Ring;
And the bonny Earl of *Murray*,
Oh! he might have been a King.

He was a braw Gallant,
And he play'd at the Ba',
And the bonny Earl of *Murray*,
Was the Flower amang them a'.

He was a braw Gallant,
And he play'd at the Glove,
And the bonny Earl of *Murray*,
Oh! he was the Queen's Love.

Oh! lang will his Lady,
Look o'er the Castle-*Down*,
E'er she see the Earl of *Murray*,
Come sounding through the Town.

Moray's murder took place in 1592, and while logic suggests that a ballad about it would have emerged while the event was still hot copy, Thomson's is the earliest version we have, which leaves us with a hiatus of almost a century and a half. One way of accounting for such a hiatus is to deny its existence by claiming that the ballad was *not* written in 1592 but in 1733 or thereabouts. No question about it, a great deal of eighteenth-century ballad activity did consist of patching-up and piecing-out 'imperfect' texts or even occasionally making them up out of the whole cloth, and a fair swatch of twentieth-century ballad scholarship has been devoted to identifying these impostures (though 're-creations' would be a more charitable term).[2] But only Robert Chambers – who traced just about all the best-known ballads back to Lady Wardlaw (d.1827) – suggested that 'The Bonny Earl of Murray' was such a text, and there is general scholarly agreement as to both its antiquity and excellence. David Fowler, for example, based his *A Literary History of the Popular Ballad* on the assumption that 'a given ballad took the particular shape it has about the time it was written down', yet he accepted 'The Bonny Earl's' antiquity, even seeing it as a source upon which eighteenth-century imitators drew heavily.[3] Where Thomson found it we do not know,[4] but it's at least a good guess that it was taken down from singing somewhere back along the line, if not by Thomson then by his source – or *his* source.

King James VI and I at age 29 (1595). (*Scottish National Portrait Gallery.*)

Above: George Gordon, 6th Earl of Huntly. From a pencil and wash drawing by Charles Kirkpatrick Sharpe, after an unknown artist. *Scottish National Portrait Gallery.* (Computer enhancement by Alaric Faulkner.)

Left: Medallion image of Huntly on one of the magnificent fireplaces in Huntly Castle.

A likeness of James Stewart, 2nd Earl of Moray. (Computer generated from Death Portrait by Alaric Faulkner.)

Doune Castle. *Photograph by Valentine of Dundee.* (R.C.A.H.M.S.)

Darnaway Castle as it appears today. (R.C.A.H.M.S.)

Donibristle as it might have appeared before the fire. According to Alexander Fenton, the surrounding wall was more to protect against animals and the like than to act as a defense against attack. The long central complex included the living quarters and a possible byre; on the right is a stackyard and barn, while the nearest buildings may be horse barns, servant quarters, or both. (From the Death Portrait insert. Computer enhancement by Alaric Faulkner.)

Donibristle in flames. (From the Death Portrait insert. Computer enhancement by Alaric Faulkner.)

The shore at Donibristle as it appears today. Compare to the shore as it appears in the illustrations above.

The Death Portrait. (*Reproduced by kind permission of Lord Moray.*)

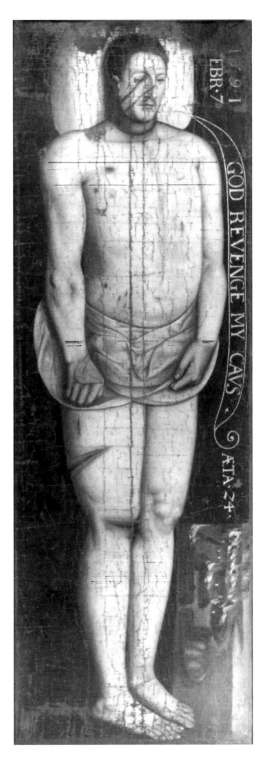

Blackness Castle, where Huntly was warded for eight days. (R.C.A.H.M.S.)

Strathbogie or Huntly Castle, as it appeared in the early nineteenth century. (R.C.A.H.M.S.)

Dyke churchyard, where the 3rd, 4th, and 5th Earls of Moray are buried. The Moray plot is the one with the iron fence.

The old Kilmadock cemetery in Doune, where Lord and Lady Doune – and very likely the Bonny Earl – are presumed to be buried.

The 'hiatus' is better explained by the fact that during the seventeenth century there wasn't enough literary or musical interest in ballads or folksongs to have encouraged anyone to write them down. That is, they were *there*; the 'folk' were singing them alright, but no-one who counted was paying any attention – except, of course, the occasional oddball antiquary, like whoever was the compiler of that famous manuscript Bishop Percy found under a bureau in Shropshire.[5] The first stirrings of the Romantic Movement, with its emphasis on the local and medieval, changed all that, and Thomson's little collection was a response to those stirrings.

SIXTEENTH-CENTURY SCOTTISH BALLADRY

Unfortunately we have no *direct* evidence that 'The Bonny Earl of Murray' was composed in 1592, but the circumstantial evidence is compelling. To begin with, there was enough ballad-singing and like activity in Scotland for officialdom to look on it as a first-rate nuisance and even to take legislative and judicial steps to control it. James Porter gives us a fair sampling:

> In 1560 Edinburgh ordered all 'vagabonds, fiddlers, pipers' without masters to depart the city on pain of burning of the cheek, and again in 1579 it held 'all minstrels, singers, and tale-tellers' as 'idle beggars' unless attached to Lords of Parliament or burghs as their common minstrels. In 1587 the same city issued an edict against 'common sangsters,' especially those who sang 'bawdy and filthy sangs.'[6]

That same officialdom also tried to control the printing of ballads. There had been presses in Edinburgh ever since Chapman and Millar set up the first one around 1508, and, as printers to the south had found that ballads in single-sheet were a profitable commodity, so did those in the Scottish capital. One Robert Lekpreuik, for example, was well-known for his enterprise in this métier, and, according to Brother Kenneth, his press produced 'a constant stream of ballads and broadsheets during the troubled times of Mary's short reign and the subsequent regencies of Moray, Lennox and Mar'.[7] In 1552 an act prohibiting the printing of 'ballads, songs, and blasphemous rhymes without license'[8] was passed, followed by another in 1567 – it even became a crime to fail to destroy such broadsides on sight! – but evidently none of this legislative activity stemmed the flow.[9] There was at least one black-letter broadside – a pretty ferocious one – lamenting the murder of Darnley (1567) and evidently a whole series on the assassination of the Regent Moray three years later.[10] Nor was

Edinburgh the only city plagued with publishing problems. 'Upon the twelfth day of August,' says William Moysie in a note dated 1579, 'one William Trumbill and William Scot was hanged at the cross of Sterling for making of certain ballads, which were thought able to sow discord amongst the nobility. And this was thought a new precedent, seeing none had been executed for the like before'.[11] I doubt that 'The Bonny Earl of Murray' was a creature of the broadside press, but the fact that there *was* an active broadside press indicates that its products found a ready market – a ballad-singing and ballad-listening public.

It is also important that 1592 comes right in the middle of an extremely creative period for Scottish historical ballads. Hodgart sums it all up nicely:

> There are about thirty, including the border ballads, which are based on sixteenth century and about twenty based on seventeenth century history . . . Some of them, like 'Edom o' Gordon', appear in manuscript quite soon after the event, and there is no reason to doubt that the others were composed at about the same time. The period between 1550 and 1650 seems to have been the one most productive of historical or semi-historical ballads.[12]

Four of these ballads, including 'The Bonny Earl of Murray', are based on incidents that happened in 1592, two of them, 'Willie Macintosh' (Child 183) and 'The Baron of Brackley' (Child 203), being based on episodes that were direct consequences of Moray's murder and another, 'The Laird of Logie' (Child 182), telling of Queen Anne helping – for reasons of the heart – one of her husband's prisoners escape execution. Three others deal with feuding between the Gordons and their traditional enemies.[13] Clearly, the Scottish ballad muse was on the *qui vive* at the time.

Finally, there is one intriguing bit of evidence that is as close as we'll ever come to direct proof that 'The Bonny Earl of Murray' appeared soon after the murder. It will be recalled that popular outrage over Moray's murder brought Edinburgh close enough to riot for King and Chancellor to think it prudent to leave town for over a month, the King claiming that he had never 'been in such danger and peril' before.[14] That outrage was not simply a thing of the moment. Abetted by constant harangues from the Kirk, it continued for some months until James in desperation promulgated the so-called Golden Act, hoping it would quiet things down. James Melvill, nephew to Andrew, made the following triumphal entry in his Diary (the italics are mine):

The fear of Bothwell's remaining always within the Country, and often times hard about the Court, together with the horror of the deed of Donibristle, which the unburied corpse lying in the Kirk of Leith, made to be not only unburied amongst the people, but *by common rhymes and songs kept in recent detestation*, as much as the public threatening of God's judgments thereupon from pulpits, obtained . . . beyond our expectations that which had cost us much pain in vain many years before, to wit, the Ratification of the liberty of the true Kirk.[15]

'It is strange to think that *The Bonny Earl o' Moray* should have helped to rivet Calvinism on Scotland,' said historian Agnes Mure Mackenzie. 'Yet so it would appear from James Melville's record.'[16] That same record makes it clear that people were singing about Moray's murder not long after the event itself. Of course, there is nothing that says for sure that the ballads we have today are the very ones – or even among the ones – that were being sung in the streets of Edinburgh in the spring of 1592, but that is at least a very strong presumption, and it is a presumption supported by all my own primary research on the ballads and songs of the American lumberwoods, where I find that topical songs invariably appeared shortly after the events they celebrated.[17] To doubt the authenticity of the extant ballads seems a cavil on the tenth part of a hair. If that often grouchy but always skeptical old scholar Joseph Ritson could conclude that '"The Bonny Earl of Murray" may reasonably be supposed contemporary with the event of his murder',[18] we may too, leaving any naysayers to bear the burden of proof.

EVOKED NARRATIVE, CONNOTATION, COMMONPLACE

Up to this point we have been talking *about* – or even *around* – 'The Bonny Earl of Murray'. We have looked at it from three points of view, all of them historical. First of all, we spent a great deal of time on 'what really happened'. Second, we considered the ballad's origin as an artifact, and we will return to this perspective in a following section on that artifact's history. Third, we have just finished looking at the ballad as agent, as an entity that played its part in human affairs. It is time now to look at the ballad for what it is in itself – a work of art, an evocative presence, both in terms of what it evokes and how.

But evoked in who? I have already said in the Prologue what images Dyer-Bennet's singing evoked in one mid-twentieth-century folkie, and I will pick this theme up again in a following section. That 'The Bonny Earl of Murray' has survived over four centuries is evidence that it has spoken to many generations, but what I want to do now is go back to the beginning and ask what would a hip and ballad-singing (or at least ballad-listening) Scot of 1592 have made of this song? To put that another way, assuming that, like all ballads, 'The Bonny Earl of Murray' had a very individual author, what associations, what connotations did that author work into his ballad for listeners and singers to pick up on, and what knowledge could he reasonably have expected them to bring to it?

To take the second question first, since he does not *tell* the story, it is clear he took it for granted that everyone knew it – that it was, as I said earlier, hot copy. That one line in the first stanza ('They ha'e slain, etc.') would call up the whole, and both singer and audience could then properly place whatever bits and pieces followed within that evoked framework. It is a technique that fits rather nicely the description of what Wilgus and Long called the 'blues ballad':

> The total story is a given, and the ballad performer, secure in his knowledge that his audience is familiar with the referent . . . selects a scene or a number of scenes for presentation and, freed from the necessity of presenting circumstantial detail, concentrates on conventionalized dramatic scenes, oblique delineations of character through action and speech, and lyrical comment by characters or the narrator.[19]

They go on to show that this idea, this way of treating a story, 'antedates the traditional type [*of ballad*] by at least five hundred years', and they point to examples in both early Irish and Welsh traditions,[20] where no form like the British ballad – 'no self-contained drama recounted in successive stages' – is to be found at all.[21] However, others have noted the 'Bonny Earl's' resemblance to Gaelic praise songs, laments and funeral dirges celebrating the virtues and mourning the loss of the deceased. Friedman, for example, says of Sir Walter Scott that 'he found in "The Bonny Earl of Murray" a ballad that had been modeled on the Gaelic coronach, and this ballad seems to have suggested to him the tone and shape of his pibrochs and clan-gathering songs.[22] But all this gets us pretty far afield. While 'The Bonny Earl of Murray' has little direct resemblance to the lavish and detailed Gaelic praise songs, its author was making use of the same framing technique – that of evoked narrative – and using it most appropriately: to frame a lament.

Not only could he count on his audience to supply the necessary history, he could also count on it to respond to a common fund of direct meanings and oblique – some of them very oblique indeed – allusions. That, of course, says no more than that he and his audience shared a world of discourse, and fortunately language is a stable enough medium to allow us to share much of that world four hundred years later. Yet in numerous ways their world was *not* our world. Playing 'at the Ba'', for example, has a rather general but no specific referent for us today, but I am sure anyone at the time not only would have known exactly what that game was but also would have understood what his playing it said about Moray's character.

On this general level, the world of discourse we have been talking about would be common to all communicative events. A word or phrase, that is, would 'mean' about the same thing whether it appeared in a book, a conversation, a joke or a song, and its connotative possibilities could be exploited in any medium or genre. On the other hand, there are formulations that have special significance in one form but not necessarily in others, and folk balladry has always been famous for this kind of genre-specific language. William Motherwell was one of the first to call attention to it back in 1827, saying that one of the 'never varying features of these compositions' was their 'ever agreeing in describing certain actions in one uniform way'.[23] Someone arriving at a gate 'tirled at the pin'; a message is delivered with the following exchange:

'What news, what news, my little wee boy?
    What news hae ye to me?'
'Bad news, bad news, my master dear,
    Bad news as you will see.'

Or a man will call for his horse:

'O saddle me the black, the black,
    Or saddle me the brown:
O saddle me the swiftest steed
    That ever rade frae a town.'

Sometimes it is a matter of a simple epithet – 'red, red gold', 'milk-white steed', 'clay-cold lips'. These words and phrases are generally called 'commonplaces', and their presence in a poem sets us squarely in the special ballad world. They have been much studied and used to support various theories of ballad origins and transmission, but by far the most comprehensive – and sensible – treatment of them is Flemming Andersen's recent *Commonplace and Creativity*, in which he introduces the concept of 'ballad formula': a special kind of commonplace, action-oriented rather than simply descriptive, and 'imbued with distinctive overtones from their various related contexts'. In other words, a formula not only tells us what happened but – through the freight it carries from association with other ballads – how to feel about what happened.[24] Since, in 'The Bonny Earl of Murray', what is implied is as important – if it isn't more important – than what is stated, I will have a great deal to say about formulas and formulaic language in the following pages.

EXPLICATION DE TEXTE: VERSION 'A'

I will go through each version stanza by stanza, even, at times, line by line, in order to explain whatever I think needs explaining, but I would like to preface that detail with two general observations. First, several scholars have paralleled the way ballads tell their stories with the cinematic technique of montage. 'They present the narrative,' says Hodgart, 'not as a continuous sequence of events but as a series of rapid flashes, and their art lies in the selection and juxtaposition of these flashes,'[25] and while that certainly describes our ballad, only one of its stanzas, the second, can properly be called narrative, the rest being descriptive. Second, while it is, like other ballads, stanzaic, the 'shots' being organized stanza by stanza, the stanza form is an unusual one, the first and third lines having three stresses (rather than the standard four) with the final foot in each case being a trochee rather than the more common iamb ('He wás a bráw Gállant'). I have found only three other ballads in Child's collection that use that form.[26] In addition, the poet set himself the task of having each third line end with 'Earl of Murray'. Without moving it entirely outside the pale, these traits certainly distance 'The Bonny Earl of Murray' from standard ballad repertoire. Much of the following discussion will clarify, if not increase, that distance, and it is time now to move on.

I.

Ye *Highlands* and ye *Lawlands*,
Oh! where ha'e ye been:
They ha'e slain the Earl of *Murray*,
And they laid him on the Green.

I know of no other Child ballad that opens with an apostrophe, even though it is a common enough device in Scottish poetry. Its usual place, though, is in song. Burns, for instance, opens some of his best lyrics in this way:

> 'Ye banks and braes o' bonnie Doon,
> How can ye bloom sae fresh and fair?'

> 'Flow gently, sweet Afton, among thy green braes,
> Flow gently, I'll sing thee a song in thy praise.'

However, a 1570 black-letter broadside on the assassination of the Regent Moray begins as follows:

> Ye Mountaines murne, ye valayis wepe,
>   Ye clouds and firmament,
> Ye fluids dry up, ye seyis so depe
>   Deploir our lait Regent.
> Ye greinis grow gray, ye gowanis dune,
>   Ye hard rocks ryve for sorrow:
> Ye mariguildis forbid the sune
> To oppin yow euerie morrow.

In fact, nine of its ten stanzas are one long apostrophe.[27] But the device is extremely rare in traditional balladry. I can think of only one example, 'The Schooner *Gracie Parker*', a shipwreck ballad from Prince Edward Island:

> St. Pierre's Isle, how can you smile
> While we poor souls lament?
> You've deprived us of our friends so dear,
> Why do you not repent?[28]

As for what is apostrophized, 'Hielands and Lawlands' is first of all a call to the people living on the Earl's domains in Moray, an area which, as Buchan points out, 'belongs to both Highlands and Lowland',[29] the fertile Lowlands (The *Laich*) along the Moray Firth, the wild Highlands to the south, and Darnaway just about on the line between them. We see the area so referred to in Moray's royal commission as a warden at the time of the Great Armada: he is to watch 'baith hieland and lawland'.[30] Specific it may be, but certainly it is also a general cry to all of Scotland: 'How did you let such a thing happen?' Fortunately, we do not have to make a choice between these two possibilities. We can have it both ways.

What are we to make of the next two lines? Obviously they are not historical. Huntly and his servants slashed Moray to death and left him on the rocks by the shore. My hunch is, though, that the poet took his inspiration here not from life but from art, not from knowing what actually happened but from having seen the so-called Death Portrait, which shows Moray's body lying (rather formally pillowed) on the ground, and while the years have turned that ground nearly black, it is a black that was once green (in fact, in the inset picture it *is* still green). The King may have refused to look at it, but certainly Lady Doune saw to it that many, both in Edinburgh and in the Moray domains to the north, did look at it in those days following the murder.

I can find no special overt or covert significance for the phrase 'laid him on the Green', save that both the color green and the idea of a 'village green' have certain peaceful connotations that crosscut the violence of the slaying and prepare a contrast for the sharp dramatic interjection of the following stanza.

2.

Now wae be to thee Huntly,
And wherefore did ye sae;
I bad ye bring him wi' you
But forbad you him to slae.

For the sake of the argument, if we consider 'The Bonny Earl of Murray' without this stanza it becomes less a ballad than a neatly proportioned lyric outcry: an introductory stanza, three incremental comments on Moray's character, and a conclusion, all consistently spoken by an impassioned persona, presumably the poet himself.[31] The present stanza breaks that almost perfect mold by suddenly shifting us out of a discursive frame into a dramatic one: we are no longer talking *about* the event but *witnessing* its aftermath, and the speaker is no longer the poet or singer but King James angrily charging Huntly with malfeasance. Then in the next stanza, we just as suddenly shift back again.

There are two ways of accounting for this breakaway. First, it was part of the original poet's plan; second, it is the result of conflation – a subsequent singer accidentally or intentionally including this stanza from another Murray ballad, and indeed there is a remarkably similar stanza in the 'B' version. Conflation is by far the more likely answer. As I have already suggested, leave this stanza out and the poem is an almost perfectly structured lament: introduction, three incremental stanzas of praise, and conclusion, all in consistent voice and each stanza's third line ending with the same phrase, 'the bonny Earl of *Murray*'. I cannot believe our poet would have been so careful and so inconsistent all at once, but I will return to this question later on.

3.
He was a braw Gallant,
And he rid at the Ring;
And the bonny Earl of *Murray*,
Oh! he might have been a King.

'Repetition,' said Edson Richmond, 'is not only the hallmark of folk poetry, it is the very sum and substance of its being.'[32] *Mutatis mutandis*, the same could be said of any art form, but no question about it, ballads are particularly noted for their dependence on special kinds of repetition.[33] Perhaps the best known is what Gummere called *incremental repetition*, where 'each increment in a series of related facts has a stanza for itself, identical, save for a new fact, with other stanzas'.[34] Usually this device is employed to move the narrative along stepwise by the stanza – or occasionally by the half-stanza – but in the present ballad it has no narrative function at all. Rather it is used – over the space of three stanzas – to comment on the Earl's character in some rather subtle ways.

Since we are told the Earl was 'a braw gallant' three times, we can assume those words are important. What, then, did they mean in the late sixteenth century? *Braw* meant then pretty much what it means today – anything from 'brave' to 'splendid' by way of 'beautiful' – but to call a man a *gallant* was not only to say that he was dashingly well suited to fashionable society but also to suggest that he was something special with the ladies, even, perhaps, a wooer or a paramour. Here, of course, the only direct statement is that he rode at the ring, a proper activity for a young gallant. But the allusion, oblique as it may be, prepares the ground for what will come in stanza five.

Riding at the ring was a form of tilting or the quintain, in which a mounted horseman tried to spear a suspended ring on the point of his lance. In his *Sports and Pastimes of the People of England* (1801), Joseph Strutt speaks of it as 'a fashionable pastime in former days',[35] and we know that it was something of a passion with young King James. 'This day he ran for the golden ring on the pied horse,' wrote Robert Aston to Leicester in June of 1580. 'There were six who challenged all comers. The King was a defendant, and ran right bravely.'[36] Another intelligencer a year later speaks of it twice: 'The King ran that day [*Tuesday*] at the ring, and,' he adds, 'for a child ... did very well ... On Thursday the

King dined at Leith, and after dinner he ran at the ring and beheld such other pastimes as were to be seen'.[37] And, according to Willson, when he arrived in England in 1603 he was rather annoyed to discover that other riders were more skilful at this sport than he was.[38]

Might Moray have been King? If we ignore history and take the ballad simply on its own terms, yes, had the Bonny Earl graduated from 'Queen's love' to 'Queen's husband' he would then have been King indeed (or the next best thing to it), and I am quite sure that is how most people singing or hearing the ballad down the years have interpreted that line. It is only when we let our knowledge of history get in our way that we have any trouble with it, because in no way was he in the direct line of succession. However, his father-in-law, the Good Regent, *was* the eldest son of James V; had he been legitimate, then he, not Mary, would have succeeded his father, and – all else being equal – the Bonny Earl would have succeeded him. But that is to let contingency tease us out of thought. It is worth mentioning only as something that might have been on the edge of the makar's mind. Whatever his reasons may have been, if his purpose in creating this ballad was incendiary – and I think it was – then raising the killing from a common bloodfeud occurrence to a possible matter of state would certainly have fanned the flames.

All of which raises two interesting and closely related final points. First, one does not have to be a Freudian (at least not much of a one) to see that lance-and-ring can have erotic connotations. If we accept that idea, then 'rid at the Ring' can imply Moray's sexual prowess, especially when taken together with his being a 'braw Gallant'. Second, in saying that he 'might have been a King' (and whoever took that phrase down from oral tradition could easily have mistaken 'the' for 'a') is the ballad suggesting that Moray was quite as good at what James did as James was himself – and not only on horseback? On its own, that seems far-fetched; taken together with what follows – both overt statement and glancing metaphor – it works.

4.
He was a braw Gallant,
And he play'd at the Ba',
And the bonny Earl of Murray,
Was the Flower amang them a'.

Monday, 5th March, 1990, and a group of us from the School of Scottish Studies had driven down from Edinburgh to Denholm to watch the playing of the annual Ba' Game. It had been explained to me that there were two sides – where you lived in town determined whether you were an Uppie or a Doonie – and the object of the game was to get control of the ball and put it in the other side's goal or 'hail', some distance out of town, by whatever means necessary, restraint being limited, as Brian Shuel says, to 'Knock a man down but don't 'urt 'im'.[39] It was a gray day with a small cold intermittent rain, which probably explained why no more than a score of young men had gathered on the green (the number would double later on), but soon a publican came out carrying a small beribboned leather ball, which he tossed into their midst. A scrum formed and, save for an occasional grunt, nothing much seemed to happen, but finally someone broke loose and started down the green, the others in hot pursuit. Someone brought him down, which led to another scrum, until finally a lad got free and disappeared up the road, traffic be damned, a lorry having to veer onto a sidewalk to miss him and his pursuers. That was that until the players drifted back, and the whole process began again as another publican threw up another ball.

Two or three wet rounds of that were enough for me that day, and I headed for the nearest pub, where, warmed by a couple of pints before a grand fire, I recalled that the Bonny Earl had played 'at the Ba'', and I began to wonder a rather obvious wonder. Back at the School, a little research revealed that while the game varied from village to village, ever since the sixteenth century – and probably long before that – some variation of it had been known in villages from the north of England to the Orkneys under such names as Hurling, the Hood Game, Hand Ba', Shrovetide Football, Street Football, or even just Football or The Ba'. It was usually seasonal, played either at New Year or Shrove Tuesday (actually the game I watched came a week after Shrove Tuesday), and it might involve as many as a hundred or so young men – and some not so young – on each side.[40]

The evidence is also pretty clear that it was very much a pastime of the commons: townspeople, farm laborers, apprentices, tradesmen, etc., although in Sir David Lyndsay's 'Ane Pleasant Satyre of the Thrie Estaites' (c.1540) even the village parson, admitting his neglect of spiritual matters, joined in:

> I wait thair is nocht amang you all,
> Mair ferlie can play at the fut-ball.[41]

But members of the first estate showed up from time to time and when they did they evidently took the game as seriously as any villager. In fact, in 1583 the young Earl of Bothwell challenged the Master of Marischal to a duel over an incident during a game of football in which one kicked the other, and George, Fifth Earl of Huntly – the ballad Huntly's father – died in 1576 of a fit while playing football. There is even a tradition that King James V himself, though carefully disguised, once joined in the game at Jedburgh.[42]

Obviously, then, there was precedent for the Bonny Earl's playing at The Ba', but just as obviously the ballad poet saw this playing as significant.[43] Here was a man, he seems to be telling us, who not only was expert at knightly pursuits but also delighted in common rough-and-tumble on the village green – a real guy, not one of your standoffish aristocrats![44] It is a theme found so often in the lives of great men who have become popular heroes as to make further documentation of it superfluous. In passing, though, I will add that both the Death Portrait and contemporary descriptions show Moray to have been a big and powerful man, a splendid asset to the Uppies, if it didn't turn out he was a Doonie.

To take connotation even further, playing at the ball has a special place in the language of ballads, as Flemming Andersen has demonstrated. The following stanza from 'Little Musgrave and Lady Barnard' (Child 81) is typical:

> Four and twenty handsome youths
>   Were a' playing at the ba,
> When forth it came him Little Munsgrove,
>   The flower out ower them a'.

Andersen cites eleven ballads in which this formula is employed in one form or another, and his comments are very much to the point here:

> The PLAYIN AT THE BA family, with its favourite initial position, is thus employed as prelude to a love affair, as formulaic signal of adultery or abduction with sexual intent (typically when centring on one person in a group) and without this discriminating function we see a context-bound exploitation of the formula: forewarning of violent death.[45]

In a footnote he speaks of the stanza's use in 'The Bonny Earl of Murray' as 'very successful from a poetic point of view' and as having 'great imaginative force', but due to its 'lack of *narrative* purpose' he feels that 'its formulaic status is dubious'.[46] Given his definition of the ballad formula as action-oriented, it *is* dubious, but there need be no question that the poet was employing that formula for all its connotative freight of adultery and violent death, reinforcing the sexual suggestions of the foregoing stanza and further preparing for the direct statement of the next.

5.
He was a braw Gallant,
And he play'd at the Glove,
And the bonny Earl of Murray,
Oh! he was the Queen's Love.

To 'play at the glove' almost certainly could have been taken in two ways in the sixteenth century, and just as certainly the ballad-poet used this ambiguity to his advantage. First of all, it refers to a game very similar to riding at the ring, except that a glove was used as the mark. King James himself refers to it in a masque he wrote in which several nymphs arrive with Mercury to announce a coming tournament:

We heir are sent by goddis above
with thir oure brether deir,
Quho ar prepairid for gluife or ring
or any sporte with speir.[47]

Furthermore, the English intelligencer Nicholson reported that following the baptism of the King's daughter Margaret, the rest of that day and the following 'were spent in feasting, dancing and running at the ring and glove'[48] By playing this game, Muray is once again shown as a competent knight and horseman.

But once again the ambiguity: playing at the glove suggests dalliance. Gloves, especially gloves for women, were becoming increasingly stylish in the late sixteenth century. The gift of a fine pair was common in courtship, and the wearing of a lady's glove, say tucked in one's belt or even in one's hat, was a customary love token.[49] The glove often connotes courtship in ballads. In several versions of 'The Two Sisters' (Child 10), for instance, the young man courts one of the sisters with 'glove and ring' or just 'with a glove', and 'Child Maurice' (Child 83) sends his page to Lady Barnard, thus:

'Here is a glove, a glove,' he said,
'Lined with the silver grey;
You may tell her to come to the merry greenwood,
To speak to Child Nory.'

Interestingly enough, in both ballads glove and ring are linked as love-tokens, but it is far more important that in both ballads the death of a rival is the result of jealous rage; in the former one sister kills the other, in the latter the husband kills what he mistakenly assumes is his wife's paramour. Is it chasing a good idea into the woods to suggest that 'The Bonny Earl of Murray' works what Toelken calls a 'field of metaphorical possibility'[50] for all it is worth to suggest the King's culpability for Moray's death?

In the ballad, Moray is 'the Queen's love'. Was there any justification for such a statement? The only evidence (beyond the ballad itself) is the following passage in Sir James Balfour's *Annales of Scotland*:

> The 7 of February this year, 1592, the Earl of Murray was cruelly murdered by the Earl of Huntly, at his house in Donibristle, in Fifeshire, and with him Dunbar, Sheriff of Murray; it given out and publicly talked that the Earl of Huntly was only the instrument of perpetrating this fact, to satisfy the King's jealousy of Murray, whom The Queen, more rashly than wisely, some few day's before had commended in the King's hearing, with too many epithets of a proper and gallant man.[51]

Could 'bonny' and 'braw gallant' or their equivalents have been among those too many epithets? That would give their repeated emphasis in the ballad a special poignancy, to be sure, but obviously I can't put the idea forward as anything more than an intriguing possibility.

'Balfour may have had gossip, or he may have had a ballad, for his authority,' says Child, adding with a good Bostonian bristle that 'the suggestion deserves no attention'.[52] Granted that Balfour was writing about something that happened eight years before he was born, and granted too that he is often inaccurate, it is still true, as James Haig said in a Memoir, that he checked 'either personally, or by deputy, every document of any moment known to exist throughout the kingdom'.[53] He was, at the very least, thorough, and among his close friends was Sir Robert Aytoun, Secretary to Queen Anne. Furthermore, he admits Child's charge that his source in this case may have been 'gossip'; he was, he says, reporting what was 'given out and publicly talked'.

Later historians have claimed that Anne was quite up to shenanigans that would discomfit her husband. 'Courtiers did not scruple to draw her into the plottings of Scottish politics nor to set her against the King in the rivalries of the moment,' says Willson, adding that 'She had a quick temper, . . . and in her childish tantrums she could be violent, spiteful, indiscreet and quite ingenious in her efforts to annoy'.[54] Henderson is much more specific, suggesting that 'since the Queen was evidently desirous to make the most of this opportunity of ruining Maitland', whom she hated because he had opposed James's marrying her, 'she supplied occasion for the rumour that she had a partiality for Moray'.[55] Even so, Keith Brown is of course correct when he says that jealousy was 'an unlikely motive' for James's leniency with Huntly.[56] He had more pressing political – and possibly personal – reasons for that. But whatever the truth may be in regard to the King's jealousy or his Queen's indiscretion, there need be no question that there was talk going around – plenty of it – and that the talk was being believed. The ballad both fed and fed on that fact.

6.
> Oh! lang will his Lady
> Look o'er the Castle-Down,
> E'er she see the Earl of Murray,
> Come sounding through the Town.

From a strictly denotative point of view, this stanza is a puzzle: Who was meant by 'his Lady'? Could it have been his love, the Queen? Probably not; she would have had no place at Castle Doune. The most acceptable candidate would have been Moray's wife, who might well have been at Doune, but at the time of the murder the Countess Elizabeth had been dead for almost three months. Is it possible that the ballad's makar didn't know that? Yes, it is possible, but, considering how otherwise well-informed he seems to have been, I find it hard to believe. I think it most likely he had Moray's mother, Lady Doune, in mind. Granted, it was less poetic to have a mother waiting than either a wife or a lover, but at least it would have been the 'truth' and besides, the poet knew if he played it right he could have the best of all three. He did play it right, and once again we turn to Flemming Andersen's study of ballad formulas for an explanation of how.

Andersen brings together almost three dozen ballads employing the motif of someone looking 'o'er the castle wall' and seeing someone approaching. It takes various forms, but 'Captain Car' (Child 178) furnishes one good example:

> The lady stood on her castle-wall,
> She looked vpp and downe;
> She was ware of an hoast of men,
> Came rydinge towards the towne.

And 'Young Waters' (Child 94) another:

> The queen luikt owre the castle-wa,
> Beheld baith dale and down,
> And then she saw Young Waters
> Cum riding to the town.

Usually the one looking out is a woman, and about half the time it follows the given stanza form exactly – even to the 'down/town' rhyme.[57] Almost always, says Andersen, the formula has a 'presaging function . . . signalling violent confrontation, often associated with death',[58] and while this stanza in 'The Bonny Earl of Murray' is hardly a presage of violent death to come, it is a powerful comment on the death that has been, carrying, as it does, the sad freight of its congeners elsewhere. Andersen's note is very much to the point:

As we saw in the discussion of PLAYIN AT THE BA . . . the ballad of 'The Bonny Earl of Murray' is prone to making non-traditional [*i.e. non-narrative*] use of formulaic diction. In the present context we see a near-formula accentuating the poem's tragic scene in the last stanza.[59]

That last-stanza placement brings to mind 'Sir Patrick Spens' (Child 58), close in spirit if not in text:

> O lang, lang may their ladies sit,
> Wi their fans into their hand,
> Or eir they se Sir Patrick Spence
> Cum sailing to the land.
>
> O lang, lang may the ladies stand,
> Wi thair gold kems in their hair,
> Waiting for thair ain deir lords,
> For they'll se thame na mair.

Looking from the quiet of the castle wall to the violence beyond – Queen, wife, mother, any one or all three, it doesn't matter – a woman waits, as women have always waited. It is a perfect ending to a fine song. As I said before, our makar played it right.

In sum, 'The Bonny Earl of Murray' laments the death of a popular hero – a fine figure of a man. While the overriding tone is one of sorrow for a man unjustly cut down in his prime, there is a kind of baffled anger as well, baffled in that it is never clearly focused on any retribution or even on a villain. Huntly is named and is clearly the perpetrator, and the King's complicity – along of course with his cuckoldry – is the song's main connotative freight, but the emphasis is on Moray himself, the handsome gallant, and the sense of loss that he is no more.

DIGRESSION: HOW SOME MODERNS SAW IT

So much, then, for what this ballad would or could have meant to its time or – as I put it earlier on – to a hip and ballad-singing Scot of 1592. But what has it conveyed to those who came to it cold, for whom the nuances of ballad style and metaphor were not almost a reflex and for whom the particulars of the murder were not the common knowledge of the streets? Since this ballad has come down through four centuries, that would include most of us who have ever experienced it in any form. Certainly that describes my situation when I first heard Dyer-Bennet sing it in Town Hall, although to be sure I already knew a thing or two about ballads at that time. How did it strike others who probably had far less preparation than I could claim?

'In perfect pleasure I was to hear her sing, and especially her little Scotch song of Barbary Allen,' wrote Samuel Pepys of the actress Mrs. Knipp back in 1666.[60] That was the type of data I needed, but while such come-by-chance commentary is rare enough for any ballad or even for ballads in general, it simply doesn't exist for 'The Bonny Earl'. Even so, since I felt the question deserved *some* kind of answer, I decided to involve my students in a small experiment.

Although I had provided them with no specific preparation – that is, I had not lectured or assigned any readings on ballads – I asked my Introduction to Folklore classes simply to listen carefully to my singing of 'The Bonny Earl'. I sang it twice; then I distributed 5×8 cards and asked each student first to write down the story line as he or she understood it, then to note down whatever images the singing brought to mind. They were assured that there were no 'right' or 'wrong' answers, that this was in no way a test, and to reinforce that point I asked that they not sign their names. I carried this exercise out in classes over three semesters and thus accumulated some three hundred cards. It didn't seem worthwhile to submit the responses to this rather naïve venture to any sort of rigorous statistical analysis, but some of the results are well worth remarking here.

First of all, considering how little overt plot or even narrative there is in this ballad, most students 'got' what story there was to get: that Moray had been killed by someone who had been ordered only to apprehend him; that he was accomplished, handsome, and much admired; and that he was beloved of the Queen. On this last point, some made a rather clear connection between this love and his death, and it was commonly assumed that the 'lady' of the final stanza was the Queen. There was a good deal less certainty on who was responsible for the death. Even though Moray was 'the Queen's love', very few spoke of the King's jealousy, and even fewer saw a King involved at all. The Queen was simply the Queen, and evidently Moray was seen as a suitor who, in time, might have become King by marriage. I must say I found this view of it surprising, though logically I shouldn't have: no King as such is mentioned in the ballad. It's just that I and others like me have been blinkered by our knowledge of history.

Stanzas 3, 4 and 5 were troublesome: just what was it the Earl 'played' at? Actually most students made no mention of these details at all, which I interpret as evidence that they were puzzled by them, but for those who did comment, 'play' brought all kinds of sports to mind. Certainly no U.S. citizen can be faulted for seeing allusions to the Great American Game in references to ball and glove, but many of those who did pick up on this were bothered by its presence in a Scottish ballad (I had identified the ballad as Scottish before I sang it). A few saw 'ball' as a reference to dancing. No question about it, though, all of the allusive richness of these three stanzas was entirely – and not surprisingly – lost on this modern audience.

On the other hand, the final stanza – the lady looking from the castle – still had power, and most students identified the Queen as that lady. Some said she was waiting for the funeral cortège; others said she saw his ghost or spirit approaching; but for most she was just looking – waiting and alone.

I wasn't at all sure what my second question – 'What images do you see?' – would bring me. Occasionally I have tried asking it of singers I have collected from, though never with any great success. I still think it's a good question, and I know I myself always 'see' things both when I'm singing and when I'm listening to a song, but it's evanescent and montaging stuff, even harder to describe than dreams. Therefore I rephrased the question to my classes: 'When you think back on what you've heard, what images come to mind?' And the results have been interesting.

The most common image of all was one of rolling green hills. 'I see lush green hills with castle ruins and old broken-down stone walls,' said one student in a rather typical response. To some extent, words like 'highlands' and 'lowlands', along with 'green' – a *very* important word – triggered this response, but so did such extrinsic matters as my saying that the ballad was Scottish. What my students were seeing, that is, was what they thought a Scottish landscape ought to be: green, mountainous, and with requisite ruins. Some reported a village green, where the Earl's body was surrounded by mourners, but even this scene was usually only foreground to those far green hills.

Running a very close second was the Queen-looking-from-the-castle image I have already mentioned. 'I see a Queen in a small window high up in a castle, waiting for her love,' said one student. Another saw her 'on the parapet of a tower looking over a little town', adding that 'it was a rather sad image'. The most striking images, then, occur in the opening and closing stanzas, and certainly their position partially accounts for their power. I was surprised, though, that only one student found that dramatic second stanza evocative, perhaps because it is too harsh and specific to carry the overall sad and soft-edged freight of this song.

I was also surprised at another image reported by several people: a man *singing* the song. Often he is seen in the aforementioned typical landscape: 'Cold rainy day in an old town on a cobblestone street,' began one such description. 'Off in the distance is a very large field of grass, very green. People are walking through the street slowly, with their heads hung down. A man is standing on the corner singing the ballad.' Another saw an old man beneath the castle wall, 'and when the last line is sung the old man points up to a window in the castle where a woman is looking out'. A couple even said that I was that old man. I should have expected that, considering my own experience. Often when I sing a song I have collected, I see the singer – sometimes even seeing him where he was when he sang that particular song – along with or overlaid on whatever scene the song itself evokes.

No report of this kind would be complete without some mention of what I have come to call 'mondegreens', because that was the way author Sylvia Wright as a child heard the first stanza of 'The Bonny Earl' from her mother's reading of the ballad aloud:

They hae slain the Earl Amurray,
And Lady Mondegreen.[61]

Everyone has their favorites. I, for example, used to wonder why we proudly hailed Watso in our National Anthem. Inevitably my students came up with a few in this experiment. Several set the whole song by the seaside, because the castle was in the dunes. Several others said that the King had sent his hunter to murder Moray, but perhaps that intrinsic fluff had an extrinsic assist from the ever-popular 'Snow White', especially the ever-reviving Disney version. Both of these were easy mistakes to explain, but I was brought up short by three students who said it was Badger who had done the deed. It took me a good deal longer than perhaps it should have to realize that came from the second stanza: 'I *bade ye* bring him to me'. Murphy's Law.

To bring this digression to a somewhat orderly halt, this ballad − even though shorn of both its historical context and the rich connotations of its ballad language − still can work a magic on modern audiences, and that's a pretty good showing after four hundred years.

EXPLICATION DE TEXTE: VERSION 'B'

In 1808, seventy-five years after Thomson printed *his* version, the Scottish antiquary John Finlay published an entirely different one in the second volume of his heavily annotated *Scottish Historical and Romantic Ballads, Chiefly Ancient*. He did not come across it, he said, 'until the former ballad [*version 'A'*] in Vol. 1. was printed off; but it appeared to me . . . so satisfactory and interesting, that I willingly give it a place here'.[62] His text follows:

THE BONNIE EARL O'MURRAY

Open the gates,
  And let him come in;
He is my brother Huntly,
  He'll do him nae harm.

The gates they were opent,
  They let him come in,
But fause traitor Huntly
  He did him great harm.

He's ben and ben,
  And ben to his bed,
And with a sharp rapier
  He stabbed him dead.

The lady came down the stair
  Wringing her hands,
'He has slain the Earl o' Murray
  The flower o' Scotland.'

But Huntly lap on his horse,
  Rade to the king,
'Ye're welcome hame Huntly,
  And whare hae ye been?

'Whare hae ye been?
  And how hae ye sped?'
'I've killed the Earl o' Murray
  Dead in his bed.'

'Foul fa' you, Huntly,
  And why did ye so;
You might hae ta'en the Earl o' Murray,
  And saved his life too.'

'Her bread is to bake,
  Her yill is to brew,
My sister's a widow,
  And sair do I rue.

'Her corn grows ripe,
  Her meadows grow green,
But in bonny Dinnibristle
  I darena be seen.'

This version has only been reproduced half a dozen times, but Finlay's presentation set the pattern for all that follow: not only do all subsequent printings reproduce his text, they always present it as an afterthought. It never, that is, appears independently but only as an adjunct to the 'A' version – a sort of dinghy bobbing in its wake. David Buchan spoke of it as 'unregarded'; he is right, and he was right again when he suggested that it is in many ways the better *ballad* – at least the more ballad-like ballad – of the two.[63] Following out Hodgart's analogy of ballad narrative technique with cinematic montage and looking at the text as a shooting script should help to make that point abundantly clear.[64]

I.

Open the gates,
And let him come in;
He is my brother Huntly,
He'll do him nae harm,

The ballad begins *in medias res* – no introduction, no attribution, and certainly no apostrophe – just someone speaking, and if we assume, as we are supposed to, that the speaker is Moray's wife, we discover the surprising fact that Huntly and Moray were brothers-in-law. In fact, of course, they were nothing of the sort, but for the moment that is so much irrelevant historicism. We are in the world of the ballad, and in that world the Countess trustingly orders the gates opened to what everyone in the audience would have recognized as her husband's bloodfeud enemy. Few ballads I know begin more dramatically – or more shockingly.

The gates they were opent,
They let him come in,
But fause traitor Huntly
He did him great harm.

Here the camera shifts from a close-up of the Countess to a shot of the gates opening and the 'fause traitor Huntly' entering the castle, framing the move in that standard ballad device, incremental repetition, repeating here in action the command given by the Countess in the first stanza. The two stanzas are almost mirror images of each other, right down to the rhyme words, but the story has moved ahead:

He's ben and ben,
And ben to his bed,
And with a sharp rapier
He stabbed him dead.

The camera follows Huntly from room to room on his bloody mission. Finlay footnoted 'ben' as meaning 'farther in', which is correct, but according to the *Dictionary of the Older Scottish Tongue* it had the more specific meaning of 'in or towards the inner part or end of a house'. The poet's repeating that word three times brings us to Moray's bedside, where we witness Huntly stabbing him, an act that makes him *flagrante delicto* guilty of *hamesuken*.

These were violent times, and for one nobleman to kill another, especially if the two were in feud, was, if not an everyday matter, at least not an extraordinary turn of events. But, as Keith Brown made plain, 'The violence in Scottish society was neither anarchic nor without restraints',[65] and *hamesuken*, assaulting or killing a man in his own house, went so far beyond the acceptable as to call obloquy down on the perpetrator's head. James Maidment criticized this ballad for 'having so little resemblance to the real facts of the event it was intended to commemorate'.[66] If we assume as he did that the poet intended a chronicle, his criticism was just, but if we assume as I do that this ballad was one of the 'common rhymes and songs' whose purpose was to keep the murder 'in recent detestation', then he simply missed the point. The poet wanted to feed the public outrage, and to do that he made his Huntly as villainous a villain as he could: invited into the castle in good faith by his own sister, he murders her husband in his bed – a black and double betrayal if there ever was one!

> The lady came down the stair
>   Wringing her hands,
> 'He has slain the Earl o' Murray
>   The flower o' Scotland.'

Now the camera cuts to the grief-stricken Countess in a very ballad-like setting. It would be overkill to identify 'coming down the stair' as one of Flemming Andersen's ballad formulas; it occurs in a number of ballads, granted, but it carries no consistent connotative freight, although in 'Bonnie James Campbell' (Child 210) we do get the following in a very similar context:

> And down cam his sweet sisters,
>   greeting sae sair,
> And down cam his bonie wife,
>   tearing her hair.[67]

Still, the most we can claim is that it *is* a ballad commonplace, that its use here helps to keep us squarely in the ballad world, and that the brief scene of which it is a part heightens the brutality of Huntly's deed. In addition, 'the flower o' Scotland' contrasts Moray nicely with 'fause traitor Huntly', again in keeping with the ballad world-view, where subtleties of character are all but unknown.

> But Huntly lap on his horse,
>   Rade to the king,
> 'Ye're welcome hame Huntly,
>   And whare hae ye been?'

Up to now the action has been at Donibristle. The first two lines of this stanza – a nice example of that ballad technique Gummere called 'leaping' – serve as a kind of transitional pan shot of Huntly riding that brings us to the next important scene: the meeting with the King. This confrontation – the climax of the ballad and a nice example in its turn of what Gummere called 'lingering' – extends for two-and-a-half stanzas and is developed wholly through unintroduced dialogue between the two principals, a technique used by many ballads to heighten drama and immediacy.

> 'Whare hae ye been?
> And how hae ye sped?'
> 'I've killed the Earl o' Murray
> Dead in his bed.'

Dividing a stanza between two speeches might seem to be courting trouble, but it is perfectly standard ballad technique, and neither singers nor listeners seem to have any problem with it, so long as the break comes – as it does both here and in the preceding stanza – halfway through. The King in his speech gives no indication that he either knows what has happened or commissioned Moray's death. Huntly's announcement evidently comes as a complete surprise.

> 'Foul fa' you, Huntly,
> And why did ye so;
> You might hae ta'en the Earl o' Murray,
> And saved his life too.'

There is a suggestion here that the King wanted Moray taken, but – unless we want to credit him with more duplicity than the ballad form is designed to bear – his shock at his death is too clear to be questioned. The 'A' version, though basically a lament over Moray, contains as we have seen some unsavory allusions to the King's complicity and can be thought of as anti-James. There is none of that in the present version. But if it cannot be thought of as anti-James, it is solidly anti-Huntly, and the King's anger simply reinforces that tone.

This stanza, by the way, is very close to stanza two of the 'A' version, which, as I pointed out, probably was not part of the original lament. There doesn't appear to be much doubt that here we have it in its original context, and some singer, by accident or by choice, made the transfer. Beyond that, though, there is no possibility that

the two are variants of the same ballad. They are far too different
for that.

> 'Her bread its to bake,
>   Her yill is to brew,
> My sister's a widow,
>   And sair do I rue.

> 'Her corn grows ripe,
>   Her meadows grow green,
> But in bonny Dinnibristle
>   I darena be seen.'

To follow out and conclude our montage analogy, the camera is now
on Huntly solus, brooding, with voice-over and cutaways to ripening corn
and desolate kitchen before the final fadeout. All very well for film, but
for balladry these final two stanzas are a bit of a puzzle, and it will be
best to take them up together. Here we have the villain Huntly, guilty
of hamesuken, having murdered his brother-in-law in his bed, suddenly
bemoaning his sister's widowhood and fearing to return to the scene of
his crime after hearing the King condemn his act. That would not have
been in character for George Gordon, Sixth Earl of Huntly, nor – worse
yet from an artistic standpoint – does it seem to be in character for the
Huntly of the song. Moreover, these stanzas make a strangely lamentational
ending for a ballad that has been so very dramatically action-oriented, yet
if we accept the idea that the main thrust of this piece was less to tell a
story than to heat up public indignation, perhaps we can accommodate
them. Certainly they show a bereft widow, her housework undone and
with no-one to carry out the coming harvest, and a lily-livered brother
who cannot – or dares not – help her, having also been (we must not forget)
the cause of her plight. The acceptance of these stanzas would have been
aided by the commonplace quality of their language. Baking and brewing,
usually portrayed as women's work, are linked in several ballads,[68] and
in 'Bonnie James Campbell' (Child 210), another coronach-like piece,
we find 'My corn's unshorn,/ My meadow grows green', for instance.
Acceptance simply requires one not to think too critically about what one
is singing; that is never very difficult, and in the emotional maelstrom
created by Moray's murder it would have been even less difficult.

'The core of the action,' says David Buchan, in speaking of this
ballad, 'contains the actual event, and even the detail of the actual

place, Donnibristle [*sic*], but the presentation of that core involves some fictional heightening.'[69] His point is that this combination of factual core and heightening fiction is common in feud ballads, and he could not have chosen a better example. Beyond the 'core' of Huntly's murder of Moray, *everything* is 'fictional heightening'. Huntly was not Moray's brother-in-law, he did not kill him in his bed, he did not ride to the King, and – just to nit-pick – February in Scotland is hardly a time of ripening corn. The whole ballad is no more than a tissue of fictions dramatically presented in traditional ballad form and calculated to ensure that Huntly's act was – there is no improving on James Melvill's wording! – 'kept in recent detestation'. Together with its better-known – though less ballad-like – congener, it appears to have done its job rather well.

NOTES

1   See Roger Fiske, *Scotland in Music: A European Enthusiasm* (Cambridge University Press, 1983).

2   See David Fowler, *A Literary History of the Popular Ballad* (Durham: Duke University Press, 1968), esp. p. 239f; M.J.C. Hodgart, *The Ballads* (London: Hutchinson University Library, 1950), pp. 108ff; T.F. Henderson, *The Ballad in Literature* (Cambridge University Press, 1912), p. 120; Albert B. Friedman, *The Ballad Revival* (University of Chicago Press, 1961), Chs. 7–11, though the whole book is to the point.

3   Fowler, pp. 5, 243. For Chambers's extreme view, see his *The Romantic Scottish Ballads: Their Epoch and Authorship* (Edinburgh, 1849). He later modified his claim. See his *Popular Rhymes*, p. vii.

4   But see below, p. 114

5   See Friedman, *Ballad Revival*, pp 29–30; Thomas Percy, *Reliques of Ancient English Poetry* (first published in 1765), ed. by Henry B. Wheatley (New York: Dover, 1966), pp. lxxxi–xci.

6   James Porter, 'The 'Mary Scott' Complex: Outline of a Diachronic Model', in Porter, *The Ballad Image*, p. 68.

7   Brother Kenneth, 'The Popular Literature of the Scottish Reformation', ed., in David McRoberts, *Essays on the Scottish Reformation 1513–1625* (Glasgow: Burns, 1962), p. 180.

8   Wormald, p. 106.

9   Brother Kenneth, p. 180. For further licensing legislation, see *RPC.*, ii, pp. 387, 727; iii, pp. 583, 587.

10 The Darnley broadside and one of those on the Regent Moray can be found in James Froude, *History of England* (London: Longmans, Green, 1866), ix, pp.82–85n, 584–86. See also *C.S.P.Scot.*, iii, pp.65–66 (Feb 1570).

11 *Memoirs*, p.24.

12 Hodgart, *The Ballads*, p.70. See also David Buchan, 'The Historical Ballads of the Northeast of Scotland', *Lares* 51 (1985), 443–451.

13 'Captain Car or Edom O Gordon' (Child 178), 'The Fire of Frendraught' (Child 196), 'James Grant' (Child 197).

14 Calderwood, p.146.

15 *The Autobiography and Diary of Mr. James Melvill*, ed. Robert Pitcairn (Edinburgh: The Wodrow Society, 1842), p.294.

16 *The Scotland of Queen Mary and the Religious Wars 1513–1638* (London: 1936), p.228.

17 See my *Larry Gorman* (1964, 1993), *Lawrence Doyle* (1971), *Joe Scott* (1978), '"The Teamster in Jack MacDonald's Crew": A Song in Context and Its Singing', *Folklife Annual* 1985, 74–85.

18 Joseph Ritson, *Scotish Songs* (1794). in two volumes, Vol.I, p.98.

19 D.K. Wilgus and Eleanor R. Long, 'The *Blues Ballad* and the Genesis of Style in Traditional Narrative Song'. In Edwards and Manley, *Narrative Folksong*, p.443.

20 Wilgus and Long, pp.467–69.

21 Herschel Gower 'Traditional Scottish Ballads in the United States' (Ph.D. dissertation, Vanderbilt University, 1957), p.184.

22 Friedman, *The Ballad Revival*, pp.316–17; Hodgart, *The Ballads*, p.12. For more on the related Gaelic forms, see Francis Collinson, *The Traditional and National Music of Scotland* (London: Routledge and Kegan Paul, 1966) and Alexander Carmichael, *Carmina Gadelica* (Edinburgh: Oliver and Boyd, 1954), vol. v, pp.338–367. See also J.L. Campbell and Francis Collinson, *Hebridean Folksongs* (Oxford University Press, 1981), vols. i and ii. There is a huge literature on Gaelic song, much of the best of it published by the Scottish Gaelic Texts Society (Edinburgh). For a ballad quite similar to 'The Bonny Earl', see Child 210 'Bonnie James Campbell'.

23 William Motherwell, *Minstrelsy: Ancient and Modern* (Glasgow: John Wylie, 1827), p.xix.

24 Flemming Andersen, *Commonplace and Creativity* (Odense: Odense University Press, 1985), pp.37, 102. Actually, the whole book is relevant here, especially the catalog of formulas, pp.102–296. See also Barre Toelken, *Morning Dew and Roses* (Champaign: University of Illinois Press, 1995), p.39; Roger deV. Renwick, *English Folk Poetry* (Philadelphia: University of Pennsylvania Press, 1980); and the list of commonplaces in Child, vol.V, pp.474–475.

25 Hodgart, *The Ballads*, p.28. See also Buchan, *The Ballad and the Folk*, p.53.

26 'The Boy and the Mantle' (29), 'Lamkin' (93) and 'The Laird of Wariston' (194). 'Bonnie James Campbell' (210) and 'Willie Macintosh' (183) are related but not identical, and the same can be said for the 'B' version of 'The Bonny Earl'. See Hendren, pp.91–93, 161–62.

27 For the complete text, see Froude, ix, pp. 584–86n.

28 Randall and Dorothy Dibblee, *Folksongs from Prince Edward Island* (Summerside P.E.I; Williams and Crue, 1973), p.49.

29 Buchan, *The Ballad and the Folk*, p.28.

30 *R.P.C.*, iv. p.307 (1 August 1588).

31 See Ewan MacColl, *Journeyman* (London: Sidgwick and Jackson, 1990), pp.306–308, for some interesting speculations on this matter of persona or singer. Unfortunately MacColl has his facts all wrong.

32 W. Edson Richmond, 'Narrative Folk Poetry'. In Richard M. Dorson, ed., *Folklore and Folklife* (Chicago: University of Chicago Press, 1972), p.88.

33 The best brief consideration of it I know of is in Andersen, *Commonplace and Creativity*, pp.68–78. For an interesting discussion of 'repetition with a difference', see E.K. Brown, *Rhythm in the Novel* (Toronto: University, of Toronto Press, 1950).

34 'The Ballad', in *Library of the World's Best Literature* (1896), iii, pp.1308–09. Quoted in Wilgus, *Anglo-American Folksong Scholarship*, p.27.

35 Joseph Strutt, *The Sports And Pastimes of the People of England*, New edition by J. Charles Cox (London: Methuen, 1903), p.112.

36 *C.S.P. Scot.*, v, p.447 (10 June 1580). According to Willson (p.32), the 'pied horse' was Leicester's gift.

37 *C.S.P.Scot.*, v, p.611 (Thomas Randolph to Lord Hunsdon, Governor of Berwick).

38 Willson, p.192.

39 Brian Shuel, *The National Trust Guide to Traditional Customs of Britain* (Exeter: Webb and Bower, 1985), p.153.

40 See especially John Robertson, *Uppies and Doonies: The Story of the Kirkwall Ba' Game* (Aberdeen University Press, 1967). Also Robert Scott Fittis, *Sports and Pastimes of Scotland* (Paisley and London: Alexander Gardner, 1891); Homer Sykes, *Once a Year: Some Traditional British Customs* (London: Gordon Fraser, 1967); Christina Hole, *English Sports and Pastimes* (London: Batsford, 1949), pp.50–58; Shuel, pp.153–168.

41 Quoted in Robertson, *Uppies and Doonies*, p. 206.

42 Brown, *Bloodfeud*, p. 25; Sir James Balfour Paul, *The Scots Peerage* (Edinburgh: David Douglas, 1906), vol. iv, p.540; Robertson, *Uppies and Doonies*, p.208.

43 Ewan MacColl suggests that 'the Ba' refers to tennis. I am sure that had the poet meant tennis he would have said tennis. According to the *O.E.D.*, both 'tennis' and 'ball' had been in general use – referring to two different games – for about two centuries by this time. For MacColl's suggestion, see his *Journeyman* (London: Sidgwick and Jackson, 1990), pp.306–308.

44 Playing at both the ring and the ba' occurs also in 'Lizzie Lindsay'

(Child 226B), in which a young Highland lord in disguise as a poor shepherd is courting an Edinburgh lady.

45 Andersen, *Commonplace and Creativity*, p.123. But see the whole section, pp.119–123.

46 *Ibid.*, p.123. n.13.

47 *Lusus Regius, being Poems and other Pieces by King James.* R.S. Raitt, ed. (Westminster, 1901), p.6.

48 *C.S.P. Scot*, xiii, p.450 (Nicholson to Cecil 20 Apr 1599).

49 See C. Cody Collins, *Love of a Glove* (New York: Fairchild, 1947), esp. pp. 9,11; C. Willett and Phillis Cunnington, *Handbook of English Costume in the Seventeenth Century* (London: Faber & Faber, n.d.), p.76.

50 Barre Toelken, *Morning Dew and Roses*, p.39.

51 *The Historical Works of Sir James Balfour* (Edinburgh, 1824–25), i, p.390.

52 Child, *ESPB*, iii, p. 448.

53 Prefatory Memoir to *Historical Works*, i, p.xxvi.

54 Willson, p.95.

55 Henderson, *James I & VI*, p.107. See also P. Hume Brown, *History of Scotland*, ii, p.210.

56 Brown, *Bloodfeud*, p.157. See also Burton, v, p.291; Lee, *Great Britain's Solomon*, p.74.

57 See 'Leesome Brand' (Child 15:A330), 'Lord Ingram and Chiel Wyet' (Child 66:C12), 'The Clerk's Twa Sons O Owsenford' (Child 72:A14), 'Little Musgrave and Lady Barnard' (Child 81:L17), 'Child Maurice' (Child 83:E26,F33), 'Young Waters' (Child 94:2), 'Captain Car' (Child 178: A4, B3, E3, H4,13), 'Katharine Jaffray' (Child 221:B5), 'Bonny Baby Livingston (Child 222:B21), 'Earl Crawford' (Child 229: B8,18,26), 'The Kitchie Boy' (Child 252:A15,25; B18,33; E4,9), 'Burd Isabel and Earl Patrick' (Child 257:A18,22), 'Lord Thomas and Lady Margaret' (Child 260:B3,8, 'Lord Livingston:' (Child 262:25).

58 Andersen, *Commonplace and Creativity*, p.147. The whole section, pp.138–147, is relevant.

59 *Ibid.*, p.147n.

60 Samuel Pepys, *Diary*. Entry for 2 January 1666.

61 Sylvia Wright, 'The Death of Lady Mondegreen', *Harper's*, 209, No.1254 (Nov. 1954), 48–51.

62 Vol.II, p.19. The ballad itself appears on pp.21–23.

63 Buchan, 'Historical Ballads', pp. 444–445.

64 See above, p.84.

65 Brown, *Bloodfeud*, p.22.

66 James Maidment, *Scottish Ballads and Songs, Historical and Traditionary* (Edinburgh: William Patterson, 1868), vol.i. p.238.

67 For further examples see 'The Cruel Brother' (Child 11), 'Hind Horn' (Child 17), 'The King's Dochter Lady Jean' (Child 52), 'The Laird of Logie' (Child 182), 'The Bonnie House of Airlie'

(Child 199), 'The Gypsy Laddie' (Child 200), 'The Earl of Aboyne' (Child 235).

68 See especially 'Fair Annie' (Child 62), 'The Gay Goshawk' (Child 96), 'The Laird o Drum' (Child 236), and 'The Wife Wrapped in Wether's Skin' (Child 277).

69 Buchan, 'The Historical Ballads', p.445.

CHAPTER FIVE

Through Time and Space

IN THE FIRST three chapters we were concerned with the classic
historical problem of 'what really happened', what lay *behind* the Moray
ballads. In the preceding chapter we first considered the ballads as historical
agents, as 'artifacts' that played their part in the events of 1592; then, partly
to understand their agency more fully, we moved on to some speculations
on what those ballads would have meant to their time. We will now
look at yet another history: the four-hundred-year history of the ballads
themselves.

It is one thing to show the relevance of a ballad to its own time, quite
another to show its relevance to subsequent time or times. But if a ballad
is going to persist, we have to assume that it has remained relevant,
somehow reflecting, as David Buchan said, 'the nature and quality of
the folk's emotional attitudes *over a long period of years*'.[1] The character
of the Moray ballads' tradition may, as we shall see, make them special
cases, and for sure they have not meant the same thing through the years
that they meant to 1592 Edinburgh, but they have survived, and it will
be my task now to show not only how but why.

INDIVIDUAL CREATION / COMMUNAL RE-CREATION

Although in the preceding chapter I clearly posited that each of the two
versions of 'The Bonny Earl of Murray' was the product of an individual
makar, the sad fact is that we can never know who these authors were,
nor will we ever know the authors of any of the 305 ballads in the Child
canon. Back around the turn of the century mystagogues like Francis
Barton Gummere elevated this ignorance into the theory of 'communal
composition', claiming that ballads had no authors, that they were products
of an inspired 'singing, dancing throng', even though neither Gummere
nor anyone else was ever able to come forward with so much as a single
concrete example of such a production. Faced with no authors on the one
hand and no evidence on the other, scholars turned away from the problem
of primary creation. Ballads had authors, yes, but ballads became ballads

only as the community – through 'the summation of an infinite series of individual re-creative acts' – altered and reshaped them by passing them along. 'Communal re-creation' (the phrase is Phillips Barry's[2]) was the alembic through which an individual creation had to pass to become a folksong, and while my work in Maine and the Maritime Provinces of Canada has led me to see the song's original maker as the primary alembic,[3] Barre Toelken is quite right when he says that 'Nothing is as central to the critical study of folklore as this often cumbersome but obligatory investigation of variant expressions of the same basic item'.[4] A ballad is not a single text; it is, in effect, a synergy of its variants, and, since I have brought together some fourscore redactions of the Moray ballads, it is time now to look at them from this point of view.

Immediately we have three problems. First of all, there is that hiatus we spoke of in the preceding chapter:[5] Moray was murdered in 1592, but the earliest text of the 'A' version doesn't come along until 1733, and the 'B' version doesn't appear until 1808. If we accept the analogy of a ballad as a living and developing organism (and it is a reasonable one), our first representations of this pair come at ages 141 and 216 respectively. We know nothing, that is, of the whole first third of their careers.

Second, since those first representations are not photographs but pen-and-ink sketches at best, we have no idea what allowances if any we should make for artistic license. For the 'B' version, we have Hustvedt's latter-day opinion that Finlay's texts were 'in general carefully edited'[6] and Finlay's own word that the text 'was taken down from recitation', but for the 'A' version we don't even have that much. William Thomson was no antiquarian, responsible or otherwise. He was a well-known London musician, and his *Orpheus Caledonius* was a book of songs with accompaniments. However, if he had little reason to be 'accurate', we have no particular reason to distrust him either. Besides, like it or not, these two texts, Thomson's and Finlay's, are where any historical or distributional study of 'The Bonny Earl of Murray' must begin.

There is nothing particularly unusual about either of these problems. They could be duplicated in the study of any number of Child or even later ballads, but the third problem is, so far as I can find, unique: as we go forward in time, until we come to a scattering of twentieth-century American versions, every publication of the lyrics of 'The Bonny Earl' is simply a redaction, acknowledged or not, of Thomson's or Finlay's texts. Thus, for the first third of its career we have nothing at all, and for the second two-thirds all we have is a purely literary or musico-literary tradition that (save for occasional changes in spelling and punctuation) is very faithful to its originals. We don't appear to have very exciting material for a traditional kind of ballad study.

CONTEXT AND PERFORMANCE

But perhaps we have been looking at the wrong thing: the naked text, the ballad in and for itself. If all the contextual and performance studies of the past three or four decades have taught us anything – and they have taught us a great deal – they certainly have made the point that no item of folklore exists in a vacuum. A ballad, for instance, is held quietly in someone's mind until, under certain specific social conditions and circumstances, it is called forth into performance, at which synapse it may move to other minds. The contextualist wisdom is that we should study that performance event in all its complexity, not simply in its oral words-and-music aspect. But even if we limit ourselves to that oral aspect, we should be aware that a song performance often either carries with it or evokes a certain freight of commentary having to do, for instance, with the song's source or significance. MacEdward Leach gave a good example in his description of a Labrador song session:

> There is talk, the unending talk about the fish, the weather, the out-of-the-run events of the day. Pipes are going. An hour or so slips.by. Someone calls out, 'Uncle Peter, how about giving us a song?' Uncle Peter smiles, 'What'll it be?' And then he answers his own question, 'I'll sing "Jimmie Whelan"; that one is a good song. Many a time my father sang that one. Some of you'll mind him singing 'Jimmie Whelan.' He learned me that song when I was just about as big as the lad there.'[7]

After the song is over, says Leach, 'there is no applause or extravagant praise. Rather there are quiet remarks here and there, "That's sure a good song," or "A song like that, it's got more truth than a preacher's sermon"'. Further along, Leach remarks that when a local song is sung, 'the listeners immediately identify with the song and live in it. When it is over, then every omitted detail must be brought forth and reminisced', leading him to suggest 'that song may be just a stimulus, prompting memory and leading the listeners to re-live the event'.[8]

My own experience in Maine and the Maritimes has been similar: A song was frequently embedded in commentary about where it had been learned, who used to sing it, what this-or-that phrase meant, where the action had taken place, what 'really' happened, etc. John McDowell, too, in his study of Mexican corridos, found that performances often involved 'a conversational prologue and epilogue allowing performers and audience members to indulge in commentary about the songs', and – calling the commentary *informative*, the song *commemorative* discourse – he felt that much could be learned from studying 'the peculiar bond linking these contrastive discourse styles'.[9] I wholeheartedly agree, only adding – again from my own experience – the two rather obvious observations that the informative discourse will thicken in proportion both to the song's topicality and to the presence of an outsider in the audience, especially one – a junketing folklorist, say – who is obviously interested in what's going on.

But Leach and McDowell were talking about *oral* tradition (and so was I), and since there is no reliable record of an oral tradition for 'The Bonny Earl's' first 300 years – let alone any 'informative discourse', thick or thin – it would appear that all we have gained through this contextualist excursion is double reason for scholarly despair. How can we possibly turn this darkness into some measure of light?

We can begin by accepting the fact that while most ballads have been carried forward by a predominantly oral tradition, 'The Bonny Earl of Murray' has been carried forward by a predominantly written – or, more accurately, printed – one.[10] That it began in the oral tradition and traveled some while in it is an article of faith, since, as we have seen, it can't be positively demonstrated, but it is an important philosophic underpinning to all that follows. That it has re-entered the oral tradition from time to time in various ways is something that *can* be demonstrated, and we will take that up in due time, but without any question both versions of the ballad owe their continued existence not to being sung but to being reprinted in one collection after another, where, however, they are always represented as songs or ballads, never as poems; not art song but folk song.

At this point an interesting analogy suggests itself. If we accept print as 'The Bonny Earl's' predominant medium, then the various books in which the ballad was published become equivalent to 'performance events' and the individual texts to 'performances'. Sometimes those texts will be simply the words, or words plus tune, but far more often there will also be introductory material – quotations or even interpretive essays – and occasional footnotes to explain the ballad or set it in historical context, a coupling that is quite parallel to McDowell's commemorative and informative discourse, the essay as prologue, say, the footnotes as epilogue. Since 'The Bonny Earl of Murray' is both topical in content and often oblique in its technique, this prologue/text/epilogue presentation is beautifully suited to it, and I will work with it in the following pages as we follow the ballad through the two and a half centuries since William Thomson first presented it to the world in 1733.

THE EIGHTEENTH CENTURY

To begin with, the last half of the eighteenth century witnessed a veritable explosion of concert activity in Britain. Simon McVeigh, in a recent and readable book,[11] has documented this explosion for London, and we can be sure that regional centers in the hinterlands followed the capital's lead with their own concerts, singly and in series, public and private. In addition, there was a great deal of musical activity in the comfortable drawing-rooms of the well-to-do everywhere, especially since singing and playing the piano or harpsichord were looked on as necessary female 'accomplishments' needing display. Jane Austen's novels, for example, are full of references to everything from full-scale concerts to after-dinner entertainments, as when Mary, with minimal persuasion, is 'glad to purchase praise and gratitude by Scotch and Irish airs', or, on another occasion, Miss Bingley, 'after playing some Italian songs . . . varied the charm by a lively Scotch air'.[12] And, as I have already suggested, it was in the repertoire of this singing tradition that 'The Bonny Earl of Murray' was to live for almost two centuries – and, in fact, lives yet.

As the quotations from Austen's novels suggest, 'Scotch' songs formed a significant part of that repertoire, though contemporary opinions as to their aesthetic worth varied widely.[13] Even so, according to Roger Fiske, they were so much the rage in early eighteenth-century London that 'the English almost forgot that they had any traditional or folk-songs of their own',[14] Nor was that enthusiasm limited to England, as the wealth of Scottish material in the bibliographies of Stenhouse, Laing and Dick can attest.[15] In addition, James Porter points out that the proliferation of Scottish family manuscripts coming down to us from the first half of the century shows that there was a keen interest in musical performance among both the Scottish gentry and the merchant and professional classes. These manuscripts, he continues, 'contain a wealth of Scots tunes arranged for voice and instruments such as treble recorder, violin, or harpsichord',[16] and the same can be said of the published collections from both sides of the border.

Obviously, Scottish or English, people in polite society wanted 'Scotch' songs they could sing and play in their drawing rooms. Given that enthusiasm, it is not surprising that a flood of publications catered to it, nor is it surprising that many of the compilers – either out of ignorance or cupidity – used the rubric 'Scotch song' rather too inclusively. What is surprising from the point of view of this study – though perhaps *disappointing* is a better word – is how seldom 'The Bonny Earl of Murray' turns up in these early collections. In Edinburgh, only the Italian Francis Barsanti included it – tune with continuo – in his 1742 *Collection of Old Scots Tunes*;[17] in London, with the exception of William Thomson, only the Scot James Oswald included it – tune only – in the sixth volume of his 1753 *Caledonian Pocket Companion*.[18] But Thomson's exception, as we have seen, made all the difference, though it is worth noting that even he didn't get around to including it until his second edition of 1733.

The 1725 edition of *Orpheus Caledonius* was especially important as the first such collection to publish not only tunes (with continuo) but full sets of words as well, most of which Thomson took directly from the first edition of the Scotsman Allan Ramsay's *Tea-Table Miscellany* of the year before. In addition, Thomson probably capitalized both on the fact that he himself really was a Scot – earlier collections of 'Scotch' tunes had been brought out by Englishmen – and on his already having a considerable reputation at Court 'on account of his Scots songs' (his subscription list included just about everybody who was anybody at the time).[19] At any rate, the book was a great success, and the two-volume 1733 octavo edition – the one in which 'The Bonny Earl' appears – was even more successful, establishing, as Fiske says, 'the basis of the Scotch song repertoire for half a century and more'.[20] Aside from his choice of title, which was perhaps a glancing reference to Playford's earlier (1698) publication of Purcell's songs as *Orpheus Britannicus*, Thomson doesn't seem to have had any particular patriotic or historic programme. To be sure, the tone of 'The Bonny Earl' makes it a bit singular in that collection dominated by songs of love and dalliance, but there it is, and, for all practical purposes, there it began its career.

It next appears in 1737 in the first printing of Volume IV of Allan Ramsay's *The Tea-Table Miscellany*, and, so far as I can determine, it appeared in every printing (more than two dozen!) of that amazingly popular book thereafter. *The Tea-Table Miscellany*, as Sigrid Rieuwerts suggests, may have been aimed at an upper-class female audience, but while it carried far beyond that, its bulk and fine binding – the eleventh edition (1750) has a stamped leather cover and over 480 gilt-edged pages, for example – probably kept the price up to around six shillings, thus limiting its circulation to the more affluent classes. By no means was it a chapbook for the workingman's pocket. Even so, it was 'perhaps the most widely read book of poetry in the eighteenth century', copies of it literally being read to death on both sides of the Tweed.[21] Ramsay subtitled his book 'A Collection of Choice Songs, Scots and English', but he printed no music, though he headed the words with the name of the tune when that was known. Nonetheless, 'The Bonny Earl of Murray' obviously had a good start – perhaps 'rebirth' would be more accurate – in life, having been included in two of the early century's most popular anthologies.

In McDowell's terms, all the performances we have discussed so far are purely commemorative, with no informative discourse either before or after – song without context. With Bishop Percy's *Reliques of Ancient English Poetry* (1765), all that changes.[22] Although his 'Bonny Earl' (all but identical with Thomson's and Ramsay's) bears the subtitle 'A Scottish Song', it is no longer just a song; it is a poem to be read in the context of its history, and its 'performance' in the *Reliques* includes both informative and commemorative modes. Two years before publication, Percy had sent 'The Bonny Earl', along with several other pieces, to David Dalrymple (Lord Hailes), his 'trusted mentor', as Friedman says, 'in everything to do with Scottish history and poetry',[23] and apparently Dalrymple recommended he read William Robertson's recently published (1759) *History of Scotland*, which Percy summarized in his headnote, adding to it some material about the Death Portrait, the story of Buckie forcing Huntly to stab the helpless Moray, and a comment that, while James never punished Huntly, 'I know not any reason for supposing he was jealous of Murray with his Queen' – all in all a very readable and informative essay.[24]

The *Reliques* was so successful that Percy had to bring out a second edition two years later, and with it came some interesting changes in commentary and arrangement, the most important of which for our purposes has to do with the ballad 'Young Waters', in which a Queen praises a young knight too highly and the King has him put to death.[25] The ballad appeared in an earlier position in 1765, but in the 1767 edition it comes immediately after 'The Bonny Earl' with the the following transition:

> It has been suggested to the Editor, that this ballad covertly alludes
> to the indiscreet partiality, which Q. Anne of Denmark is said to
> have shewn for the *bonny Earl of Murray*; and which is supposed to
> have influenced the fate of that unhappy nobleman. Let the reader
> judge for himself.[26]

In order to help the reader judge for himself, there follows at length the
quotation from Balfour (whom Percy calls 'a contemporary writer, and
a person of credit') about the Queen's commending Murray 'with too
many epithets of a proper and gallant man' in the King's hearing.[27]
Significantly, too, Percy's statement (quoted above) that he doubts the
King's jealousy has been eliminated. That 'Young Waters' almost certainly
has no relevance to Moray's murder is beside the point; Percy thought it
might have and arranged things so that the reader (an important word here)
would segue smoothly into its consideration. In fact, the whole of 'Young
Waters' here can be seen as part of the informative discourse embedding
'The Bonny Earl'.

The Bonny Earl's' inclusion in the *Reliques* added significantly to its
Both the headnote and the placement of 'Young Waters' remain the
same through future editions, but Percy made two small changes in the
text for the third (1775) edition by slightly antiquing the spelling, changing
his earlier 'whair' and 'whairefore' to 'quhair' and 'quhairfore'. 'Quh' and 'wh'
would have been pronounced exactly the same, but clearly for Percy the
former had the medieval patina he wished for his readers. This was, after
all, *ancient* poetry he was offering them. We today tend to see the *Reliques* as
a reference work, forgetting that Percy meant it as a work to be read.

'The Bonny Earl's' inclusion in the *Reliques* added significantly to its
wide distribution, but it did a good deal more than that: it gave it a literary
respectability neither Thomson's nor Ramsay's works could offer. It is no
exaggeration to say the *Reliques* became one of the most influential books
in all English literature – a cornerstone, in fact, for the entire Romantic
Movement. In Germany, for example, Herder – certainly one of the high
priests of that movement – was wildly enthusiastic, including over two
dozen translations from it (one of them of 'The Bonny Earl of Murray') in
his influential *Stimme der Völker* (1778–79).[28] The enthusiasm for it in its
own country can be felt in young Walter Scott's delight when he saw there
'pieces of the same kind which had amused my childhood . . . considered
as the subject of sober research, grave commentary, and apt illustration',[29]
but perhaps it can best be exemplified by Wordsworth's confession:

> Contrast . . . the effect of Macpherson's publication [*of Ossian*] with

the Reliques of Percy, so unassuming, so modest in their pretensions! – I have already stated how much Germany is indebted to this latter work; and for our own country, its Poetry has been absolutely redeemed by it. I do not think that there is an able writer in verse of the present day who would not be proud to acknowledge his obligations to the Reliques; I know that it is so with my friends; and, for myself, I am happy in this occasion to make a public avowal of my own.[30]

Once again, as with Thomson and Ramsay, 'The Bonny Earl of Murray' found itself published in the right place.

Over the next thirty years, the *Reliques* was republished three times, the last time in 1794, each time with various changes, but 'The Bonny Earl' remained the same. During that thirty-year period it also appeared in several other collections, always in the Thomson/Ramsay/Percy text but in various editorial settings. The Scot David Herd included the words only in his *Ancient and Modern Scots Songs* (1769); so did the Englishman John Pinkerton in both his *Scottish Tragic Ballads* (1781) and *Select Scottish Ballads* (1783), and three Edinburgh publishers – Neil Stewart (1780), James Johnson (1788), and William Napier (1790) – brought out collections including both words and music (tune and accompaniment) but nothing more.[31] Finally, to close out the century, Joseph Ritson's two-volume *Scotish Songs* appeared in 1794, the same year as the fourth edition of Percy's *Reliques*. It is well-known that the two men were implacable scholarly enemies, Ritson unequivocally condemning Percy's creative restorations. 'That Mr. Ritson was most scrupulously honest, according to the strict letter of the law, I am very ready to grant,' wrote his contemporary Robert Jamieson; 'but,' he continued, 'I can see no extraordinary merit in that, any more than in his atrabilious, furious, and obstreperous abhorrence of forgery of every kind.'[32] That sets the tone of the two men's differences rather well, which makes it fascinating to find Percy's irascible nemesis reproducing not only his rival's 'Bonny Earl' headnote (albeit with full credit) but his text, antiqued spelling and all.

THE NINETEENTH CENTURY: EARLY TO MID

In the eighteenth century the 'drawing room' or 'concert' tradition of 'The Bonny Earl of Murray' had been carried forward by men like Johnson and Napier, and, as we shall see, it would be carried forward by others in the new century.33 But meanwhile a second tradition had developed: starting with Ramsay, 'The Bonny Earl' became a poem to be read. Then through Percy it became literature, something to be taken seriously, a vestige of an earlier time needing explication, and the poem, embedded in that explication, became one with it – a new form. Ritson picked up on it, but it was to have its main development in the nineteenth century.

With the possible exception of Francis James Child himself, no-one did more explicating than John Finlay in his *Scottish Historical and Romantic Ballads, Chiefly Ancient* (1808).34 His text is Percy's, very accurately reproduced, followed by footnotes – the first we have seen, by the way – on the 'ring', 'glove' and 'castle Down' references, the whole headed up by a long introduction. His chief historical source is David Moysie, but he works some odd and tempering changes on that writer's savage protestant indignation: Moysie's 'the earl of Huntly with his bloody retinue most treasonably raised fire' becomes 'the Earl of Huntly raised fire', for example, and, worse yet, 'having the execution of a bloody conspiracy in their heart' winds up as 'having another purpose in their head'. Such changes would be surprising anywhere, but they are especially surprising in the work of a man who otherwise shows himself a careful and dependable scholar.

Finlay redeems himself, though, in his second volume, which evidently he didn't put together until after the first volume had gone to press. Under the title 'The Bonnie Earl o' Murray. A Different Ballad from That in Vol.I', he prints (very accurately, I should add) almost ten pages of material from Archbishop Spottiswoode's *History of the Church of Scotland*, detailing everything from Bothwell's Holyrood raid through the murder and beyond. Then he prints the 'B' version, 'taken down from recitation'.35 It is hard to tell which was more important for Finlay, the informative history or the commemorative ballad, but fortunately that decision is irrelevant to our purpose. It is their combination that interests us.

The Percy/Finlay pattern of presenting the words in the context of an extensive historical essay, often with long passages from Balfour and others, appears right through the century in a series of anthologies that fed on each other freely.36 It would be rather tiresome to go over each of them here, but a couple of general comments come to mind. As their titles make clear, these are mostly 'national' collections, which means that their compilers saw themselves as taking up where Burns had left off in glorifying the Scottish muse, especially the folk muse. Some, like Motherwell, were quite scrupulous in their editing, while others, like Aytoun and Gilchrist, were quite ready to make repairs and even combine versions to make a ballad over into what they thought it ought to be. Yet while other well-known ballads suffered various improvements at their various hands, both versions of 'The Bonny Earl' came through it all virtually unscathed. Even Allan Cunningham limited himself to no more than making the 'A' version into a three-stanza song by combining stanzas 1 and 2, 3 and 4, and 5 and 6 and changing 'he might have been a King' to 'Was a man to make a king'.

The reasons for this stability are not far to seek. First – and this is less a documented 'reason' than a speculation on my part – the two extant versions did not invite improvement; each was too well-known and respected for what it was to permit much tinkering, and, more important perhaps, they were too intrinsically different to invite amalgamation. It is true Finlay had wondered whether 'they may at one period have been united', and no less a critic than Child would soon wonder the same thing,[37] but anyone who tried to fuse them must quickly have discovered their polarity. Having said that, though, I still find it surprising that someone like Allan Cunningham, who once boasted to his brother, 'I could cheat a whole General Assembly of Antiquaries with my original manner of writing and forging ballads',[38] didn't try it. Perhaps we should be grateful.

But the second reason is not a speculation. Whatever else they were, and how variously scrupulous or creative they may have been with their sources, men like Cromek, Gilchrist, Cunningham, Motherwell, Aytoun and Maidment were interested in publishing new versions of old ballads, either from manuscript or from oral tradition, whenever they could find them. Over the years they did find valuable versions, for which we are in their debt, but what they didn't find was new variants of 'The Bonny Earl of Murray'. Yet since their books had words like *ancient, historical* and *legendary* in their titles, 'The Bonny Earl' – along with some learned informative text – made an appropriate and creditable inclusion, and include it they did. It was, after all, a fine ballad, even if it wasn't in active oral tradition among the ballad-singing folk at the time.

CHILD AND THE ACADEMIC TRADITION

Between 1857 and 1859, Francis James Child, then in his early thirties and a Professor at Harvard, brought out an eight-volume collection entitled *English and Scottish Ballads*, compiled, as he said in his Preface, 'from the numerous collections of Ballads printed since the beginning of the last century'.[39] It could have been thought of as the collection to end all collections – the biggest thing since *The Scots Musical Museum* – but almost immediately Child was dissatisfied with it, as he made clear in a letter to the Swedish ballad scholar Svend Grundtvig:

> Ever since I attempted an edition of the English and Scotch ballads, I have had the intention of making some day a different and less hasty work. I had at the time neither leisure nor materials, and as you, better than anybody, could perceive, but a very insufficient knowledge of the subject. The collection was made as a sort of *job* – forming part of one of those senseless huge collections of *British Poets*.[40]

What chiefly bothered him was that he had been forced to work from other people's *collections*, not from the original sources, the manuscripts on which these collectors drew, and he spent the rest of his life both gathering and studying those manuscripts and finally publishing the results of that study in his magnum opus, *The English and Scottish Popular Ballads* (1882–98). 'The Bonny Earl of Murray' appears in both works, but, of course, in the interim, Child found no manuscript behind his printed sources: *The Tea-Table Miscellany* and Finlay.

It *is* odd, as Bronson points out,[41] that he missed the version in Thomson's *Orpheus Caledonius*, but obviously – and quite forgivably – he just never happened on that volume. For both his earlier and later collections, Child reproduced his sources quite accurately (give or take some minor punctuation changes), though it is hard to tell which edition of Ramsay's collection he consulted for the earlier 'A' version. The one change for which he could be criticized comes in the later collection's 'A' version, where he indicates the repetition of the last two lines of the stanza only after the final one, where Ramsay marks it after each stanza. A small matter, but I remember that years ago I found it confusing, and I imagine someone coming on it fresh today would still find it a bit of a puzzlement.

There is no need here to give a full review of Child's tremendous influence on ballad study, but if Ramsay can be said to have given 'The Bonny Earl' wide distribution and Percy to have given it literary respectability, Child can be said to have assured it a place – along with 304 other ballads – in the Groves of Academe. Through him and his successor George Lyman Kittredge ballads came to be more accepted as a legitimate area of scholarly research, as the flood of early twentieth-century ballad publications proves only too well. Ballads even entered the *literary* canon and became anthologized; for example, Arthur Quiller-Couch included more than a dozen in his *Oxford Book of English Verse* (1900), 'The Bonny Earl of Murray' being one of them. Equally significant, no self-respecting college literature anthology would ever again be without a selection of ballads (usually as an annex to the medieval section), and over the next half-century or so at least a dozen special ballad anthologies appeared, a few for the general reader but most of them aimed at the academic market, and 'The Bonny Earl of Murray' had a place in most of them.[42]

MUSIC: THE THOMSON TRADITION CONTINUES

At this point it is necessary to swing back in time to the early nineteenth century. If, as we have discovered, 'The Bonny Earl' was not being sung by farm servants 'in the bothies and farm-kitchens, at feeing-markets and harvest home suppers',[43] we can be sure that on proper occasions it continued to be sung in the front parlor by the farmer's wife or daughter, and, as we have seen, it had often been included in collections of Scottish songs arranged for just such presenters and just such presentation. The eighteenth-century works of Thomson, Barsanti, Oswald, Stewart and Napier included it, and they were still around, and so did James Johnson's twice-reprinted *Scots Musical Museum*. It also appeared in new works like Robert Archibald Smith's six-volume *The Scotish Minstrel* (1821–1824) and, of course, in Edward Rimbault's *Musical Illustrations of Bishop Percy's Reliques of Ancient English Poetry* (1850). All of them used (with only the slightest variations) the words found in Thomson, Ramsay and Percy, and all of them used Thomson's tune set to some simple accompaniment, arranged so that it could also be played as a piano solo if the performer so desired. No-one was striving for any great originality or expressiveness in these settings, and anyone with basic instrumental competence could have handled them.

The same cannot be said for the tune itself, or rather it can be said only after some very careful qualifications. Most melodies in British-American oral tradition fall within a range of an octave to an octave and a third, and my own experience has been that songs at the top of this range are apt to be thought of as hard ones to sing.[44] Thomson's tune for 'The Bonny Earl' has a range of an octave and a *sixth* and, just to make matters worse, a leap downward of an octave and a fourth between the third and fourth phrases, both of which features would always have pushed the average (read 'folk') performer's voice to its limits. These traits also cast doubt on the tune's traditional provenance; I am quite sure, for instance, that it is not the one that echoed in the angry streets of 1592 Edinburgh. But Thomson wasn't interested in the untrained or 'folk' voice. He knew that his singers – by virtue of the twin facts that they could read music and that they were even venturing to sing in the music-room ambience – had probably had some voice training and would welcome opportunities for a little pretension and display. Hence almost half the tunes in his book have a range of an octave and a fifth or more. However, for 'The Bonny Earl of Murray' this was *the* tune, the only tune there was, and as such it went virtually unchanged from anthology to anthology for over 150 years. It wasn't until 1894 that George Eyre-Todd dared to tamper with it in print by dropping that soaring fifth phrase an octave, but it wouldn't surprise me to know that singers along the way had seen that possibility and gratefully taken advantage of it.45

MUSIC: CHRISTIE'S SINGULAR TUNE

However, two interesting tune changes took place during the last quarter of the nineteenth century. First of all, in 1876, one W. Christie, M.A., Dean of Moray, published the first of his two volumes entitled (to give it in full) *Traditional Ballad Airs, Arranged and Harmonized for the Harmonium. From Copies Procured in the Counties of Aberdeen, Banff, and Moray.* Like Allan Cunningham, Christie combined stanzas 1 and 2, 3 and 4, 5 and 6 (using the standard text), but unlike Cunningham he gives us a tune to fit that doubled form. Christie's footnote to this version is interesting:

> This air was sung to 'The bonny Earl of Murray' by the Editor's maternal grandmother. Through her and her mother it can be traced in this form as far back as the year 1760. A set of it, 'Frennett Hall,' is given in Johnston's [*sic*] Scots Musical Museum, III, 296. The smooth Melody sung in Buchan will contrast favourably with the set in the 'Museum.' The Editor's paternal grandmother sang the air in this form to the ballad of 'Young Grigor's Ghost.'46

Here are the first two stanzas as he has them:

Ye High-lands, and ye Law-lands, O where have you been? They have slain the Earl of Mur-ray, And they laid him on the green. "Now wae be to thee, Hunt-ley! And where-fore did you sae? I bade you bring him wi' you, But for-bade you him to slay."

Christie takes some pride in the fact that this tune has come down on both sides of his family, and I find it interesting that it is the women, not the men, to whom he credits its preservation. As a good local antiquary, he is of course concerned to show that his version is not only 'old' but quite as good as, perhaps even better than, versions to be found elsewhere. However, since his chief interest was in the music, not only did he often fail to publish the full texts of his ballads, he just as often pieced out his tunes to get a better textual fit. But while he didn't make any cuts in 'The Bonny Earl of Murray', he did do some rearranging to make the text fit his tune. Hustvedt claimed that Christie was 'reputed to have treated the melodies rather arbitrarily',[47] and Gavin Greig several times comments on his habit of adding a second strain to his tunes, 'which,' he says indignantly, 'seems to be the outcome of his very original process of "arranging".'[48] That sort of arranging is almost certainly what he did with 'The Bonny Earl of Murray', which means that while we may be reasonably safe in accepting the first half of Christie's tune as traditional, we would do well to be more circumspect about the second half. It is also worth remarking that – with one oddball exception – no other version of 'The Bonny Earl' makes use of the Christie tune.[49]

MUSIC: MALCOLM LAWSON'S TUNE

The second change makes its appearance in an 1885 collection edited by
A.C. MacLeod and Harold Boulton, *Songs of the North*.[50] The subtitle
claims that the contents were 'Gathered Together from the Highlands
and Lowlands of Scotland', and here is 'The Bonny Earl of Murray' as
it appears therein:

THE BONNIE EARL O' MORAY

Ye Hielands and ye Lawlands,
O, whar ha'e ye been?
They ha'e slain the Earl o' Moray,
And laid him on the green.
He was a braw gallant,
And he rade at the ring;
And the bonnie Earl o'Moray
He might ha'e been a king.
O, lang will his ladye look frae the Castle Doune
Ere she see the Earl o' Moray come soundin' through the toun.

O, wae betide ye, Huntly,
And wherefore did ye sae?
I bade ye bring him wi' you,
And forbad' ye him to slay.
He was a braw gallant,
And he played at the glove;
And the bonnie Earl o' Moray,
He was the Queen's love.
O, lang will his ladye look frae the Castle Doune
Ere she see the Earl o' Moray come soundin' through the toun.

Here we have the standard Thomson/Ramsay/Percy text rearranged into two symmetrical verses with stanza 6 serving as a refrain, the whole being set to a very stirring tune. Its range, running as it does from the fifth below the tonic to the third above, is only a major sixth, well within any singer's compass. 'This has a mournful beauty,' says Bronson.[51] He is right, and most settings of it – Dyer-Bennet's among them – pick up on this quality, making it, very appropriately, into something of a dead march for the pipes. But, Bronson adds, it is 'not very folklike, or at any rate balladlike', and he is right again. Whether we think of each stanza as a progression of four long eight-beat phrases followed by two more in the refrain (thus ABCD/EF) or – and this is the way it has always felt to me – as two progressive four-phrase tunes with a third for the refrain (thus abcd/efgh/ijkl), I know of no other ballad air in the entire British-American repertoire that is so structured. Even though it is claimed in the headnote as a 'Traditional Melody arranged by Malcolm Lawson', we have to wonder about the extent of Lawson's creativity. He was an established English conductor and composer – especially of church music and song settings – of the time.[52] Did he make the tune himself, either creating it out of whole cloth or working it up from a fragment? Possible. Or did the editors give it to him, having in turn been given it by someone as 'traditional' (and we should also keep in mind that Sir Harold Boulton was himself a well-known composer)? Also possible. There are, I am sure, other possibilities, but until a true bill is found for a predecessor I will credit the tune to Malcolm Lawson. And he should be proud of his work.

It does create one problem, though: its two strophes can only accommodate five of the Thomson/Ramsay/Percy text's six stanzas. Most singers, having learned it in the Lawson pattern in the first place, would see no problem – that's the way the song is sung – but some I talked to were quite aware of the omission and concerned by it ('*How* does that fit in now?' mused Sheila Douglas as we talked about the song after she sang it for me). Since most versions follow the Lawson pattern (136/256) closely, what always gets left out is one of the three 'braw gallant' stanzas, usually stanza 4 ('And he played at the ba"), but a few – Goss's, for instance, and Hermes Nye's – break the pattern by keeping the stanzas in their original order (123/456) and not using stanza 6 ('Lang may his lady') as a refrain, an arrangement that 'works' but is obviously not entirely satisfactory. A half-dozen, though, solve the problem by adding another strophe while keeping stanza 6 as a refrain. All but one of them simply repeat stanza 1; the exception solves it by bringing in a stanza from the B version, thus:

> His lady she came doon the stair
> A wringing o' her hand,
> 'They hae slain the Earl of Murray,
> The flour o' Scotland.'
> He was a braw gallant,
> And he played at the ball;
> Oh the bonny Earl of Murray
> Was the floor among them all
> Oh lang may his lady look frae the castle Doune
> E'er she see the Earl of Murray come soundin' through the toon.[53]

This, too, is a solution that 'works', but it hasn't caught on. Whatever else we may say about the Lawson arrangement, and however people adjusted the original stanzas to fit it, it makes a ballad that was already heavily lyrical even more so. It is not what happened that counts; it is how we feel about what happened.

MUSIC: THE LAWSON TUNE TAKES OVER

As I said earlier on, Christie's tune doesn't appear in any other British collection. Thomson's tune, on the other hand, does show up a few times more. I have already mentioned George Eyre-Todd's including it – in modified form – in his *Ancient Scots Ballads* (1894),[54] and John Goss reproduced it in its original form in his very popular *Ballads of Britain* (1937) along with both the Christie and Lawson tunes. Norman Luboff and Win Stracke included a bastardized version in their *Songs of Man* (1965), not only lowering that troublesome next-to-last phrase but having the final a low flatted seventh – an ersatz dramatic touch found nowhere else that I know of in British or American folksong, and certainly not in Scotland.[55] And, aside from John Purser's citation of it as 'a remarkable example of the wide vocal range which the ballads expect of their singers' in his recent *Scotland's Music*, and a couple of textbook reproductions, that's about it for the 'old' tune.[56] From here on in, with one exception, the Lawson tune takes over.[57]

The score of published versions of this arrangement I have brought together take two forms: the time-honored one of published sheet-music and the new one of electronic recordings. Beyond satisfying a certain compulsive sense of neatness, there is no particular point in taking them up separately, considering how many crossovers there have been and how many published versions were put out by people who were active folksingers themselves. For example, the first recorded version, released in England somewhere in the mid-thirties, was of baritone Alex Carmichael singing Alfred Moffatt's 1925 interpretation, and Dyer-Bennet's 1955 recording – the same version I heard him sing in Town Hall in 1949 – was published with full piano and guitar score in 1971. The Clancy Brothers and Tommy Makem published their version in 1969, but they had already recorded it, having sung it on both sides of the Atlantic for years. John Langstaff, too, had been singing the song in concert long before he published it (with John Edmunds's spare and tasteful piano setting) in 1969. No question about it, with its new and very singable tune 'The Bonny Earl of Murray' moved easily from score to recording to concert stage (both classical and folk) and back again time after time.

Yet, through the early 'fifties and during the great folksong revival of the late 'fifties and the 'sixties, it can never be said to have attained what might be called standard repertory status. It was, to be sure, both recognized and respected in coffee-house and hootenanny circles, but it wasn't all that often sung, and even the later enthusiasm for Irish and Scottish folk music didn't change that much, making my own fascination with it somewhat singular, perhaps. 'Yes, it's a fine song,' Jean Redpath reassured me recently. 'Very powerful. But it has this concert-platform-baritone-with-heavy-vibrato quality about it now.' Hamish Henderson agreed. 'Yes,' he said, 'it's an art song. It's become that. There's a kind of little core of them, you might say. "The Queen's Marys" is another one, the short version. It's the same as "The Bonny Earl of Murray." It became a popular song for art singers, and consequently it changed its character a wee bit.'[58] Both of them are quite right, but if 'The Queen's Marys' became an art song, it did so relatively recently, while art song had been 'The Bonny Earl's' proper milieu for over two centuries, as we have seen, and those versions of it that do occur in later revival tradition can well be thought of as garden escapes.

However, unless we insist on striking some impossibly purist stance, garden escapes, wherever they are found, are *there*, very much part of the local flora, and they are often extremely beautiful and interesting. To carry this metaphor one step further, since 'The Bonny Earl' was originally brought over the wall *into* the garden, we shouldn't be surprised if it shows a certain hybrid vigor when it escapes back *out* of it, and indeed it does. For example, normal British-American ballad style is solo and unaccompanied, yet several of the most interesting versions I have found are those sung by contemporary Scottish folk groups featuring several voices – often in harmony – and various 'folk' instruments both in accompaniment and in display in breaks between stanzas.[59] I confess to having been rather sniffish about such arrangements in the past, but, if we consider them in the totality of 'The Bonny Earl's' history, there is absolutely no reason to consider them less 'traditional' or 'authentic' than any of the ballad's other manifestations.

Among those other manifestations, two deserve special mention. There have been several twentieth-century concert settings of the Lawson tune, but certainly none has been anywhere near as successful as Benjamin Britten's (1943), which – if my own forty years of moderately steady concert and recital-going count for anything – seems to have driven all the others from the platform, not to mention that there have been at least two dozen recordings of it released between 1956 and 1993.[60] But, just as certainly, no version has reached as many folksong enthusiasts as Ewan MacColl's several *a cappella* recordings, the first of which appeared in 1956. 'With his fine voice and unashamedly dramatic as well as authentic style of singing . . .,' said Ailie Munro, MacColl 'had a powerful and seminal influence on the whole Scottish scene'.[61] MacColl's influence was indeed powerful and seminal, but while his use of 'callant' (i.e. fellow) for 'gallant' does turn up in a few later versions, his variant tune for the first section never seems to have caught on at all:

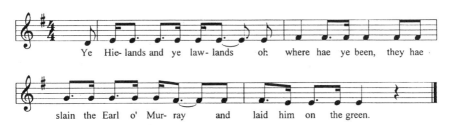

Ye Hie-lands and ye law-lands oh where hae ye been, they hae

slain the Earl o' Mur-ray and laid him on the green.

> Ye hielan's and ye lawland's,
> O, whaure hae ye been?
> They hae ta'en the Earl o' Murray
> And laid him on the green.[62]

That failure is evidence of just how solidly the Lawson tune had become established as the proper one for 'The Bonny Earl'. Not even Ewan MacColl could shake it loose!

THE ORAL TRADITION: SCOTLAND

Before we get started on either this section or the next, a splendid irony should be brought to light. I have been working along the way with John McDowell's idea of the bond between informative and commemorative discourse in ballad performance – the ballad itself as commemorative, talk about it before and after as informative. McDowell developed this concept to illuminate what he found in live performances, but I adapted it for what it could show us about 'The Bonny Earl's' *printed* tradition. Now that I have come to the point of considering the ballad's *oral* tradition, I find I am forced to deal with the commemorative aspect only, because collectors collected items, not performances, and only in a very few cases do we find any informative discourse at all.

One further fact ought to be made absolutely clear: while there has been a rich twentieth-century Scottish ballad harvest, no collector working among the country or traveling folk has reported 'The Bonny Earl of Murray' from tradition. John Ord didn't find it; nor did Gavin Greig or the Reverend James Duncan, and such contemporary workers as Kenneth Goldstein, Flemming Andersen, John Niles, and James Porter assure me they haven't found it either.[63] There is no questioning that record; it is just too clear, and, truth to tell, it should not surprise anyone who has read this far. What should be more surprising are the nine exceptions I found in the School of Scottish Studies Archives, but, as we will see, even they turn out to be not very surprising surprises at that.

All nine are in the Lawson tradition. Five follow his two-strophe-with-refrain pattern faithfully, and, while the other two break from that, their tunes show the Lawson bloodline clearly. The earliest – and in some ways the most interesting – was collected in 1952 from Willie Mathieson, a retired farm servant from Aberdeenshire, well into his seventies, and an old-song enthusiast if there ever was one. All his life he had been collecting songs both from the men he worked with on various farms around Aberdeenshire and from books he found (Roberts's *Legendary Ballads* was a prime source), writing them down in three large ledger books he carried in his kist wherever he went. In 1952 Hamish Henderson began interviewing him, ultimately recording his entire repertoire. Here is his singing of 'The Bonny Earl', and since the tune varies from stanza to stanza I have included the whole of it:

3. He was a braw - gal - lant And he rode at the ring,
The bon - nie Earl o' Mo - ray, he might hae been a king.

4. He was a braw - gal - lant And he played at the ba',
The bon - nie Earl o' Mo - ray Was the flour a - mong them a'.

5. He was a braw gal - lant And he played at the glove,
6. The bon - nie Earl o' Mo - ray, he was the Queen's true love.

Oh land will his la - dy Look ower the Cas - tle Downe,
Ere she see the Earl o' Mo - ray Come soon - din' through the town.

Obviously Mathieson is not sure of his tune. A note says, 'Tune imperfect. Heard when at school', and we can almost feel him groping for it stanza by stanza or even phrase by phrase, the result being that while no stanza is the same as any other all have a rather clear family resemblance. Hamish Henderson's comments are revealing:

To be absolutely honest with you, he wasn't really — as a singer — that tremendously good, old Willie. I mean he could carry a tune right enough, especially with the bawdy ones that he hadn't written down. But he wasn't really a first-class singer. You see, gradually as we went on recording he wanted to record more and more. He didn't want to stop recording . . . He was sort of diving into his memory.[64]

It seemed very likely – and Henderson suggested as much to me – that Mathieson recorded 'The Bonny Earl' in one of those later sessions, well after he had run through his 'active' repertoire. Here he was going back over sixty years to dredge up a song he had learned in school and that in all likelihood he hadn't heard sung in the bothies since. It was a reasonable scenario, but unfortunately it didn't fit the facts. Not only did he sing 'The Bonny Earl' in one of the earlier sessions, he even began a session with it, and while Henderson claimed he often had one of the ledgers open in front of him as he sang, comparison shows he wasn't singing 'The Bonny Earl' from his written-out text. Apparently it was simply another song he knew, but since he seldom got a call to sing it he was rusty on the tune. Had he had the chance to sing it over a few times the tune might have come back – I have seen it happen this way with other singers – as the ballad became familiar to him once again. Or it might have settled down in some variant form, but certainly its Lawson parentage would have remained clear. We'll have to leave it at that.

The second 'deviant' is really not very devious. Hamish Henderson recorded it in 1960 from the singing of one John MacNeil, a native of Motherwell who was then living in London. Henderson had heard him often at Cecil Sharp House ceilidhs, and Peter Kennedy persuaded him to record his repertoire. His version of 'The Bonny Earl' combines the Lawson tune-strophe (ABC/ABC) with the straight-ahead Thomson/Ramsay/Percy text (123/456). Henderson asked MacNeil if he had learned the ballad at home before coming to London. No, he claimed, 'We didn't have much singing around us'. The first authentic ballad singing he ever heard, he said, was from a London friend of his, a fellow artist named Robert MacBride, around 1946. 'I didn't ever sing 'The Bonny Earl of Murray' before that time, Hamish,' he said. 'No, it was the magic of MacBride's singing that sort of took my attention straight to it and kept it there.' The ways of tradition are roundabout – and endlessly fascinating.

All the rest of the Scottish oral versions follow Lawson religiously. In 1952 Francis Collinson recorded a Lexie Matheson at a ceilidh in Plockton,

Ross-shire, and her operatic singing of it (which the School's transcriber was inspired to call 'a very beautiful and heartfelt performance') could have been straight from Lawson's sheet music – ritards, crescendos and all – save that it was unaccompanied. Then in 1953 Hamish Henderson recorded from one Patty Ward – an Edinburgh schoolgirl and the daughter of some close friends of his – a version which that same transcriber described as 'in a more straightforward, child-like style', but even so it is almost note-for-note Lawson. The same can be said of a 1961 singing (which the transcriber found even more beautiful than Mrs. Matheson's version) by a 'member of the company' at a ceilidh at Delgatie Castle, Aberdeenshire, on the occasion of the Clan Hay Gathering.

In 1959 Henderson recorded the well-known Scottish poet Tom Scott singing it at Linburn in a ceilidh organized for the benefit of blind and disabled veterans. 'Tom Scott didn't have really folksongs,' said Henderson, 'He had a good voice and he sang things, well, he sang things like "The Bonny Earl of Murray." And I was very keen in many of the ceilidhs to have not only traditional singers and revival singers but also to have poets.'[65] His performance has that 'concert-platform-baritone-with-heavy-vibrato' quality that Jean Redpath spoke of, but it was obviously a crowd-pleaser, since he was asked to repeat it later in the program. Seven years later he published 'The Bonny Earl' in *The Oxford Book of Scottish Verse*, which he helped edit, claiming that it was 'still sung in Scotland, as heard by the editors'.[66] Perhaps he had recently heard either Ewan MacColl or Sheila Douglas sing it at a ceilidh, since he follows their use of 'callant' for 'gallant' here, while both his 1959 singings have 'gallant'. It's an interesting change.

We can conclude this description of the Scottish oral tradition with a version sung by Archie Fisher and a group at a 1974 festival at Kinross. Twenty years later, when I asked Fisher about his singing of it, he responded as follows:

> The song actually was one of the songs my father used to sing, but he didn't sing it as a traditional song . . . He was a tenor and he sang classical music; he sang opera. And although it has got into traditional groups . . . it was treated as an art song. It was very much a drawing-room song at the time, and Scottish baritones and tenors sang it. . . . Since then the song has kind of dropped out of the folk repertoire, neglected rather than rejected . . . I learned it from my father just as a vignette from Scottish history.

'The Bonny Earl of Murray' has become neither purely art-song nor purely folk-song in Scotland. It belongs to a métier somewhere in between, sharing aspects of both, and thus can be at home in the classical concert, in the folk revival, or in the ceilidh. That is an interesting position to occupy, and it shares it with good company, like 'The Queen's Marys' and even 'My Love is Like a Red, Red Rose'.

THE ORAL TRADITION: THE UNITED STATES

If the Scottish oral tradition presented us with no real surprises, the American tradition is rather various and baffling. It is not, once again, a rich tradition. Considering all the ballad-collecting that has gone on in the century since Child and the thousands upon thousands of ballad versions that have been found in the United States and Canada, six texts and a 'trace' make 'The Bonny Earl of Murray' a very rare find indeed. Rare or not, these American versions are well worth a careful look, and while in general they support some conclusions already drawn, they interestingly question some others.

Herschel Gower established three stages of the Scottish ballad in America: the emigrant, the transitional, and the naturalized.[67] Emigrant texts are those that are still essentially Scottish, having been collected from someone recently arrived from Scotland; transitional texts, while they can be said to have entered American tradition, frequently maintain Scottish dialect and are usually directly traceable to a Scottish source; and naturalized texts, while still clearly versions of Scottish ballads, have lost almost all trace of their provenance. So long as we make allowances for certain borderline shadings, these stages apply rather well to American versions of 'The Bonny Earl of Murray'.

By far the most Scottish of the versions – in fact it is hardly to be considered American at all – is that collected (along with three others) in December, 1906 by one Claude H. Eldred 'from Mrs. McLeod of Dumfries, Scotland, when she was on a visit to her relatives at Lake Mills, Wisconsin'. Eldred – an upper-class transfer student from the Normal School at River Falls – was enrolled at the time in one of ballad scholar Arthur Beatty's classes at the University of Wisconsin, and evidently he collected these texts as part of an assignment.[68] When Beatty published them in the *Journal of American Folk-Lore* a year later, he claimed that they were 'undoubtedly traditional, as the reciter could not read or write, nor could her parents before her', adding that 'she had learned the ballads from her parents, but she was not always sure of the words in particular cases'.[69] Thus, the text we have here was not sung but recited – with no great confidence – by a Scotswoman in the United States on a visit only, and it was collected by the student of an early and enthusiastic ballad scholar. It would be helpful to know more about the circumstances of collection, but ninety years later we are fortunate to know as much as we do, and the text is an extremely interesting one:

CHILD, NO. 181.
Oh mourn, oh mourn, ye Lowlands,
   Oh mourn, ye Highlands a',
They have slain the Earl o' Murray,
   On the greensward ha' he fa'.

Oh shame be to ye Huntly,
   To treat your brother sae,
To meet him wi' your claymore,
   An' in his bed to slay.

Oh, your lady will be sorrowfu'
   Whe [*sic*] ye to hame have sped,
An' she learns the Earl o' Murray
   You have murdered in his bed.

An' your corn will often ripen,
   An' your meadow grass grow green,
Ere you in Dinnybristle town
   Will daurna to be seen.

Mrs. McLeod's version draws on both the 'A' and 'B' traditions. Like 'A', it begins with an apostrophe, but its three other stanzas are clearly from 'B', and the fusion is different enough from either to suggest that it had had an independent life for some time. On the other hand, that fusion may have taken place in Mrs. McLeod's admittedly imperfect memory, as she tried hard to please an enthusiastic college student. All four Child-ballad versions she recited for Eldred are offbeat enough to make this a real possibility. 'Her text differs considerably from the two versions in Child,' says Gower, but, he adds, it is 'nearly as compelling as either'.[70] I agree, whichever way it came into existence.

Another 'text' – if text it is – that should certainly not be considered American under any circumstances is that tentatively reported by Barry, Eckstorm and Smyth from Maine, but this one too must be seen in the context of how it was collected. Quite apart from their collecting complete texts whenever and wherever they could, the editors also tried to gather what they called 'traces' by loaning a prospective informant the Sargent-Kittredge one-volume abridgment of Child to see what ballads – and even what specific stanzas – he or she recognized; they then printed the identified stanzas or lines from Child as what they called 'jury texts'. As a field technique, the method may be open to question, but many fieldworkers (myself among them) have used similar approaches – check-lists, finding aids, etc. – and besides, all materials so gathered by Barry and his colleagues were placed in a separate chapter. They made no attempt to pass this material off for other than what it was, though I agree with Wilgus that sometimes they seemed 'to attach more importance to it than is warranted',[71] largely, we can be sure, through their enthusiasm to demonstrate that the South didn't have a monopoly on Child ballads in America.

One of the people they worked with in this way was Charles L. Donovan, a sixty-six year old retired sea captain of Jonesport, Maine, who had 'commanded seven vessels, making foreign voyages and employing sailors of many nationalities', and who was sure 'that what he remembers of these old songs came to him from seamen who sailed under him, which explains,' the editors added, 'why he recognizes only the outlines of the story and does not know the text'.[72] That makes sense; a captain, even a captain as well-read in and curious about matters historical as Captain Donovan was,[73] would not have been so close to his men as to *learn* the songs they sang, though he might well have *recognized* them in a general way.

Among the numerous ballads the Captain recognized was 'The Bonny Earl of Murray', for which he fingered stanzas 1, 2 and 3 of 'A' and 1, 2, 3, 6 and 7 of 'B', calling the resultant song 'The Tragedy of Huntley'.[74] 'Captain Donovan is entirely sure when his texts are "right,"' say the editors, 'and we have much confidence in his identification.'[75] We today should be far more cautious than they were, but even so, here is one more suggestion of a combined version, a second straw in the wind, let us say.

A rather more significant straw was collected in 1934 by Helen Hartness Flanders from Mr. George Edwards of Burlington, Vermont. 'Mr. Edwards knew this song from childhood days in Yorkshire, England,' says the headnote. 'His grandfather sang many border ballads to teach him history.' We can call this version an emigrant text so long as we realize that the emigration took place in two stages: first to the north of England, then to the United States. The text follows:

THE EARL OF MURRAY

Ye Highlands and ye Lowlands,
Oh, where have ye been?
They have slain the Earl of Murray
And they laid him on the green!

'Woe be to thee, Huntly!
And wherefore did ye sae?
I bade ye bring him to me
But did not say "To slay."'

Now Huntly leaped upon his horse
And hie'd him to the King.
'I welcome you, brave Huntly.
Will you tell me where you've been?'

'I come from Dinnisbristle,
And that is where I've been;
And I have killed the Earl of Murray,
And I dare not be seen.

'He was a gallant nobleman
And played at the ball.
Oh, the bonny Earl of Murray
Was the flower among them all.'

The false-hearted Huntly
With his wicked cruel band,
He has slain the Earl of Murray –
The noblest in the land.[76]

Once again we have stanzas from both versions, plus one we have never seen before, the whole being sung to a tune that is almost *sui generis*.[77] It is a very strange mix, but no stranger than some of the other Child-ballad fragments Mr. Edwards communicated to Mrs. Flanders, many of them unique in American tradition.[78] Most of these fragments – and several of his more complete texts – are suspiciously close to versions found in Child, and, in a letter to Mrs. Flanders, Edwards confessed to sometimes omitting words and stanzas which in his opinion 'crowded the music', were incongruous or superfluous, or contained sentiments he 'did not like to use in a mixed audience'.[79] He seems to have been an articulate, educated man, tremendously interested in Mrs. Flanders' work and wanting to help her in every way he could. Under these circumstances it is very likely that from time to time he let his enthusiasm outrun his circumspection, and we should keep this in mind when we consider his version of 'The Bonny Earl of Murray'.

Having said that much, I still find it fascinating that three 'emigrant' versions in American collections, however flawed and dubious they may be, point to the possibility of a Scottish version that combined 'A' and 'B', while nothing in Scottish tradition even suggests any such fusion. That such a version, if it existed at all, was the stem from which 'A' and 'B' branched out is something I very much doubt. It is far more likely either (1) that some inglorious but not-so-mute Allan Cunningham worked out a judicious conflation – though why that version wouldn't have turned up in Scottish tradition is beyond me – or (2) that the three extant conflations have each only their coincidental reasons for being. Gower said that Mrs. McLeod's version suggested 'that many American texts of the Child ballads may very well be variants of texts never collected in Britain ... Variations must have taken place before the songs left Scotland'.[80] For 'The Bonny Earl of Murray', maybe, maybe not. That's about as far as the available evidence will let us go.

The two following versions are clearly what Gower would call 'transitional': both were learned in America from 'Scotchmen', yet both have retained Scottish dialect. Both also use the Lawson tune and the general format dictated by it, which means they don't go back beyond 1885, but each shows evidence of independent oral tradition. The first was collected by Elsie Clews Parsons from the singing of May Folwell Hoisington in Rye, New York, who called it 'Highlands and Lowlands' and claimed she had learned it in 1906 'from a Scotchman who had heard it from a kinsman of the Murray family':[81]

I.

Ye highlands and ye lowlands,
Oh where ha' ye been?
They have slain the Earl of Moray
And have Laid him on the green.
He was a bra' gallant
And he playéd at the glove
And the bonny Earl of Moray
He was the queeny's love.

2.

Ye highlands and ye lowlands,
Oh where ha' ye been?
They ha' slain the Earl of Moray
And have laid him on the green.

He was a bra' gallant
And he playéd at the ring
And the bonny Earl of Moray
He might ha'e been the King.

3.

O wae's me for ye, Huntley,
And wherefore did ye sae?
I bade ye him to capture
And forebade ye him to slay.
He was a bra' gallant
And he playéd at the ring
And the bonny Earl of Moray
He might ha' been the king.

4.

Oh lang may his lady
Look fra' the castle doon
Ere the bonny Earl of Moray
Comes sounding through the toon.

Though Ms. Hoisington said she learned the piece in 1906, it isn't clear exactly when Parsons collected it from her, but since her great interest in folklore didn't develop until about 1915, it would almost certainly have been after that date. Nor is it clear who Ms. Hoisington was. She may have been a local friend, or she may have been one of the staff at Lounsberry House, the Clews family mansion in Rye, but whichever way it was, it is of some interest that she ultimately published some poetry of her own[82]

The second comes from Long Beach, California, where it was collected in 1959 as sung 'by Fred Williams of upper New York state', who learned it 'from an old Scotchman in Buffalo'.[83] Since Williams's tune varies from the preceding only in the first section, that is all I give here. 'The timing,' says editor Bronson, 'seems doubtful but I have not ventured to adjust it.' Neither have I:

[1]

Ye heelands and ye lowlands,
Oh where hae ye been.
They hae slain the Earl of Moray
An' laid him on the green.

He was a braw gallant
An' he played at the glove
And the Bonny Earl of Moray,
He was the Queen's love.
Oh, lang will his lady,
Look frae the castle doon,
Ere she see the Earl of Moray
Come stumblin' frae the toon.

Ye hee-lands and ye low-lands, Oh - where hae ye been. They hae slain the Earl of Mor-ay. An' laid him on the green. He was a braw gal - lant An' he played at the glove And the Bon-ny Earl of Mor -ay He was the Queen's- love. Oh, lang will his la- dy, Look frae the cas -tle doon, Ere she see the Earl of Mor - ay Come stumb - lin' frae the toon.

[2]
Away ye Huntley
And wherefore be dead
I bade ye bring him wi' ye,
And forbade ye him to slay.
    He was a braw gallant
    An' he rayed (*sic*) the ring.
    And the Bonny Earl of Moray,
    He must have been a king.

> Oh, lang will his Lady
> Look frae the castle doon,
> Ere she see the Earl of Moray
> Come stumblin' frae the toon.

A look back over the Lawson-derived tunes found in oral tradition shows that most of their variation occurs in that first section, partly, I am sure, because it *is* the first stanza and partly, I am also sure, because the strong inverted major phrase that opens the second section serves to settle things down.

In 1953, when Flanders and Olney published a version of 'The Bonny Earl of Murray' in *Ballads Migrant in New England*, they gave it the following headnote: 'The following was copied from the written back pages of an old receipt book belonging to Mrs. Charles L. Olney, Springfield, Vermont. M. Olney, Collector, February, 1939'.[84] What followed appeared to be a rather faithful redaction (lacking stanza 4) of version 'A', even to the repeated last two lines, but, except for the word 'Bonnie', it was one that had been completely englished; 'braw' had become 'brave', for example, and 'sae' had become 'see', even though that made little sense. I would have unhesitatingly called it a 'naturalized' version, but when it was reprinted in *Ancient Ballads* ten years later along with its tune, I began to wonder:

That tune is unquestionably from Scotland, being the one the Reverend Christie published back in 1876 as having been handed down in his family, but Christie's four-phrase tune, which fits his two-stanza strophe, has been changed to three-phrases to fit the one-stanza-with-repeat form by eliminating the third phrase.

We cannot know for sure where or when this change took place. It is certain that it didn't happen in Scotland, else why the English wording? My best guess is that someone – probably an American, even possibly Mrs. Olney – had the Thomson version in one of its many redactions and, finding its octave-and-a-sixth range too much to handle, retrofitted it with Christie's far more singable tune altered to suit. If that is how it was, eliminating Christie's third phrase brought the new tune's range down to a simple octave, well within any singer's compass. This little scenario is pure speculation, of course, but one thing is certain: a change like that did not come about as 'the summation of an infinite series of individual re-creative acts'; it happened all at once, the result of *one* re-creative act.

The last of our seven American versions turns up in the Frank Brown Collection from North Carolina. It was collected in 1927 by Mrs. Maude Minish Sutton, one of Professor Brown's most prolific fieldworkers, from 'Aunt Becky' Gordon of Henderson County, one of her most prolific informants, and it is the only version that can truly be called 'naturalized' (I have changed the stanzas from two-line to four-line for comparative purposes):[85]

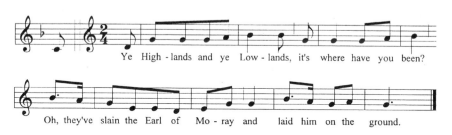

Ye High-lands and ye Low-lands, it's where have you been?
Oh, they've slain the Earl of Mo-ray and laid him on the ground.

I.

Ye Highlands and ye Lowlands,
    it's where have ye been?
Oh, they've slain the Earl of Mo-ray
    and laid him on the ground.

2.

Oh, he was a handsome feller,
    and wore a leather glove.

Oh, the bonny Earl of Mo-ray
he was the Queen's love.

3.

He was a noble rider,
  a-ridin' through the town,
And all the pretty ladies
  they watched him up and down.

4.

He was a gallant player,
  a-playin' at the ball;
Oh, the bonny Earl of Mo-ray
  was the flower of them all.

5.

He was a handsome feller
  and wore a golden ring.
Oh, the bonny Earl of Mo-ray
  he ort to a been king.

With the exception of the one word 'bonny', the diction has been completely Americanized. 'Green' has become 'ground', 'braw gallant' has become 'handsome feller', and the usual final stanza ('Lang may his lady') has been entirely made over into the present stanza 3 (in which the rhyme words have been kept, though their pronunciation has been changed). It is interesting that the one dramatic stanza ('Oh wae be to you, Huntly') is the one that is omitted. Only in the most oblique sense can there be said to be any story here at all now; an already lyrical ballad has become even more lyrical – perhaps as lyrical as its original author intended it to be! As for the tune, Bronson sees it as derived from Thomson, and his analysis is well worth quoting here:

> The first two phrases suggest Thomson's first; the third of this suggests Thomson's third when lowered an octave; the closing phrases of both are not unlike. The range of the Thomson tune is so extreme that tradition would naturally find easier equivalents for the upper octave, and sheer coincidence seldom goes beyond a phrase. The change of meter is a common phenomenon.[86]

If he is correct, this tune has gone from essentially mixolydian (though hexatonic) to pentatonic, and its range has been reduced from that ferocious octave-and-a-sixth of Thomson's to a mere major sixth. Extreme changes indeed – extreme enough perhaps to raise the scholarly eyebrow!

What, then, do we know about the circumstances of its collection? Mrs. Sutton was not a professional folklorist; she collected for the fun of it, and over the years contributed hundreds of items to Dr. Brown's collection, including 154 song-texts and 112 tunes. 'She took down songs in longhand, words only . . . with inconsistent phonetic spellings of dialect,' says Dan Patterson. 'She may not have gotten the song texts word perfect,' he adds, 'but she would not in my opinion have made up song texts.'[87] She delighted too in providing vignettes of her collecting work. Of Aunt Becky she had the following to say about the day she collected 'The Bonny Earl':

> On her narrow porch she sat, bunching and tieing galax leaves. As she counted and tied the glossy leaves in bunches of a hundred each, she sang me the old ballad of the 'Cruel Brother.' . . . She also sang that day a fragment of 'The Bonny Earl of Moray,' and I thought of James Stuart of Donne [*sic*] whose tragic murder the old tale commemorates . . . The old woman singing the ballad on Blevins Creek three hundred and fifty years later, used the same identical phraseology in which Sir James Balfour wrote of the death of the luckless earl.[88]

Mrs. Sutton loved what she was doing, and neither I nor Professor Patterson see any reason not to accept her text as reasonably accurate. As for the tune, Patterson has the following to say:

> The manuscript for this transcription is preserved in the Brown Papers at Duke, with no data concerning who wrote it down. Maude could not have taken it down. She was virtually tone deaf. She had a friend, Vivian Blackstock, however, who taught music and who went with her on several trips in Henderson County in the late 1920s to take down the tunes for ballads from the singers Maude had gotten ballad texts from [*and who*] took some tunes down from Aunt Becky. I assume she was the musician who wrote down this one.[89]

I see no reason for not accepting Blackstock's transcription (assuming of course that it *is* hers) as reasonably accurate. Were subtle details of pitch or modality crucial, we might have some cause to question it, but Aunt Becky's tune is so simple and straightforward as to make its transcription quite within the limits of the skills we might expect any competent 'music teacher' to possess. In short, we can accept both text and tune as valid, and they show us a unique version, far different from any other found in America. In fact it is different from anything found anywhere.

But, unlike the version in Mrs. Olney's Vermont receipt book, its differences represent the kinds of changes we would expect to find if a ballad has been in oral tradition for a long time, far longer than the century or less we can credit to any of the other oral versions found in either America or Scotland. 'Aunt Becky's' version, then, may well be the last and lingering representative of a line going well back beyond the nineteenth-century Lawson-inspired tradition, a true survivor indeed.

A SUMMING UP

The ballads we know as 'The Bonny Earl of Murray' were conceived in anger born of bloodshed in 1592, and, as 'common rhymes and songs', they served to keep that anger alive. For a long time after that – almost a century and a half for 'A', over two centuries for 'B' – we know nothing about them at all save that somehow they survived. In 1733 William Thomson included 'A' in a book of Scottish songs meant for a fashionable audience, and four years later Allan Ramsay included the words in Volume IV of his *The Tea-Table Miscellany*, thus assuring its being widely distributed throughout that same audience. Then in 1765 Thomas Percy included it in his *Reliques of Ancient English Poetry* along with a learned introduction, and this format became standard for a host of eighteenth-and nineteenth-century redactions, including John Finlay's, which in 1808 brought out the first appearance of the 'B' version. The inclusion of both versions in Francis James Child's monumental *The English and Scottish Popular Ballads* (1882–98) assured them a place in the literary canon. Throughout this period, the ballad existed either as a poem to be read and studied in the context of its history or as a song to be sung in concert or at entertainments in polite society, but later American tradition suggests that there was a parallel if limited oral tradition among the lower classes as well.

Through the eighteenth and most of the nineteenth centuries Thomson's was the only tune known for 'The Bonny Earl', although it is doubtful if it was the tune the ballad was originally sung to. But two new tunes emerged: Christie's in 1876 and Lawson's in 1885, both of them far more singable than Thomson's. Christie's claimed to come from North-Eastern tradition, but not only is it unique there, it never caught on in any wider tradition. Lawson's, on the other hand, in spite of its unfolklike structure, rather effectively drove all others out of circulation and has become the tune that everyone uses today.

Except among revivalists – and even there infrequently – the ballad is not found in Scottish folk tradition today, nor does it appear to have had a place in that repertoire – except as an occasional 'escape' from concert tradition – for several hundred years. Yet it has maintained itself. It had the good luck to be included in the right anthologies, to be sure, and it was well adapted to concert and drawing-room performance, being short, well-shaped, and very Scottish. But beyond that, it had great integrity, and a sophisticated audience could see it as a fine poem, not *telling* a story so much as, in a little, shadowing one forth: murder, treachery, youth, and a queen's love:

> . . . old, unhappy, far-off things,
> And battles long ago.

NOTES

1 Buchan, 'History and Harlaw', p.37. The italics are mine.
2 Phillips Barry. 'Communal Re-Creation', *Bulletin of the Folk-Song Society of the Northeast*, No. 5 (1933), 5. The entire history of the individualist-communalist 'ballad war' has been extremely well-told in D.K. Wilgus, *Anglo-American Ballad Scholarship Since 1898* (New Brunswick, N.J.: Rutgers University Press, 1959), pp.3–122.
3 See especially *Joe Scott*, pp.422–23.
4 Barre Toelken, 'Ballads and Folksongs'. In Elliott Oring (ed.), *Folk Groups and Folklore Genres: An Introduction* (Logan: Utah State University Press, 1986), pp.157–58.
5 See above, pp.78–79.
6 Hustvedt, p.61.
7 MacEdward Leach, *Folk Ballads and Songs of the Lower Labrador Coast.* (Ottawa: National Museum of Canada Bulletin No.201, 1965), p.9.
8 *Ibid.*, p.10.
9 John H. McDowell, 'Folklore as Commemorative Discourse', *Journal of American Folklore* 105 (Fall, 1992), 404.
10 For the importance of the word 'predominantly' in this comparison I refer the reader to Charles Seeger's brilliant if sometimes opaque essay, 'Oral Tradition in Music', in Maria Leach (ed.) *Standard Dictionary of Folklore, Mythology and Legend* (New York: Funk & Wagnall's, 1950), vol.ii, pp.825–29.

11 *Concert Life in London from Mozart to Haydn* (Cambridge: Cambridge University Press, 1993).

12 *Pride and Prejudice* (1813), Chs. 6 and 10. See also Ch. 18. For a good description of a private concert, see the same author's *Persuasion* (1818), Ch. 20. See also McVeigh, pp. 44–49.

13 See McVeigh, p.133.

14 Roger Fiske, *Scotland in Music: A European Enthusiasm* (Cambridge University Press, 1983), p.ix. See also Derek B. Scott, *The Singing Bourgeois* (Milton Keynes: Open University Press, 1989), pp.92–99.

15 See *The Scots Musical Museum* (Hatboro, Pa: Folklore Associates, 1962), Vol.i, pp.xxvi–cxxxiv for the Stenhouse and Laing material, and James C. Dick, *The Songs of Robert Burns* (Hatboro, Pa: Folklore Associates, 1962), pp.xxv–xliii.

16 James Porter, 'The "Mary Scott" Complex: Outline of a Diachronic Model' in Porter, *The Ballad Image*, p.71.

17 Others appeared later in the century, like *A Collection of Scots Songs* [n.d.], published by Neil Stewart.

18 I would like to thank Patricia Shearman for the loan of her copy of Oswald's book, which has been in her family for several generations and includes an additional 38 hand-written tunes.

19 Henry George Farmer, Introduction to the 1962 edition of *Orpheus Caledonius*, pp.[I]–[III].

20 Fiske, p.16.

21 Friedman, *The Ballad Revival*, p.144. See also Rieuwerts, p.83. I would like to take this opportunity to thank Sigrid Rieuwerts for carefully checking the only extant copy of the 1737 printing for me at the Huntington Library. For further information on Ramsay, see Oliphant Smeaton, *Allan Ramsay* (Edinburgh: Anderson and Ferrier, 1896; reprinted AMS Press, 1979) and Burns Martin, *Allan Ramsay* (Cambridge: Harvard University Press, 1931; reprinted Greenwood, 1973).

22 In the 1765 edition, 'The Bonny Earl' is found in vol.ii, pp.210f, but since the 1966 Dover reprint of the fourth edition of 1794 is more generally available, my references are to that edition.

23 Friedman, *Ballad Revival*, p.200. See also A.F. Falconer, *The Correspondence of Thomas Percy and David Dalrymple, Lord Hailes* (Baton Rouge: Louisiana State University Press, 1954), pp.29, 101.

24 Percy, *Reliques* (1765 edition), ii, p.210.

25 See Child, ii, pp. 342–45 (No. 94).

26 Percy, *Reliques* (1767 edition), ii, p.212.

27 See above, p.92.

28 *Fünftes Buch: Englische Lieder*. 'Murrays Ermordung' appears as No.14. Herder's version was given an elaborate setting for voice and piano by Brahms. See *Lieder und Romanzen*, Opus 14 (1861).

29 Quoted in T.F. Henderson's Prefatory Note to Sir Walter Scott,

Minstrelsy of the Scottish Border (Edinburgh: Oliver and Boyd, 1932), i, pp.ix–x.

30 William Wordsworth, 'Essay Supplementary to the Preface [*of the Lyrical Ballads*]' (1815). See William Knight (ed.), *The Poetical Works of William Wordsworth* (Edinburgh: William Paterson, 1883), vol.iv, pp.352–53.

31 David Herd, *Ancient and Modern Scots Songs* (Edinburgh: Martin and Wotherspoon, 1769), pp.32–33; John Pinkerton, *Scottish Tragic Ballads* (London: J. Nichols, 1781), p.60, and *Select Scottish Ballads* (London: J. Nichols, 1783), vol. i, pp.88–89; Neil Stewart, *A Collection of Scots Songs Adapted for a Voice and Harpsichord* (Edinburgh: c.1780); James Johnson, *The Scots Musical Museum* (Edinburgh: James Johnson, 1788), vol.ii, p.185; William Napier, *A Selection of the Most Favourite Scots Songs* (Edinburgh: W. Napier, 1790), p.73; Joseph Ritson, *Scotish Songs* (London: J. Johnston, 1794), vol.ii, pp.372–374. Johnson's massive work was heavily annotated by William Stenhouse in an edition brought out in 1853, but he added nothing to what Percy had.

32 Robert Jamieson, *Popular Ballads and Songs* (Edinburgh, 1806), vol. i, p.xv.

33 For a good summary of this tradition, see Scott, *Singing Bourgeois*, especially pp. 1–59.

34 vol.i, pp.77–84.

35 Finlay, vol. ii, pp.11–23.

36 Those collections in which 'The Bonny Earl of Murray' appears are R.H. Cromek, *Select Scottish Songs, Ancient and Modern* (London: Caddell and Davies, 1810), vol. ii, pp.156–57; John Gilchrist, *A Collection of Ancient and Modern Scottish Ballads, Tales, and Songs* (Edinburgh: Blackwood, 1815), vol. i, pp.89–92; Allan Cunningham *The Songs of Scotland, Ancient and Modern* (London: John Taylor, 1825), vol. ii, pp.180–81; William Motherwell, *Minstrelsy: Ancient and Modern* (Glasgow: John Wylie, 1827), pp.78–82; Robert Chambers, *Scottish Ballads* (Edinburgh: William Tait, 1829), pp.69–71; Alexander Whitelaw, *The Book of Scottish Ballads* (Glasgow: Blackie, 1845), pp.16–17; W.E. Aytoun, *The Ballads of Scotland* (Edinburgh: Blackwood, 1858), vol.i, pp.241–43; James Maidment, *Scotish Ballads, Historical and Traditionary* (Edinburgh: William Patterson, 1868), vol.i, pp.234–39; John S. Roberts, *The Legendary Ballads of England and Scotland* (London: F. Warne, 1868), pp.403–4; *The Ballad Minstrelsy of Scotland* (Glasgow: Maurice Ogle, 1871), pp.530–32.

37 Finlay, vol. ii, p.20; Francis James Child, *English and Scottish Ballads* (Boston: Little Brown, 1860), vol. vii, p.120.

38 Quoted in Hustvedt, p.63.

39 vol.i, p.vii.

40 Hustvedt, p.246. Grundtvig was in the process of compiling his great collection of Danish ballads, and he had already published a set of

translations of British ballads, which included 'The Bonny Earl of
Murray'. See his *Engelske og Skotske Folkeviser* (Copenhagen: Wahlske
Boghandlings, 1842–46), vol.i, pp.52–55.

41 Bronson, *The Traditional Tunes*, vol.iii, p.159.

42 Francis Barton Gummere, *Old English Ballads* (Boston: Ginn & Co:
1894), pp.155, 334; Helen Child Sargent and George Lyman Kittredge,
English and Scottish Popular Ballads (Boston: Houghton Mifflin, 1904),
pp.443–44; R. Adelaide Witham, *English and Scottish Popular Ballads*
(Boston: Houghton Mifflin, 1909), pp.82–83, 164–65; Maude M.
Hall. *Ballads and Other Narrative Poems* (Boston: Allyn and Bacon,
1909), pp.87–89, 377–79; Walter Morris Hart, *English Popular Ballads*
(Chicago and New York: Scott, Foresman, 1916), pp.559, 313–4;
William Dallam Armes, *Old English Ballads and Folk Songs* (New York:
Macmillan, 1919), pp.125, 189–90; John E. Housman, *British Popular
Ballads* (London: George Harrap, 1952), pp.217–18; MacEdward
Leach, *The Ballad Book* (New York: Harper, 1955), pp.491–93;
Bartlett Jere Whiting, *Traditional British Ballads* (New York: Appleton-
Century-Crofts, 1955). pp.83–84; Albert B. Friedman, *The Viking Book
of Folk Ballads of the English Speaking World* (New York: Viking, 1956),
pp.264–65; Ruth Manning-Sanders, *A Bundle of Ballads* (Philadelphia:
Lippincott, 1959), p.36; Matthew Hodgart, *The Faber Book of Ballads*
(London: Faber & Faber, 1965), pp.144–45, 255; MacEdward Leach,
The Book of Ballads (New York: Heritage Press, 1967), pp.90–91; James
Kinsley, *The Oxford Book of Ballads* (Oxford, 1969), pp.594–96, 704;
Michael Brander, *Scottish and Border Battles and Ballads* (London: Seeley
Service, 1975), pp.95–98. To these books should be added Kenneth S.
Goldstein's four-volume LP record set, *The English and Scottish Popular
Ballads* (Riverside RLP 12–621–629), which appeared in 1958.

43 Alexander Fenton, 'Introduction' to *Ord's Bothy Songs and Ballads*
(Edinburgh: John Donald, 1990), p.xii.

44 See, for example, Bruno Nettl, 'Preface to the Musical Annotations',
in Helen Hartness Flanders, *Ancient Ballads Traditionally Sung in New
England* (Philadelphia: University of Pennsylvania, 1960), vol. i, p.35;
Jan P. Schinan, *The Music of the Ballads* (Durham, N.C: Duke University
Press, 1957), vol. iv, p.362; Alan Lomax, *Folk Song Style and Culture*
(Washington, D.C: American Association for the Advancement of
Science, Publication No. 88, 1968), pp.63–64, 214–15, 334; Ives, *Joe
Scott*, pp.259–60.

45 George Eyre-Todd, *Ancient Scots Ballads* (London: Bailey & Ferguson,
1894), pp.127–30.

46 Christie, vol. i, p.202.

47 Hustvedt, p.125.

48 Patrick Shuldham-Shaw and Emily Lyle, *The Greig-Duncan Folk Song
Collection* (Aberdeen: Aberdeen University Press, 1981–90), ii, p. 543.
For a second example, see iv, p. 526.

49 For the oddball exception, see below, p.142.
50 (London: Field & Tuer, 1885), pp.142–46.
51 Bronson, *The Traditional Tunes*, vol.iii, p.159.
52 James D. Brown, *Biographical Dictionary of Musicians* (Paisley and London: Alexander Gardner, 1886), pp.378–79.
53 Rory and Alex McEwen, *Folksong Jubilee*. 12' LP, EMI Records: CLP 1220.
54 (London: Bayley and Ferguson, 1894), pp.127–31.
55 (Englewood Cliffs: Prentice-Hall, 1965)
56 (Edinburgh and London: Mainstream, 1992), p.116.
57 The exception is a nearly through-composed tune and arrangement by that talented and tragic genius Ivor Gurney (1890–1937), appearing first as sheet music in 1921 and later in Sidney Northcote's anthology *Baritone Songs* (London and New York: Boosey and Hawkes, 1950), pp.120–22.
58 Interview 22 June 1992. NA 2324.010.
59 See, for example, Rory and Alex McEwen and Isla Cameron, *Folksong Jubilee*, 10' LP record, EMI Records: CLP 1220 (1958); The Galliards, *Scottish Choice*, 10' LP record, Decca ACL 1065 (1961); The Corrie Folk Trio and Paddie Bell, *More Folk Songs for the Burds*, Waverley ELP 132 (1963); The Ian Campbell Folk Group, *Four Highland Songs*, Transatlantic EP 146 (1966); Five Hand Reel, *Earl O' Moray*, 12' LP, RCA PL25150 (1978).
60 Benjamin Britten, *Folksong Arrangements. volume I: British Isles* (London: Boosey and Hawkes, 1943), pp.6–7. Other settings of the Lawson tune include those by Fritz Kreisler (1917), Alfred Moffat (1921), Malcolm Davidson (1925), S.E. Lovatt (1947), Hugh S. Roberton (1952), and Bob Sharples (1963).
61 Ailie Munro, *The Folk Music Revival in Scotland* (London: Kahn & Averill, 1984), p.46.
62 Kenneth S. Goldstein, *The English and Scottish Popular Ballads*. Riverside Records RLP 12–627, vol.iv, side 2, band 1. Other singings, in which he alternates the variant with the standard tune, appear in Ewan MacColl, editor, *The English and Scottish Popular Ballads*, Folkways FG 3509 (1961), and Ewan MacColl and Peggy Seeger, *Blood and Roses*, vol.iv. DISC ESB 82 (1986). MacColl claimed he learned the song 'while he was in the army from a Private MacDonald who had learned it at school'.
63 John Ord, *The Bothy Songs and Ballads* (Paisley: Alexander Gardner, 1930); Gavin Greig, *Folk-Song of the North-East* (Peterhead: 'Buchan Observer' Works, 1914; reprinted 1963); Gavin Greig and Alexander Keith, *Last Leaves of Traditional Ballads and Ballad Airs* (Aberdeen: The Buchan Club, 1925); Shuldham-Shaw and Lyle, *The Greig-Duncan Folk Song Collection*. volumes 1 through 4 have been published, and four more are projected. With the help of Dr. Emily Lyle I have

checked the unpublished Greig-Duncan materials at the School of Scottish Studies.

64 Interview 22 June 1992. NA 2324.005.

65 Interview 22 June 1992. NA 2324.006.

66 (Oxford: Oxford University Press, 1966), p.296.

67 Herschel Gower, 'The Scottish Palimpsest in Traditional Ballads Collected in North America', in Walker and Welker, pp. 142. See also his doctoral dissertation 'Traditional Scottish Ballads in the United States (Vanderbilt University, 1957).

68 My thanks to the Registrar's Office at the University of Wisconsin-Madison and to the Alumni Office at University of Wisconsin-River Falls for this information.

69 Arthur Beatty, 'Some New Ballad Variants', *Journal of American Folk-Lore* 20 (1907), 154-56.

70 Gower, 'The Scottish Palimpsest', p. 137.

71 Wilgus, *Anglo-American Ballad Scholarship*, p. 203.

72 Phillips Barry, Fannie Hardy Eckstorm and Mary Winslow Smyth, *British Ballads from Maine* (New Haven: Yale University Press, 1929), p. 435.

73 *Ibid.*, p.465.

74 *Ibid.*, p.469.

75 *Ibid.*, p.435.

76 Flanders, *Ancient Ballads*, vol.iii, pp.188–89.

77 Bruno Nettl (Flanders, *Ancient Ballads*, vol.iii, p.188) suggests, without much conviction, that it may possibly be related to the North Carolina tune (see below, p.143).

78 See *ibid.*, vol. i, pp.239–41 'St. Stephen and Herod' (Child 22); p.242 'Willie's Lyke-Wake' (Child 25); vol.iii, p.43–44 'The Gay Goshawk' (Child 96); p.117 'Robin Hood and the Bishop' (Child 143); pp.133–34 'Gude Wallace' (Child 157); pp.149–50 'The Rose of England' (Child 166).

79 *Ibid.*, vol. ii, pp. 197–98.

80 Gower, 'The Scottish Element', p.151.

81 Elsie Clews Parsons and Helen H. Roberts, 'A Few Ballads and Songs', *Journal of American Folklore* 44 (1931), 296–97.

82 I am grateful for Rosemary Lévy Zumwalt's support in this surmise (letter, 26 March 1996). See also her *Wealth and Rebellion: Elsier Clews Parsons, Anthropologist and Folklorist* (Urbana: University of Illinois Press, 1992), especially pp. 184–209. On the other hand, there is Hoisington property shown on a 1929 map out around Kirby Pond, a rather nice part of Rye, and there is a small handset volume of verse, *Seven Poems* (1951) and two unpublished poems by May Folwell Hoisington in the collection of the Rye Historical Society. I am grateful to Sandra Tashoff, the Society's Librarian/Archivist for this.

83 Bronson, *The Traditional Tunes*, vol. iii, p. 161. It was collected,

Bronson notes, 'by Dorothea Jean Kirkhuff and Phyllis Klein. Transcribed for the editor by Edward Cray'.

84 P.133.

85 Belden and Hudson, *Brown Collection*, vol. ii (1952), p. 160; Schinan, *Brown Collection*, vol.iv (1957), p.83. The full date was 8 October 1927. Ms. Gordon was from Stateline Hill, Henderson County, N.C.

86 Bronson, *The Traditional Tunes*, vol. iii, p.160.

87 Personal communication, 3 October 1995. See also Patterson's article, 'A Woman of the Hills: The Work of Maude Minish Sutton,' *Southern Exposure* V (Summer-Fall 1977), 105–110.

88 Maude Minish Sutton, 'Ballad Hunting' (unpublished, in the possession of Daniel Patterson, n.d.), p.7.

89 Personal communication, 3 October 1995.

Speculations

'HUMAN KIND,' SAID T.S. Eliot, 'cannot bear very much reality,' and of none of the dimensions in which we live and move can that be said more truly than of time. Within us and around us, constant and irreversible, it bears us on in an eternal now, both past and future being no more than extensions of mind trapped in that now. Yet those extensions are among humankind's defining achievements, allowing us not only to escape – however temporarily – the tyranny of the now but also to comprehend it more fully.

It is the past that concerns us here. We examine it partly to help us decide who we are, partly to explain why things are as they are, partly for the sheer hell of it, but, whatever our motivation, the reality of the past is beyond us for two reasons. First, since the past has no material existence – it isn't *there* – we can't examine it at all. The best we can do is sort out its detritus in order to reconstruct a version of it, and that brings us to the second reason: immediate experience, the moment present and passing, is so infinitely rich and complex that not even the best poetry or Proust's bit of *madeleine* can come anywhere close to claiming wholeness of vision, and since the past is an accumulation of all the present moments that ever were, whatever we reconstruct will be a simplification, a simulacrum of the reality. As Renford Bambrough said, 'The ideal limiting case of a reproduction is reduplication, and a duplicate is too true to be useful', adding that 'Anything that falls short of the ideal limit of reduplication is too useful to be altogether true'.[1] Even so Coleridge, who says in 'Kubla Khan' that could he revive the Abyssinian maid's song he 'would *build* that dome in air' – giving us not a description but the thing itself!

Whether we take Coleridge's remarkable statement at face value – and that poet *was* well read in hermetic lore – or as a metaphor for the creative process, it comes to the same thing for our purposes: full description would be more incomprehensible than the reality itself – and quite as unresponsive to the questions we normally address to time past. It is not so much that we cannot *bear* very much reality as that, seamless and amorphous, it is useless to us in its raw form. Unable to step out of the constant flow, we seek emblems of fixity, and that is what we ask of History: to create for us the sense that certain past actions fall together in patterns we call events – limited shapes of time moving from identifiable beginnings to recognizable ends – and by so doing to make the past part of the present. The historian sifts the detritus, and, through careful selection and arrangement, gives us those emblems, constructs which – though they build no domes in air and are far too useful to be true – sustain us in our individual and collective human journey.

It was one such construct, a song, that led me to poking around in some old Scottish sources like Moysie and Birrel for the ostensible purpose of illuminating some of that song's references, like who Huntly was or 'the Queen's love' business, but my search soon went well beyond that, ultimately leading me to create – for the sheer hell of it, really – a proper history. Taking Moray's murder as my focus, I went back in time to tell what brought it about, then forward to show what happened because of it, cause and effect, a closed construct quite as independent and self-sufficient as the ballad itself – and just as artificial. That account – going, as it does, far beyond what is necessary to 'explain' the ballad – has to be its own excuse for being, but, just as the ballad led to it, it leads back to the ballad, an intersection that certainly enriches our experience of both.

The two accounts are the same, then, in that each is a representation of something that 'really happened', to be judged not only on its truthfulness (how well it measures up against the available detritus) but on its aesthetic integrity (how complete and satisfying it is in itself) as well. But there is one important difference: while my account was constructed four hundred years after the event, the ballad was contemporary with it and is thus *part* of the detritus, no less a historical document requiring evaluation and interpretation than is a state paper or the account in Moysie's *Memoirs*. Historians, however, with their traditional disdain for oral traditions, have paid it slight attention or else cast it in the role of anti-history – that which must be swept aside in the name of Truth. Keith Brown, for instance, in his fine book *Bloodfeud in Scotland*, speaks of it only as 'the romantic ballad that immortalized the relatively unimportant Moray', and Michael Lynch in his recent *Scotland: A New History* dismisses it with a contemptuous wave, claiming that 'the only relationship which the well-known ballad bears to reality is that the Earl was indeed bonnie'.[2]

In all fairness, though, I should point out that Brown is perfectly correct in what he says, and he neither uses nor abuses the ballad in his account. Moray *was* a rather minor figure, amounting to little if anything in his own right, and he was entirely out of his league with someone like Huntly, who amounted to a great deal. 'The murder of Moray,' says Maurice Lee, 'was an enormously important event, not because of the removal from the scene of one young and rather lightweight earl, but because James refused to do anything about it.'[3] I should say in passing that even with 20/20 hindsight it is hard to see just what James could or should have done, but if ever anyone had greatness thrust upon them it was the murdered Moray. A strapping, handsome young gallant, tall in the saddle, a bruiser in football and good at knightly games, he was in many ways a quintessential popular hero, and when he was brutally butchered the people rewarded him with a measure of immortality.

On the other hand, Lynch's remark is more clever than correct. To be sure, the two ballads are wrong in details (Moray could never have been King, Huntly wasn't Moray's brother-in-law, etc.), but, as we have seen, in their expression of outrage they bear a very close relation to the reality, having, in fact, helped create it. Even the 'Queen's love' business in the 'A' version can show that the gossip was in the streets at the time, and – no question about it – nothing has done more to keep that bit of gossip alive than that ballad. Lynch's quip is a better example of a historian expecting the wrong things from oral tradition than it is of anything else. 'Where balladry is of genuine value,' said Friedman, and he was referring specifically to historical ballads, 'is in revealing the public reaction to political events and in helping to reconstruct the political and social atmosphere.'[4] And 'The Bonny Earl of Murray' does that very well.

While historians generally mistrust oral tradition, they seem to have been quite ready to accept its authority in the present instance for one specific detail: the Earl's epithet. Over and over again in historical literature he is 'the Bonny Earl', even though there is not a shred of evidence – except for the 'A' version of the ballad – that he was ever so known in his time. A contemporary source (Moysie) speaks of him as 'being the lustiest youth', and a near-contemporary source (*The History of King James the Sext*) says he was 'a comely personage, of a great stature and strong of body like a kemp', but neither describes him as 'bonny'. Certainly, too, the Death Portrait shows him as a fine physical specimen, but the word 'bonny' doesn't appear until 1765 when Percy in the first introductory essay to the ballad claimed that 'if this picture did not flatter, he well deserved the name of the bonny *Earl*.[5] Scott picked up on that lead, saying that 'Murray was so handsome and personable a man, that he was generally known by the name of the Bonnie Earl of Murray', and a half century later Gregory in his *History of the Western Highlands* (1881) also claimed that he was 'commonly called' "the Bonny Earl"'.[6] Then the redoubtable T.F. Henderson, in his *Dictionary of National Biography* article on Moray (1897–98), said that 'his personal beauty and accomplishments gained him the name of 'the bonny earl',[7] and the even more redoubtable Andrew Lang used the epithet time and again in speaking of him, though, to be sure, nowhere does he claim that Moray was so known in his time.[8] On the other hand, John Hill Burton, writing at about the same time, *does* claim that he 'was known in his day as 'the bonny Earl of Murray', and Paul suggests the same thing in his *Scots Peerage* (1897).[9] No need to labor the point further: while he has been known as 'the Bonny Earl' down the centuries, there is no evidence that he was ever called that in his lifetime. And it's at least worth a mention that in the 'B' version he does not bear that epithet at all. It is, then, entirely the creation of the 'A' version's makar, who drew it from the common store of ballad epithets – a lovely example of folklore *becoming* history.

Let us now move from history to the ballad itself. Several times in the course of this book I have emphasized (when I haven't simply taken it for granted) both the richness and subtle possibilities of ballad language – especially in such resources as metaphor and connotation – and the ballad makar's skill in employing it. Such an emphasis (or such an assumption) will of course be questioned by those who may still bear an allegiance to some form of Herder's *Naturpoesie/Kunstpoesie* dichotomy, wherein folksong is seen as 'spontaneous', 'naïve', 'simple', the 'natural' expression of the 'folk' – something quite different from 'art song', which is the product of an individual poet exercising craft and careful thought. I don't know any folklorist – certainly no folksong specialist – who still subscribes to Herder's cleavage, but even so it's surprising how often and in what various guises it continues to surface.[10]

As I pointed out in the previous chapter, 'individual creation/ communal re-creation' has been pretty much dogma for over half a century, and – though the whole subject of origins has gone rather out of style – it remains dogma today, with the emphasis clearly on the second half of that formula as the source of ballad whatness. Friedman states that point of view very well:

> For ballad tradition is not, as some individualists seem to think, simply a means of transmitting ballads. And the result of such transmission need not always be degeneration. Tradition in the healthy days of balladry was a constructive, creative process. Guided by a superintending pattern, it was capable of remaking all manner of diverse material into ballads. This pattern, the essential traits of ballad style, is balladness.[11]

On the other hand, I have written three books and a couple of articles based on two premises: first, in folksong as in art-song, the original maker, not some superorganic process, is the primary shaper; second, both folk and fine artists face the same problems – especially in resolving the tension between tradition and innovation – and they solve them in the same ways.[12] Obviously, I continue both premises in the present book. 'All cultural changes are initiated by individuals,' said Homer Barnett.[13] That in the present instance we cannot identify that individual doesn't mean he or she wasn't there, working it over, making it happen, putting this in, leaving that out. 'I see motion,' said St. Thomas Aquinas somewhere, 'I infer a motor.' It's the same way with art.

If we can't know specifically who created 'The Bonny Earl of Murray', can we make some reasonable guesses about him? Yes, but first we should briefly reconsider whether we are dealing with one ballad or two; that is, are the 'A' and 'B' versions simply variants of a common original? Both Finlay and Child raised this question, and I raised it again in regard to the curiously conflated American 'emigrant' versions, but while I cannot flatly rule it out, the two preceding chapters should have made it clear that I consider such an ancestral version an extremely remote possibility.[14] All I can add at this point is the corroborative judgment of the Chadwicks, who speak of version 'A' as an 'elegy' while 'B' is 'a narrative poem, much occupied with speeches.' The two versions,' they conclude, 'would seem to have been independent poems originally, though the surviving text of A has borrowed one stanza from B.'[15] Thus, since we are dealing with two separate ballads having almost nothing in common save their subject, we will, of course, have to make two separate guesses about their authors.

We have little enough to go on with either version, but since 'B' is by far the more, ballad-like, it is also the less individual – the more anonymous – of the two. Even its 'fictional heightening' by having Huntly stab Moray

– whom it casts as his brother-in-law! –' dead in his bed' is not so much an individualizing trait as it is the sort of thing David Buchan claimed we could expect in feud ballads.[16] 'B' is so close in its metric, its style, its date and its mix of fact and fiction to 'Willie Macintosh' (Child 183) as to make me wonder about common authorship, but I will content myself with a more modest possibility: a common geographical tradition, that of the Northeast of Scotland. Slender as the evidence is, that possibility takes on more flesh if we allow Motherwell's claim that 'Bonnie James Campbell' (Child 210) – another feud ballad – has to do with a Campbell killed in the battle of Glenlivet in 1594 or even Maidment's far less likely suggestion that it has to do with the murder of Campbell of Calder.[17] And, more intriguing yet, that would create the possibility of all three ballads being related specifically to the Huntly-Moray feud. A true bill? By no means. Grounds for a modest presumption? Perhaps. And I wonder again in passing about common authorship.

If by my guess the much neglected 'B' version came from country north of the Grampians and The Mounth, my further guess is that the more famous 'A' version came from well south of that ridge, probably, in fact, from the streets of Edinburgh itself. My evidence – no less presumptive and probabilistic than before – is drawn from both style and content. As for style, we have seen that 'A' is almost not a ballad at all, or rather it can only be called one by grace of the Wilgus-Long concept of 'blues ballad'. It is a lyric lament that achieves its effect through a combination of ballad techniques (incremental repetition, 'O lang will his lady', etc.) and a very unballadlike apostrophic opening. Its most balladlike stanza ('Now wae be to thee, Huntly!'), since it jars the otherwise almost perfectly balanced lyric structure, was no part of the original author's plan but rather the interpolation of a later singer. More about that in a moment.

As for its content, the song shows its makar to have had no special 'insider' knowledge. No one in any way close to the Earl – say a member of his household or one of his tenants – would have had his three-months-dead Countess watching in vain for his return, for example. On the other hand, he had probably seen the Death Portrait (which we know was being shown around Edinburgh) and heard the gossip about the Queen, but otherwise knew the Earl only as one would a popular hero – handsome, a footballer, good with weapons and the darling of the ladies. Finally, since I hazard that this was one of the 'common rhymes and songs' being sung in the streets at the time, I see the author as an Edinburghian, say a burgess or tradesman, something of a reader (at least of broadsides) but still close enough to the oral tradition to be able to manipulate ballad techniques – albeit in unballadlike, non-narrative ways[18] – with skill and ease. He may even have launched his little five-stanza lament as a broadside.

But if I emphasize the individual creator's role, in no way am I denying the creative role that can be played by subsequent tradition. Were that my argument, 'The Bonny Earl of Murray' would be a poor illustration, because the ballad as we know it – and as it has been known to us for over 250 years – is not its makar's work alone, which brings me back to that aberrant, pattern-breaking second stanza. In Chapter 3 I wondered whether it was part of the poet's intention or the result of a later conflation, and I gave my reasons for believing that some subsequent singer, either through error or genius, slipped this stanza in, probably transposing it from the 'B' version. Its jolting shift of both tone and point of view gives the ballad a vibrancy its otherwise lyric 'perfection' would have lacked. Perfection is all very well in its way, but breaking molds can create new perfections, and 'The Bonny Earl of Murray' as we have it is a case in point. The original makar, had he known about this change at the time, might well have viewed it as poetic vice, but viewing it from the perspective granted us by four centuries – and hearing it sung to its fine though unfolklike nineteenth-century tune – we can see it as a vice more than redeemed by its virtues.

O felix culpa!

NOTES

1 Quoted in Peter Munz, *The Shapes of Time* (Middletown: Wesleyan University Press, 1977), p.17.
2 Brown, *Bloodfeud*, p.144; Michael Lynch, *Scotland: A New History* (London: Century, 1991), p.233.
3 Maurice Lee, Jr., *Great Britain's Solomon* (Urbana: University of Illinois, 1990), p.74.
4 Friedman, *The Ballad Revival*, p.75.
5 Percy, vol.ii, p.210 (1765 edition).
6 Scott, *Tales of a Grandfather* (1827–29), p.353; Gregory, p.244.
7 *D.N.B.*, vol.18, p.1194.
8 Lang, *History*, vol.ii, p.355ff.
9 Burton, vol.v, p.289; Paul, *Scots Peerage*, vol.vi, pp.316–17.
10 It has shown up especially in the folk art/fine art distinction. The most elaborate – and by far the best – treatment of this subject known to me is Henry Glassie, *The Spirit of Folk Art* (New York: Harry Abrams, 1989).

11 Albert B. Friedman, *The Viking Book of Folk Ballads of the English-Speaking World* (New York: Viking, 1956), p.xxxiii.
12 *Larry Gorman, Lawrence Doyle, Joe Scott.* See also my 'Joe Smith: The Poet as Outlaw', in Porter, *The Ballad Image*, pp.148–70, and '"The Teamster in Jack MacDonald's Crew": A Song in Context and its Singing'. *Folklife Annual* 1985, 74–85.
13 H.G. Barnett, *Innovation: The Basis of Cultural Change* (New York: McGraw Hill, 1953), p.39.
14 See above, pp.143, 167.
15 H. Munro and N. Kershaw Chadwick, *The Growth of Literature* (Cambridge University Press, 1940), vol.iii, p.684, n.3.
16 Buchan, 'The Historical Ballads', p.445.
17 Quoted in Child, iv, p.142. For the Calder murder see above, p.34–35.
18 See Andersen, *Commonplace and Creativity*, p.147n.

Epilogue

FEBRUARY 7, 1992. All day it had been riding on my mind that this was the four hundredth anniversary of Moray's murder, and I wanted to mark it, make the day somehow special. But I had no idea how to do it. I had thought about a party. Bobby and I liked giving parties on slightly offbeat occasions like St. David's Day or William Carlos Williams's hundredth birthday, but we agreed that celebrating an obscure bloodfeud killing – or any killing at all, for that matter – was a bit of a bad joke, and we had abandoned the idea early on. At the moment I was grateful we had. It would not have answered my present mood, but since I still didn't know what *would* answer it – and since my puzzlement wasn't helping me saw any academic wood – I left the office a little early and set off through the gathering winter dark for my home in Bucksport.

What was left of a chill if splendid sunset did nothing to dispel my bafflement as I crossed the river and headed south on the final leg of my trip, and there was still a far down glow in the west as I turned in the driveway. The house, though, was dark. Bobby would be late tonight, I remembered. I threw a couple of logs in the stove and went into my study.

But I didn't turn on the light, not right away. Easing myself down in the big chair where I sometimes read, sometimes snooze – sometimes, by turns, do both – I let the dark possess me. The house was quiet, but it *was* a quiet house. Occasionally a pipe would hammer as the heat came up or a radiator would whistle some, but tonight even those sounds made it seem quieter than usual. It was far from unpleasant, but neither was it quite the answer, at least not a sufficient answer. I had to reach out, I had to *share* this presence of the past, but with whom? Who would enjoy or be amused – in the best sense of that word – by my including them in it? Even as I asked, I knew: Richard Dyer-Bennet.

We had met and spent the most of two days together when he came to the University to sing thirty years before, and we'd hit it off very well. On the strength of that I had written him several months back asking his permission to dedicate this book to him, and we'd had some small correspondence. I turned on the light, checked my little book, and went in the other room to call, feeling, as I always did at times like this, a little apprehensive about presuming.

A woman answered my ring, and I asked to speak to Richard Dyer-Bennet.

A slight pause. 'This is his wife,' she said. 'Who is this calling, please?'

'My name is Sandy Ives. I'm calling from Maine, and —'

'Oh yes,' she said, 'I know who you are.' Another pause. 'I don't quite know how to tell you this, but Dick died recently. You didn't see it in the papers?'

Now it was my turn to pause. 'No,' I said at last. 'I guess that's not the sort of thing makes it into the *Bangor Daily News*.' I groped for something more to say. 'When did it happen?'

'In December,' she said. 'It was lymphoma.'

'I feel diminished,' I said. The word was entirely accurate.

'Yes,' she said. 'So do I.'

'We are all diminished,' I said. 'The world is the less without his presence.' Then I told her why I had called in the first place. 'I just thought that if he didn't know, he of all people alive ought to.'

'It would have pleased him,' she said.

'Perhaps he knows all about it anyhow,' I said.

Another pause. 'I wish I could believe that,' she said.

'I wish I could too,' I said.

And that was about it.

The dark seemed rather melodramatic now. I walked around the house turning on lights, checking the thermostat, closing the damper on the stove – things like that, but mostly just to be moving, seeing familiar objects in their familiar places, touching them, putting a book back on the shelf . . . the reassurance of my own quiet footfalls. I thought of putting Dick's 'Bonny Earl' on the player.

But what need? I was hearing it, as I will always be hearing it as once again I was on that moor before the swart tower from whose battlement a lone lady forever looked into the distance . . .

Bobby would be home soon.

Bibliography

A work marked with an asterisk (*) contains a set of the words. One marked with a hash mark (#) contains a tune or tunes. Citations of such works will also indicate an A or B text, the volume and page reference, and whether there is an historical essay or notes.

Acts and Proceedings of the General Assemblies of the Kirk of Scotland. In three volumes (Edinburgh, 1845).

The Acts of the Parliaments of Scotland. T. Thomson and C. Innes, editors (Edinburgh, 1814–75).

Adam, R.J. *The Calendar of Fearn: Texts and Additions 1471–1667* (Edinburgh: Scottish History Society, 1991). Fifth Serires, Vol.IV.

Andersen, Flemming G. *Commonplace and Creativity: The Role of Formulaic Diction in Anglo-Scottish Traditional Balladry* (Odense: Odense University Press, 1985).

——, and Thomas Petit. '"The Murder of Maria Marten": The Birth of a Ballad?' In Richmond, *Narrative Folksong*, pp. 132–78.

*Armes, William Dallam. *Old English Ballads and Folk Songs* (New York: Macmillan, 1919). A, p.125, with notes pp.189–90.

*Aytoun, William Edmundstoune. *The Ballads of Scotland* (Edinburgh and London: William Blackwood, 1858). AB pp.241–43, with essay.

Balfour, Sir James. *The Historical Works of Sir James Balfour*. In 4 volumes. J. Haig, editor (Edinburgh, 1824–25).

**The Ballad Minstrelsy of Scotland* (Glasgow: Maurice Ogle, 1871). AB, pp.530–31, with essays.

Barnett, H.G. *Innovation: The Basis of Cultural Change* (New York: McGraw-Hill, 1953).

#Barsanti, Francesco. *A Collection of Old Scots Tunes* (Edinburgh: Alexander Baillie, 1742). P.14, tune only.

*Beatty, Arthur. 'Some New Ballad Variants'. *Journal of American Folklore* 20 (1907), 154–56. AB combined.

Border Papers. *Calendar of Letters and Papers Relating to the Affairs of the Borders of England and Scotland*. Joseph Bain, editor. In two volumes (Edinburgh: General Register House, 1894–96).

*Belden, Henry M. and Arthur Palmer Hudson. *Folk Ballads from North Carolina*. Brown Collection: Volume II (1952). Pp.160–61, words only, with headnote. See Schinan for tune.

Birrel, Robert. 'The Diary of Robert Birrel', in *Fragments of Scottish History*. J.G. Dalyell, editor (Edinburgh, 1798).

Bold, Alan. *The Ballad* (London: Methuen, 1983).

Brander, Michael. *Scottish Border Battles and Ballads* (New York: Potter, 1975). A, pp.95–98, with essay.

Brereton, Henry Lloyd. *Gordonstoun: Ancient Estate and Modern School* (Edinburgh and London: W. & R. Chambers, 1968).

Britten, Benjamin. *Folksong Arrangements*. Volume I: British Isles (Medium Voice). (London: Boosey & Hawkes, 1943). A, pp.6–7.

*#Bronson, Bertrand H. *The Traditional Tunes to the Child Ballads*. In four volumes (Princeton: Princeton University Press, 1959–72). A, vol.III, pp. 159–61. Excellent discussion of tune tradition.

The Frank C. Brown Collection of North Carolina Folklore. In seven volumes. Newman Ivey White and Paul F. Baum, editors (Durham: University of North Carolina Press, 1952–64). See Belden above for specific entry.

Brown, E.K. *Rhythm in the Novel* (Toronto: University of Toronto Press, 1950).

Brown, P. Hume. *History of Scotland*. In three volumes (Cambridge: Cambridge University Press, 1912). Originally published in 1902.

Brown, James D. and Stephen S. Stratton. *British Musical Biography* (Birmingham: S.S. Stratton, 1897).

Browne, James. *A History of the Highlands and of the Highland Clans* (Glasgow: A. Fullarton, 1840).

Brown, Keith. *Bloodfeud in Scotland 1573–1625*. (Edinburgh: John Donald, 1986).

Buchan, David. *The Ballad and the Folk* (London: Routledge and Kegan Paul, 1972).

——. 'History and Harlaw', In Lyle, *Ballad Studies*. pp.29–40.

——. 'The Historical Ballads of the Northeast of Scotland'. *Lares* 4 (Oct. -Dec., 1985), 443–51.

Burns, J.H. 'The Political Background of the Reformation, 1513–1625.' In McRoberts, pp.1–36.

Burton, John Hill. *The History of Scotland*. In eight volumes (Edinburgh and London: William Blackwood, 1897).

Calderwood, David. *The History of the Kirk of Scotland*. In 8 Volumes (Edinburgh: The Wodrow Society, 1842–49).

Caldwell, David H. (editor). *Scottish Weapons and Fortifications, 1100–1800* (Edinburgh: John Donald, 1981).

Calendar of State Papers relating to Scotland and Mary, Queen of Scots 1547–1603. Various editors. In 13 volumes (Edinburgh: General Register House, 1898–1969).

Carmichael, Alexander. *Carmina Gadelica*. In five volumes (Edinburgh: Oliver and Boyd, 1954).

Cassell's Old and New Edinburgh. James Grant, editor. In three volumes (London: Cassell, n.d.).

Cawdor, Earl of. *The Murders of Lord Moray & the Thane of Cawdor in* 1591 A.D. Privately printed, 1985.

Chadwick, H. Munro and N. Kershaw Chadwick. *The Growth of Literature.* In three volumes. (Cambridge: Cambridge University Press, 1940; reprinted 1986).

*Chambers, Robert. *The Scottish Ballads* (Edinburgh: William Tait, 1829). A,pp.69–71, with extensive essay.

———. *The Romantic Scottish Ballads, Their Epoch and Authorship* (Edinburgh, 1859).

———. *Popular Rhymes of Scotland.* New Edition (London and Edinburgh: Chambers, 1870).

Chambers, William. *Historical Sketch of St. Giles' Cathedral, Edinburgh* (Edinburgh: W. & R. Chambers, 1890).

*Child, Francis James. *English and Scottish Ballads.* In eight volumes (Boston: Little, Brown, 1857–59). AB, vol.vii, pp.119–122, with essay.

*———. *The English and Scottish Popular Ballads.* In five volumes. (Boston and New York: Houghton Mifflin, 1882–98). AB, vol.iii, pp.447–49, with extensive essay.

*#Christie, W. *Traditional Ballad Airs.* In two volumes (Edinburgh: Edmondston and Douglas, 1876). A, vol.i, pp.202–03, with essay.

*#Clancy Brothers and Tommy Makem. *The Irish Songook* (New York: Music Sales Corp., 1969). A, pp.114–15, with brief headnote.

Coffin, Tristram P. 'Mary Hamilton and the Ango-American Ballad as an Art Form'. In Leach and Coffin, pp.245–256. Originally published in *Journal of American Folklore* LXX (1957), 208–14.

Collins, C. Cody. *Love of a Glove* (New York: Fairchild, 1947).

Collinson, Francis. *The Traditional and National Music of Scotland* (London: Routledge & Kegan Paul, 1966).

Cowan, Edward J., editor. *The People's Past* (Edinburgh: Polygon, 1991).

Cowan, Edward J. 'The Darker Vision of the Scottish Renaissance: The Devil and Francis Stewart.' In Cowan and Shaw, pp.125–40.

Cowan, Ian B. and Duncan Shaw, editors. *The Renaisasance and Reformation in Scotland: Essays in Honour of Gordon Donaldson* (Edinburgh: Scottish Academic Press, 1983).

*Cromek, R.H. *Select Scotish Songs* (London: Cadell and Davies, 1810). A, vol.ii, pp.156–57.

*Cunningham, Allan. *The Songs of Scotland.* In four volumes (London, 1825). A, vol.ii, pp.180–81, with essay.

Cunningham, C. Willett and Phyllis Cunningham. *Handbook of English Costume in the Seventeenth Century* (London: Faber & Faber, n.d.).

*#Davidson, Malcolm (arranger). 'The Bonnie Earl o' Moray; Scots Folk Song' (London: Boosey & Co., 1925). For male voices.

Dalyell, J.G. *Fragments of Scotish History* (Edinburgh: Archibald Constable, 1798).

*#Diack, J. Michael. 'The Bonnie Earl o' Moray' (London: Paterson's, 1925).

A. Sheet music.

*#——. *The New Scottish Orpheus*. In two volumes (London: Paterson's, 1939). A, vol.ii, pp.28–29.

Dibblee, Randall, and Dorothy Dibblee. *Folksongs from Prince Edward Island* (Summerside, P.E.I:Rodney Clark, 1973).

Dickinson, W. Croft. *Scotland from the Earliest Times to 1603*. Third edition, revised and augmented by Archibald A.M. Duncan (London Oxford University Press, 1977).

Donaldson, Gordon. *Scotland: James V to James VII* (Edinburgh & London: Oliver and Boyd, 1965).

Dorson, Richard M., editor. *Folklore and Folklife* (Chicago: University of Chicago Press, 1972).

Doubleday, H.A. & Lord Howard de Walden. *The Complete Peerage: or a History of the House of Lords and All Its Members from the Earliest Times.* (London: St. Catherine Press, 1935).

Drinker, Henry S., translator. *Solo Songs of Johannes Brahms*. With piano accompaniment. (Association of American Choruses, n.d.).

*#Dyer-Bennet, Richard. *The Richard Dyer-Bennet Folk Song Book* (New York: Simon & Schuster, 1971). A, pp.32–37.

Edwards, Carol L. and Kathleen E.B. Manley. *Narrative Folksong: New Directions. Essays in Appreciation of W. Edson Richmond* (Boulder, Colorado: Westview Press, 1985).

*#Edwards, Jay. *The Coffee House Songbook* (New York: Oak, 1966). AB mixed.

*#Eyre-Todd, George. *Ancient Scots Ballads* (London: Bayley and Ferguson, 1894). A. pp.127–30, with essay.

Falconer, A.F. *The Correspondence of Thomas Percy and David Dalrymple, Lord Hailes.* (Baton Rouge, Louisiana State University Press, 1954).

*Finlay, John. *Scottish Historical and Romantic Ballads*. In two volumes (Edinburgh, 1808). AB, vol.i, pp.77–84; vol.ii, pp.11–23, both with extensive essays.

Fiske, Roger. *Scotland in Music: A European Enthusiasm* (Cambridge: Cambridge University Press, 1983).

Fittos, Robert Scott. *Sports and Pastimes of Scotland* (Paisley & London: Alexander Gardner, 1891).

*#Flanders, Helen Hartness. *Ancient Ballads Traditionally Sung in New England.* In four volumes, with critical analyses by Tristram P. Coffin; music annotations by Bruno Nettl (Philadelphia: University of Pennsylvania Press, 1960–1965). AB, vol.3, pp.185–89, with essay.

Fowler, David C. *A Literary History of the Popular Ballad* (Durham: Duke University Press, 1968).

Fraser, Antonia. *Mary Queen of Scots* (New York: Delacorte, 1969).

Fraser, William. *The Chiefs of Grant*. In three volumes (Edinburgh, 1883).

Fraser, Sir William. *The Red Book of Menteith*. In two volumes (n.p., 1880).

Friedman, Albert B. *The Ballad Revival* (Chicago: University of Chicago

Press, 1961).

*——. *The Viking Book of Folk Ballads of the English-Speaking World* (New York: Viking, 1956). A, pp.264–65 with essay. See also pp.xix–xx.

Froude, James A. *History of England from the Fall of Wolsey to the Death of Elizabeth.* In twelve volumes (London: Longmans, Green, 1856–1870).

*Gilchrist, John. *A Collection of Ancient and Modern Scottish Ballads, Tales and Songs.* In two volumes (Edinburgh: William Blackwood, 1815). A, vol.i, pp.89–92, with essay.

Gordon, Sir Robert. *A Genealogical History of the Earldom of Sutherland* (Edinburgh: George Ramsay, 1813).

*#Goss, John. *Ballads of Britain* (London: John Lane, 1937). A, pp.80–81. Gives all three tunes.

Gower, Herschel. 'Traditional Scottish Ballads in the United State'. Ph.D. dissertation, Vanderbilt University, 1957.

.——.'The Scottish Element in Traditional Ballads Collected in America'. In Lyle, *Ballad Studies*, pp.117–151.

.——.'The Scottish Palimpsest in Traditional Ballads Collected in North America'. In Walker and Welker, pp. 117–144.

Gregory, Donald. *The History of the Western Highlands and Isles of Scotland* (London, 1881).

Grundtvig, Svend. *Engelske og Skotske Folkeviser.* In three volumes (Kjøbenhavn: Wahlske Boghandlings Forlag, 1842–46).

*Gummere, Francis B. *Old English Ballads* (Boston: Ginn, 1894). A, p. 155, with notes p.334.

Gunnyon, William. *Illustrations of Scotish Life and Superstition from Song and Ballade* (Glasgow: Robert Forrester, 1879).

*#Gurney, Ivor. 'The Bonnie Earl of Murray; old Scotch ballad set to music' (London: Winthrop Rogers, 1921). Sheet music. See also Northcote, Sydney, below.

*#Hall, Maude M. *Ballads and Other Narrative Poems* (Boston and New York: *Allyn and Bacon, 1909). A, pp.87–89, with footnotes.

Hare, Peter H. A *Woman's Quest for Science: Portrait of Anthropologist Elsie Clews Parsons* (Buffalo: Prometheus Press, 1985).

Harker, David. *Fakesong* (Milton Keynes: Open University Press, 1985).

Harris, Joseph. (editor) *The Ballad and Oral Literature* (Cambridge: Harvard English Studies No. 17, 1991).

*Hart, Walter Morris. *English Popular Ballads* (Chicago and New York: Scott, Foresman, 1916). A,p.59, with notes pp.313–314.

Henderson, T.F. 'James Stewart, 2nd Earl of Moray'. In *Dictionary of National Biography*, Vol. 18, p. 1194.

——. *The Ballad in Literature* (Cambridge: Cambridge University Press, 1912).

Hendren, J. W. *A Study of Ballad Rhythm, With Special Reference to Ballad Music* (Princeton: Princeton Studies in English, No. 14, 1936). Reprinted New York: Gordian Press, 1966.

*Herd, David. *Ancient and Modern Scots Songs*. In two volumes (Edinburgh: Martin and Wotherspoon, 1769). A, pp.32–33.

Herder, Johann Gottfried von. *Sämmtliche Werke* (Bernhard Suphan, editor). 33 vols. 1877–1913; reprinted 1967–68.

The Historie and Life of King James the Sext (Edinburgh: Bannatyne Club Publications No. 13, 1825).

Hodgart, M.J.C. *The Ballads* (London: Hutchinson University Library, 1950).

*———. *The Faber Book of Ballads* (London: Faber and Faber, 1965). A, pp.144–45, brief note, p.255.

Hole, Christina. *English Sports and Pastimes* (London: B.T. Batsford, 1949).

*Housman, John E. *British Popular Ballads* (London: George G. Harrap, 1952). A, p.217–18, with brief essay.

Ives, Edward D. *Larry Gorman: The Man Who Made the Songs* (Bloomington: Indiana University Press, 1964; reprinted New York: Arno Press, 1977; reprinted Fredericton, N.B: Goose Lane Editions, 1993).

———. *Lawrence Doyle: The Farmer-Poet of Prince Edward Island*. Maine Studies No. 92 (Orono, Maine: University Press, 1971).

———. *Joe Scott: The Woodsman Songmaker* (Champaign, Illinois: University of Illinois Press, 1978).

———. 'Joe Smith: The Poet as Outlaw'. In Porter, *The Ballad Image*, pp.148–70.

———. '"The Teamster in Jack MacDonald's Crew": A Song in Context and Its Singing'. In *Folklife Annual 1985*, pp.74–85.

*#Johnson, James. *The Scots Musical Museum*. In two volumes. With annotations by William Stenhouse (Hatboro: Folklore Associates, 1962). Originally published in 1788. A, vol.i, p.185, with essay vol.ii, pp.172–73.

Keith, Alexander. 'Scottish Ballads: Their Evidence of Authorship and Origin'. In Leach and Coffin, pp.39–56. Originally published in *Essays and Studies by Members of the English Association*, XII (1926), 100–119.

Brother Kenneth. 'The Popular Literature of the Scottish Reformation'. In McRoberts, pp.169–184.

*#Kinsley, James, editor. *The Oxford Book of Ballads* (London: Oxford University Press, 1969). AB, pp.594–96, with notes.

*#Kreisler, Fritz (arranger). 'The Bonnie Earl O'Moray' (New York: Carl Fischer, 1917). In collaboration with Reinhold Warlich.

Lang, Andrew. *A History of Scotland from the Roman Occupation*. In four volumes (Edinburgh and London: William Blackwood, 1902). Republished 1924.

*#Langstaff, John. *Hi! Ho! The Rattlin' Bog and Other Folk Songs for Group Singing* (New York: Harcourt Brace and World, 1969). A, pp.54–55.

Lawson, Malcolm. See MacLeod and Boulton.

*Leach, MacEdward. *The Ballad Book* (New York: Harper, 1955). AB, pp.491–93, with essay.

*———. *The Book of Ballads* (New York: Heritage, 1967). A, pp.90–91.

———. *Folk Ballads and Songs of the Lower Labrador Coast* (Ottawa: National Museum of Canada, Bulletin No. 201, 1965).

——, and Tristram P. Coffin. *The Critics and the Ballad* (Carbondale: Southern Illinois University Press, 1961).

Leach, Maria (editor). *Standard Dictionary of Folklore, Mythology, and Legend.* In two volumes (New York: Funk & Wagnall's, 1950).

Lee, Maurice Jr. *John Maitland of Thirlestane and the Founding of the Stewart Despotism in Scotland* (Princeton: Princeton University Press, 1959).

——. *Great Britain's Solomon: James VI and I in His Three Kingdoms* (Urbana: University of Illinois Press, 1990).

Lindsay, Robert. *The Cronicles of Scotland.* In two volumes (Edinburgh, 1814).

*#Lovatt, S.E. 'The Bonny Earl of Moray' (London: Oxford University Press, 1947). Arranged for men's voices.

*#Luboff, Norman and Win Stracke. *Songs of Man* (Englewood Cliffs: Prentice Hall, 1965). A, p.92.

Lyle, E.B., editor. *Ballad Studies* (Cambridge: D.S. Brewer, 1976).

——. *Andrew Crawfurd's Collection of Ballads And Songs: Volume I* (Edinburgh: Scottish Text Society, 1975).

Lynch, Michael. *Scotland: A New History* (London: Century, 1991).

MacColl, Ewan. *Journeyman* (London: Sidgwick and Jackson, 1990).

Mackenzie, Agnes Mure. *The Scotland of Queen Mary and the Religious Wars, 1513–1638* (London: Oliver and Boyd, 1957). Originally published 1936.

Mackie, J.D. *A History of Scotland.* Second Edition (New York: Penguin Books, 1978). Originally published 1964.

MacQueen, John, and Tom Scott. *The Oxford Book of Scottish Verse.* (Oxford: Oxford University Press, 1966).

*Maidment, James. *Scotish Ballads And Songs, Historical and Traditionary.* In two volumes (Edinburgh, 1868). AB, vol. i, pp.234–39, with essay and notes.

*Manning-Sanders, Ruth. *A Bundle of Ballads* (Philadelphia: Lippincott, 1959). A, p.36.

Marshall, Rosalind K. *Queen of Scots* (London: HMSO, 1986).

Martin, Burns. *Bibliography of Allan Ramsay* (Glasgow: Jackson, Wylie, 1931).

——. *Allan Ramsay* (Cambridge: Harvard University Press, 1931). Reprinted Greenwood Press 1973.

McDowell, John H. 'Folklore as Commemorative Discourse.' *Journal of American Folklore* 105 (Fall 1992)

McRoberts, David, editor. *Essays on the Scottish Reformation, 1513–1625* (Glasgow: Burns, 1962).

Melvill, James. *The Autobiography and Diary of Mr. James Melvill.* Edited by Robert Pitcairn (Edinburgh: Wodrow Society, 1842).

Melville, Sir James. *Memoirs of His Own Life, 1549–1593* (Edinburgh: Bannatyne Club, 1827).

Miscellanea Scotica: A Collection of Tracts Relating to the History, Antiquities, Topography, and Literature of Scotland. In four volumes (Glasgow: John Wylie, 1818).

*#Moffat, Alfred (arranger). 'The Bonnie Earl o'Moray, old Scottish Lament' (Glasgow: Bayley and Ferguson, 1921). A. Sheet music.

*#———. *The Scottish Song Book. For Bass. A Collection of the Favourite Songs and Ballads of the North* (London: Bayley and Ferguson, c.1925). A, pp.12–13.

*Motherwell, William. *Minstrelsy: Ancient and Modern* (Glasgow: John Wylie, 1827). AB, pp.78–82, with essay.

Moysie, David. *Memoirs of the Affairs of Scotland* (Edinburgh: The Bannatyne Club. No.39, 1830).

Munro, Ailie. *The Folk Music Revival in Scotland* (London: Kahn and Averill, 1984).

*#Napier, William. *A Selection of the Most Favourite Scots Songs/ Chiefly Pastoral/ Adapted for the Harpsichord/ With an Accompaniment for a/ Violin/ by/ Eminent Masters* (Edinburgh and London: Napier, c.1790). A, pp.72–73.

*#Northcote, Sydney. *Baritone Songs* (New Imperial Edition, London and New York: Boosey, 1950). A, pp.120–22.

Ordnance Gazetteer of Scotland. New Edition. Francis Hinds Groome, editor (London: Mackenzie, n.d.).

Oring, Elliott. (editor). *Folk Groups and Folklore Genres* (Logan: Utah State University Press, 1986).

*#Orr, Robin (arranger). 'The Bonny Earl of Murray' (Glasgow: Bayley and Ferguson, 1965). Sheet music. Air and words from *Orpheus Caledonius*.

#Oswald, James. *The Caledonian Pocket Companion* (London, c.1753). Vol.V, p.14.

'Papers Relating to the Murder of the Laird of Calder'. In *Highland Pepers*. Vol.I (Edinburgh: Publications of the Scottish Hstory Society, Second Series, Vol.V, 1914). Edited by J.R.N. MacPhail. Pp.142–94.

*#Parsons, Elsie Clews, and Helen H. Roberts. 'A Few Ballads and Songs'. *Journal of American Folklore* 44 (1931), 296–301. A, pp.297.

Paul, Sir James Balfour. *The Scots Peerage* (Edinburgh: David Douglas, 1906).

*Percy, Thomas. *Reliques of Ancient English Poetry*. In three volumes. Edited with an Introduction by Henry B. Wheatley (New York: Dover, 1966). A, pp.226–28. This edition was originally published in London 1886 and is based on the fourth edition of 1794. First edition published 1765; second 1767; third 1775.

*Pinkerton, John. *Scottish Tragic Ballads*. In two volumes (London: J. Nichols, 1781). A, p.60.

*———. *Select Scotish Ballads*. In two volumes (London: J. Nichols, 1783). A, vol.i, pp.88–89.

Pitcairn, Robert. *Historical and Genealogical Account of the Principal Families of the Name of Kennedy* (Edinburgh, 1830).

———. *Criminal Trials in Scotland from 1488 to 1624*. In three volumes (Edinburgh: Wm. Tait, 1833).

Porter, James, editor. *The Ballad Image: Essays Presented to Bertrand Harris Bronson* (Los Angeles: Center for the Study of Comparative Folklore and Mythology, 1983).

———. 'The "Mary Scott" Complex: Outline of a Diachronic Model'. In Porter, *The Ballad Image*, pp.59–94.

Purser, John. *Scotland's Music* (Edinburgh: Mainstream, 1992).

Rait, Robert S. *Lusus Regius, Being Poems and Other Pieces by King James the First* (Westminster: Archibald Constable, 1901).

Rampini, Charles. *A History of Moray and Nairn* (Edinburgh and London, 1897).

*Ramsay, Allan. *The Tea-Table Miscellany*. Volume IV (Edinburgh: Allan Ramsay, 1737). All editions thereafter. A, vol.iv, pp.67–68.

'Randolph Hall Account'. A typed sheet on the table under the Death Portrait, Darnaway Castle. It is mostly from Calderwood, but there are additions. Put together by Morton, 17th Earl of Moray, December 1912.

Register of the Privy Council of Scotland. Various editors (Edinburgh 1877–1898).

Renwick, Roger de V. *English Folk Poetry: Structure and Meaning* (Philadelphia: University of Pennsylvania, 1980).

Richmond, W. Edson. 'Narrative Folk Poetry'. In Dorson, *Folklore and Folklife*, pp.82–98.

Rieuwerts, Sigrid. 'The Historical Moorings of "The Gypsy Laddie": Johnny Faa and the Lady Cassilis'. In Harris, pp.78–96.

#Rimbault, Edward F. *Musical Illustrations of Bishop Percy's Reliques of Ancient English Poetry* (London: Cramer, Beale, 1850). A, p.68.

*#Ritson, Joseph. *Scotish Songs*. In two volumes (1794). A, vol.i, pp.372–74, with essay.

*#Roberton, Hugh Stevenson. 'The Bonnie Earl o'Moray' (New York: G. Schirmer, 1952). Curwen Edition 50817. Arranged for men's voices. A. Sheet music.

*Roberts, John S., editor. *The Legendary Ballads of England and Scotland* (London: Frederick Warne, 1868). AB, pp.403–04, with essay.

Robertson, John. *Uppies and Doonies: The Story of the Kirkwall Ba' Game* (Aberdeen: Aberdeen University, 1967).

Robertson, William. *The History of Scotland*. In *The Works of William Robertson*. In twelve volumes (London, 1822). Originally published 1759.

Rodgers, C., editor. *Estimate of the Scottish Nobility During the Minority of James the Sixth* (London, 1873).

Row, John. *The History of the Kirk of Scotland from the Year* 1558 to August 1637 (Edinburgh: The Wodrow Society, 1842).

*Sargent, Helen Child and George Lyman Kittredge. *English and Scottish Popular Ballads*. (Boston: Houghton Mifflin, 1904). AB, pp.443–44, with essay.

#Schinan, Jan Philip. *The Music of the Ballads*. Brown Collection: Volume IV (1957). A, p.83, with notes. See Belden and Hudson for text.

Scot, W. *An Apologetical Narration of the State and Government of the Kirk of Scotland Since the Reformation* (Edinburgh: Wodrow Society, 1846).

Scott, Tom. See MacQueen, John.

Scott, Sir Walter. *The Tales of a Grandfather* (London: Adam and Charles Black, 1898). Originally published 1827–29.

Seeger, Charles. 'Oral Tradition in Music'. In Leach, *Standard Dictionary*, Vol.ii, pp.825–29.

#*Sharples, Bob (arranger). 'Bonnie Earl of Murray' (London: Palace Music Co., 1963). A. Sheet Music.

Shields, Hugh. 'Popular Modes of Narration and the Popular Ballad'. In Harris, pp.40–59.

Shuel, Brian. *The National Trust Guide to Traditional Customs of Britain* (Exeter: Webb and Bower, 1985).

Shuldham-Shaw, Patrick and Emily Lyle. *The Greig-Duncan Folk Song Collection*. In four volumes of a projected eight (Aberdeen: Aberdeen University Press, 1981–1990).

Simpson, Grant G. *Scottish Handwriting* 1150–1650 (Aberdeen: Aberdeen University Press, 1977).

Simpson, W. Douglas and Christopher J. Tabraham. *Huntly Castle* (Edinburgh: HMSO, n.d.).

Smeaton, Oliphant. *Allan Ramsay* (Edinburgh: Anderson and Ferrier, 1896). Reprinted New York: AMS Press, 1978.

*#Smith, R.A. *The Scotish Minstrel*. In six volumes (Edinburgh: Robert Purdie, 1821–1824). A, vol.iv, p.101, with note.

Spottiswoode, Right Rev. John. *History of the Church of Scotland*. In three volumes (Edinburgh: Spottiswoode Society, 1851).

Stenhouse, William. See Johnson, James.

#Stewart, Robert. *A Collection of Scots Songs Adapted for a Voice and Harpsichord* (Edinburgh, c.1780). A, 3rd folio, p.5.

Strutt, Joseph. *The Sports and Pastimes of the People of England*. New edition by J. Charles Cox (London: Methuen, 1903). Originally published 1801.

Sykes, Homer. *Once a Year: Some Traditional British Customs* (London: Gordon Fraser, 1977).

Thomson, Duncan. *Painting in Scotland, 1570–1650*. (Edinburgh: National Gallery of Scotland, 1975).

*#Thomson, William. *Orpheus Caledonius: or A Collection of Scots Songs*. Second edition. In two volumes (London, 1733). Reprinted by Folklore Associates, 1962.A, vol. ii, p.8.

Toelken, Barre. 'Ballads and Folksongs'. In Oring, pp. 147–174.

——. *Morning Dew and Roses: Nuance, Metaphor, and Meaning in Folksongs* (Champaign: University of Illinoius Press, 1994).

Walker, William E. and Robert L. Welker. *Reality and Myth: Essays in American Literature in Memory of Richard Croom Beatty* (Nashville: Vanderbilt University Press, 1964).

Warlich, Reinhold. See Kreisler, Fritz.

Weber, William. *The Rise of Musical Classics in Eighteenth Century England* (Oxford: Oxford University Press, 1922).

Westcott, Allan F. *New Poems by James I of England* (New York: Columbia University Press, 1911).

*Whitelaw, Alexander. *The Book of Scottish Ballads* (Glasgow, Edinburgh, London: Blackie, 1845). AB, pp. 16–17, with essay.

*Whiting, B.J. *Traditional British Ballads* (New York: Appleton Century Crofts,

1955). A, pp. 83–84.

Wilgus, D.K. and Eleanor R. Long. 'The *Blues Ballad* and the Genesis of Style in Traditional Narrative Songs'. In Edwards and Manley, *Narrative Folksong*, pp. 435–482.

*Witham, R. Adelaide. *English and Scottish Popular Ballads* (Boston: Houghton Mifflin, 1909). A, pp. 82–83, with essay and notes, p. 104–05.

Wormald, Jenny. *Court, Kirk, and Community: Scotland, 1470–1625* (Edinburgh: Edinburgh University Press, 1991). Originally published 1981.

Wright, Sylvia. 'The Death of Lady Mondegreen.' *Harper's* 209 No. 1254 (Nov. 1954), 48–51.

Zumwalt, Rosemary Lévy. *Wealth and Rebellion: Elsie Clews Parsons, Anthropologist and Folklorist* (Urbana: University of Illinois Press, 1992).

COMMERCIAL RECORDINGS OF `THE BONNY EARL OF MURRAY´

Anderson, Moira. *Great Songs of Scotland*. Enigma MID 5003 (c. 1978). Scottish National Chorus with Scottish Symphony Orchestra.

Balfour, Nemone. 'The Bonnie Earl of Moray'. Sung by Nemone Balfour. Recorded in Recording Lab., Library of Congress, Washington, D.C. LC 9605 A3 (12 January 1949).

Beaton, Alex. *Alex Beaton Sings of Scotland Forever*. Glenfinnan GRC 101 (c.1984). Cassette.

Britten, Benjamin. Since I know of over two dozen recordings of Britten's setting, I list here only a few of the most available: Decca LXT 6007 (1962); Decca SXL 6007 (1962) and 411-802-1 (1984), both sung by Peter Pears; Musical Heritage Society MHC 6792Z (1983).

Carmichael, Alex. *The Bonnie Earl O' Moray*. Columbia 5047 (c. 1935?). 10" 78rpm. Baritone with piano.

Corrie Folk Trio. *More Folk Songs for the Burds*. Waverly ELP 132 (1963).

Dunbar, Max. *Songs and Ballads of the Scottish Wars, 290–1745*. Folkways FW3006 (1956).

Dyer-Bennet, Richard. *Richard Dyer-Bennet 1*. Dyer-Bennet DYB 1000 (1955).

———. *The Essential Richard Dyer-Bennet*. Vanguard (c. 1977)

———. *The Art of Richard Dyer-Bennet*. Omega OVC 6007 (1991).

Five Hand Reel. *Earl O' Moray*. RCA Victor PL 25150 (1978). Bobby Eaglesham, Dick Gaughan, Barry Lyons, and Dave Tulloch.

The Galliards. *Scottish Choice*. Decca ACL 1065 (1961).

The Ian Campbell Group. *Four Highland Songs*. Transatlantic TRA SP10 (1966).

MacColl, Ewan. *The English and Scottish Popular Ballads*. Riverside RLP 12–627 (1956). Edited by Kenneth S. Goldstein.

———. *The English and Scottish Popular Ballads*. Folkways FG 3509 (1961).

———. *Blood and Roses, Volume IV*. ESB 82 (1986).

McDonald, Alistair. *Alistair McDonald*. Polydor 2383-404 (1976)

McEwen, Rory and Alex. *Folksong Jubilee*. EMI Ltd. HMV CLP 1220 (1958).

———. *Great Scottish Ballads*. Folkways FP 927.

MacEwen, Sydney. *Songs of the Thistle: Classical Favourites*. Phillips (1959).

McKinnon, Raun with Dick Weissman and Bill Lee. *American Folk Songs*. Parkway P-7024 (1962).

McKellar, Kenneth. *Folk Songs from Scotland's Heritage*. London TW 91331 (c.1964).

———. *The Songs of Robert Burns*. London SW99331 (1965?).

Nye, Hermes. *Anglo-American Ballads*. Folkways FP37 (1952).

O'Connell, Robbie. *Close to the Bone* (Green Linnet

O'Hara, Mary. *Mary O'Hara's Scotland Boot International ITB* 4509 (1974).

Seraffyn. *Of Love, Of War, Of Many Things*. Columbia CL 2157 (1964).

Turner, John and Chris Turner. *The Graceful Young Woman*. Fiddletree F7131 (1983).

RECORDINGS FROM THE SCHOOL OF SCOTTISH STUDIES SOUND ARCHIVE, EDINBURGH.

Mathieson, Willie. Ellon, Aberdeenshire. Collected 1952 by Hamish Henderson. SA 1952/7/B1.

Matheson, Lexie. Plockton, Ross-shire. Collected 1952 by Francis Collinson. SA 1952/90/B19.

Ward, Patty. Edinburgh. Collected 1953 by Hamish Henderson. SA 1953/235/B25.

Unidentified Choir. 1956. SA 1956/169/A2.

Scott, Tom. Edinburgh. Collected 1959 by Hamish Henderson. SA 1959/81/B9.

———. Edinburgh. Collected 1959 by Hamish Henderson. SA 1959/84/B21.

MacNeil, John. London. Collected 1960 by Hamish Henderson. SA 1960/206/B26.

Unidentified Woman. Delgatie Castle, Aberdeenshire. Collected 1961 by Dona Etherington. SA 1961/68/B22.

Fisher, Archie. Kinross Festival. Collected 1974 by unidentified collector. SA 1974/46/A10.

TEXTS FROM THE ARCHIVE OF FOLK CULTURE, AMERICAN FOLKLIFE CENTER, LIBRARY OF CONGRESS, WASHINGTON, D.C.

Kilberg, Lionel. Brooklyn, NY (1994). A (with his own tune).

Spaulding, Edith. Eaton Rapids, Michigan (1927) Gordon Mss. 2596. A&B.

Index

Note: Place names, as a general rule, have not been indexed, nor has material in the notes, unless such material contains additional text. For the most part, members of the nobility or others of rank are referred to by their official titles, not their family names. Ballad numbers (*e.g.* Child 181) refer to Francis James Child's *The English and Scottish Popular Ballads.*